# OPFOR SMARTBOOK



TheLightning 5

# RED TEAM ARMY

## Forces, Operations & Tactics

The Lightning Press
Christopher Larsen
Norman M. Wade

**The Lightning Press**

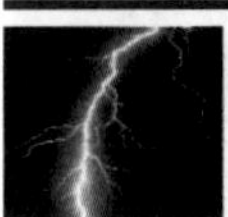

2227 Arrowhead Blvd.
Lakeland, FL 33813
**24-hour Voicemail/Fax/Order:** 1-800-997-8827
**E-mail:** SMARTbooks@TheLightningPress.com

**www.TheLightningPress.com**

# OPFOR SMARTbook 3: RED TEAM ARMY

## Forces, Operations & Tactics



**ISBN: 978-1-935886-57-0**



### Notice of Liability

The information in this SMARTbook and quick reference guide is distributed on an "As Is" basis, without warranty. While every precaution has been taken to ensure the reliability and accuracy of all data and contents, neither the author nor The Lightning Press shall have any liability to any person or entity with respect to liability, loss, or damage caused directly or indirectly by the contents of this book. If there is a discrepancy, refer to the source document. All military references used to compile SMARTbooks are in the public domain and are available to the general public through official public websites and designated as approved for public release with unlimited distribution. The SMARTbooks do not contain ITAR-controlled technical data, classified, or other sensitive material restricted from public release. SMARTbooks are reference books that address general military principles, fundamentals and concepts rather than technical data or equipment operating procedures. "The views presented in this publication are those of the author and do not necessarily represent the views of the Department of Defense or its components."



**Photo Credits**: Photos courtesy of Hae-jung Larsen and OP EASTWIND, where credited. All other public domain imagery sourced from the Ministry of Defence of the Russian Federation official website (http://eng.mil.ru).

**Printed and bound in the United States of America.**

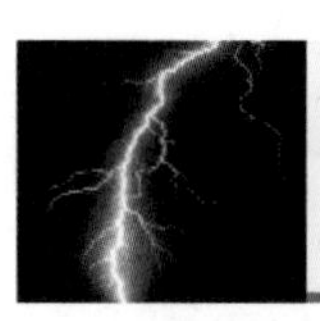

# Note to Readers

In today's **complicated and uncertain world**, it is impossible to predict the exact nature of future conflict that might involve U.S. forces. This is the nature of the contemporary operational environment (COE), and training for such an environment requires a different type of Opposing Force (OPFOR) than that of the past.

It has been nearly **thirty years** since a holistic explanation of the Soviet-based Opposing Force (OPFOR) was examined in the U.S. Army Field Manual 100-2 series. Recognizing this, "OPFOR SMARTbook 3: Red Team Army" re-examines and outlines the doctrinal operational construct and **historical foundations of Soviet-era military forces** from the FM 100-2 series, which is now out-of-print and largely unavailable.

Second, OPFOR SMARTbook 3 reorganizes that foundational material and aligns it in keeping with **contemporary military doctrinal taxonomy** to include ADRP 3-0 Unified Land Operations and ADRP 3-90 Offense and Defense (Tactics).

Third, OPFOR SMARTbook 3 **translates and bridges** the strategic- and operational-level doctrine into **tactical application at the small-unit level**.

Through this triangulation, a more modern rendition of **Red Team Armies** emerges.

## Opposing Forces (OPFOR)

From the U.S. doctrinal perspective, an enemy is an individual, group of individuals (organized or not organized), paramilitary or military force, national entity, or national alliance that is in opposition to the United States, its allies, or multinational partners. A potential adversary is sometimes designated as a threat. Once hostilities actually begin, the threat becomes the enemy. (FM 7-100 series)

An Opposing Force (OPFOR) is a training tool that should allow U.S. forces to train against a challenging and plausible sparring partner that represents the wide range of possible opponents the military could face in actual conflict. It enables training of all branches of the military and prepares forces for potential combat operations.

The Lightning Press offers three specific OPFOR SMARTbooks, plus more than a dozen related and supporting "military reference" and "national power" titles:

## SMARTbooks - DIME is our DOMAIN!

SMARTbooks: Essential reference for the Instruments of National Power (D-I-M-E: Diplomatic, Informational, Military, Economic)! Recognized as a doctrinal reference standard by military, national security and government professionals around the world, "Military Reference" SMARTbooks are designed with all levels of Soldiers, Sailors, Airmen, Marines and Civilians in mind. Our new "National Power" series is a nested collection of supporting and related titles, but with a different focus and domain scope (D-I-M-E).

SMARTbooks can be used as quick reference guides during actual operations, as study guides at education and professional development courses, and as lesson plans and checklists in support of training. Serving a generation of military and national security professionals, reference SMARTbooks have become "mission-essential" around the world. Visit **www.TheLightningPress.com** for complete details!

# Prologue: Opposing Forces (OPFOR) Doctrine and the Historical "Soviet Threat" Model

When the Army established its OPFOR program in 1976 with Army Regulation 350-2, it defined an OPFOR simply as "an organized force created by and from U.S. Army units to portray a unit of a potential adversary armed force." Thus, all OPFORs were originally threat-based, in the sense that they replicated the forces, capabilities, and doctrine of a particular country officially recognized as a threat or potential adversary. In the midst of the Cold War, the 1976 regulation identified only one potential adversary against which to train: the Soviet Union. Over time, the Army developed other OPFORs.

The Soviet threat was described in great detail in the 80s with the FM 100-2 series. The three-volume set was the definitive source of unclassifed information on Soviet ground forces and the Soviet model of combined arms warfare. Used together, the series provided a thorough reference on the Soviet Army. Initiatlly, these publications were distritubution-restricted publications limited to US Government agencies. In Sept '94, they were marked as "Approved for Public Release, Distribution is Unlimited" by TRADOC. The series is now out-of-print and largely unavailable.

## FM 100-2-1: The Soviet Army: Operations and Tactics (Jul '84)

This field manual describes the operations and tactics of Soviet general purpose ground forces. The content is based on information in Soviet writings and other open source literature. Most available information is focused on potential battle in Central Europe. This manual reflects that focus. Though Soviet military activity extends to other parts of the world, the Soviet forces opposite NATO represent a general model for Soviet forces elsewhere, as well as for forces of Soviet allies and surrogates.

## FM 100-2-2: The Soviet Army: Specialized Warfare and Rear Area Support (Jul '84)

The term "specialized warfare," used in the title of this FM, is intended to be an abbreviated, collective description of combat actions which, in US terminology, may be described as "special operations." or "operations in special conditions." Special operations include airborne, heliborne,and amphibious operations, and unconventional warfare in the enemy rear. The Soviet concept of the "rear area" visualizes modern war in an unprecedented spatial scope. This rear area concept stretches from the forward edge of the battle area (FEBA) back to the national capital.

## FM 100-2-3: The Soviet Army: Troops, Organization, and Equipment (Jul '91)

The Soviet armed forces include five separate components: the strategic rocket forces, the ground forces, the air forces, the air defense forces, and naval forces. The generic term "Soviet Army" normally includes all but naval forces. This manual concentrates on the largest of the these components, the Soviet ground forces. Highly modernized organization and equipment combine to make the Soviet ground forces the most powerful land army in the world, with unprecedented flexibility, mobility, and firepower.

In today's complicated and uncertain world, it is impossible to predict the exact nature of future conflict that might involve U.S. forces. So the military must be ready to meet the challenges of any type of conflict, in all kinds of places, and against all kinds of threats. This is the nature of the contemporary operational environment (COE), and training for such an environment requires a different type of Opposing Force (OPFOR) than that of the past.

From the U.S. perspective, an enemy is an individual, group of individuals (organized or not organized), paramilitary or military force, national entity, or national alliance that is in opposition to the United States, its allies, or multinational partners. A potential adversary is sometimes designated as a threat. In this sense, the military defines threat as "any specific foreign nation or organization with intentions and military capabilities that suggest it could become an adversary or challenge the national security interests of the United States or its allies." Once hostilities actually begin, the threat becomes the enemy.

An Opposing Force (OPFOR) is a training tool that should allow U.S. forces to train against a challenging and plausible sparring partner that represents the wide range of possible opponents the military could face in actual conflict. It enables training of all branches of the military and prepares forces for potential combat operations.

In its time, the threat-based OPFOR served the Army very well, particularly for units targeted against specific threats. The benefits of this training were borne out, for example, in Operation Desert Storm. Techniques and doctrine, including deep attack and the intelligence preparation of the battlefield, developed to cope with specific threats and honed against the OPFOR, enabled the Army to achieve decisive results on the battlefield.

More recent recent endeavors to describe threats include a strategic perspective explored in FM 7-100 Opposing Force Doctrinal Framework and Strategy (MAY 2003). Contemporary operational warfighting capabilities of the OPFOR are described in FM 7-100.1 Opposing Force Operations (DEC 2004); TC 7-100 Hybrid Threat (NOV 2010); and TC 7-100.3 Irregular Opposing Forces (JAN 2014). Additional OPFOR resources include Red Team University and the Foreign Military Studies Office (FMSO).

In the FM 7-100 series, TRADOC has created a flexible baseline for an OPFOR that can be adapted to meet a variety of different training requirements in a number of different scenarios that reflect the current operational environment. The OPFOR operational doctrine outlined represents a realistic composite of potential adversaries the Army might encounter in the real-world situations of the foreseeable future. However, the world is continually changing, as are the threats and challenges for which the Army must be prepared. The Army must remain flexible, as must the OPFOR designed to serve as a challenging sparring partner in the training environment.

Glaringly, a gap exists in our explanation of small-unit tactics, techniques and procedures of potential adversaries, threats, and enemies – particularly regarding how those tactics bridge up to operational and strategic frameworks. This gap of tactical description encompasses "state actors" within Red Team Army doctrine, as well as "non-state actors" such as insurgents, guerillas, terrorists, pirates, bandits, and crime cartels. One of the goals of this work, therefore, is to enable the development of a robust OPFOR at the small unit level in live tactical simulation, based on the construct of the historical foundations and doctrinal underpinnings of available OPFOR doctrine.

*This work does not purport to define a single military by name. However, it assumes that contemporary Red Team Army doctrine has evolved from the Soviet tradition. And while the now-defunct Soviet Army is not inherently synonymous with Red Team Army, the doctrinal underpinings, historical foundations and cultural lineage of the military forces is established. For editorial convenience, this manual may refer to the two as if synonymous. When "Soviet" is used, it is based on the historical foundations from the FM 100-2 series of the 80s and 90s (and is used in the present tense); when "Red Team Army (RTA)" is used, it refers to an amalgamation of historic enemies and current antagonists. Through a triangulation of potential, actual and historic threats, a credible OPFOR may be scripted, trained, and developed into a robust training simulation scenario.*

# References

The following references were used in part to compile "OPFOR SMARTbook 3: Red Team Army." All military references used to compile SMARTbooks are in the public domain and are available to the general public through official public websites and designated as approved for public release with unlimited distribution. The SMARTbooks do not contain ITAR-controlled technical data, classified, or other sensitive material restricted from public release. SMARTbooks are reference books that address general military principles, fundamentals and concepts rather than technical data or equipment operating procedures.

## Field Manuals and Army Doctrine 2015 Publications


ADRP 3-0, Unified Land Operations. Washington DC: Headquarters Department of the Army, May 2012.

ADRP 3-90, Offense and Defense. Washington DC: Headquarters Department of the Army, August 2012.

FM 100-2-1, The Soviet Army: Operations and Tactics. Washington DC: Headquarters Department of the Army, July 1984.

FM 100-2-2, The Soviet Army: Specialized Warfare and Rear Area Support. Washington DC: Headquarters Department of the Army, July 1984.

FM 100-2-3, The Soviet Army: Troops, Organization and Equipment. Washington DC: Headquarters Department of the Army, July 1984.

FM 100-63, Infantry-Based Opposing Force: Organization Guide. Washington DC: Headquarters Department of the Army, April 1996.

FM 100-7.1, Opposing Force Operations. Washington DC: Headquarters Department of the Army, December 2004.


## Other References


Blank, Stephen J. "Afghanistan and Beyond: Reflections on the Future of Warfare." Strategic Studies Institute. Carlisle Barracks, PA: US Army War College, June 28, 1993.

Frasche, Robert M. The Soviet Motorized Rifle Battalion. Washington, DC: Defense Intelligence Agency, September 1978.

Grau, Lester W. The Bear Went Over the Mountain: Soviet Combat Tactics in Afghanistan. Washington DC: National Defense University Press, August 2010.

Sharp, Charles C. Soviet Infantry Tactics in World War II: Red Army Infantry Tactics from Squad to Rifle Company from the Combat Regulations. West Chester, OH: George Nafziger Collection, 1998.

Sasso, Claude R. Leavenworth Papers: Soviet Night Operations in World War II. Fort Leavenworth, KS: Combat Studies Institute, December 1982.

Toppe, Alfred, BG. CMH Pub 104-3: Night Combat. Washington DC: Center of Military History US Army, 1986. Retrieved 22 May 2011. http://www.history.army.mil/books/wwii/104-3/fm.htm

# Table of Contents

## Chap 1 Red Team Armies (RTA)

# Chap 2 Offensive Operations

Chap 3

# Defensive Operations

## Chap 4 Specialized Warfare



## Chap 5 Tactical Enabling Tasks

# Chap 6 Small Unit Drills

# Chap 7 Urban & Regional Environments

Chap 8

# Rear Area Operations & Logistics

# (Red Team Armies) I. Military Doctrine

*Ref: FM 100-2-1 The Soviet Army: Operations and Tactics (Jul '84), chapter 2.*

## I. The Soviet Concept of War

To the Soviets, war is a manifestation of the class struggle. It is an expression of the conflict between the "progressive forces of socialism" and the "reactionary forces of imperialistic capitalism," which they feel will be ultimately resolved in favor of socialism. The Soviet concept of war represents a continuation of politics. In Western perceptions, war occurs when politics fail to resolve conflicts nonviolently. The Soviets feel that war is the least desirable method by which the forces of history will move toward complete victory for socialism.

The Soviet political and military theorists compare the socialist and capitalist camps by a concept called the "correlation of forces." This concept compares the relative political, moral, economic, and military strengths of both sides. In the Soviet view, the correlation of forces has been shifting in favor of the socialist camp since the Soviet defeat of Nazi Germany in World War II. Soviet Marxist-Leninist ideology requires the correlation to shift continuously in favor of socialism. The correlation of forces may be advanced by both violent and nonviolent means. When it is advanced by violent means, the military component of the correlation is the dominant factor.

## II. The Structure of Soviet Military Thought

Soviet military doctrine is the officially accepted set of concepts that delineate the ways and means to achieve military objectives in the interest of politics. This doctrine also specifies the structure of the Soviet armed forces, allocates industrial resources and output, and orients research and development efforts to support armed forces.

Military doctrine is the blueprint drawn up by the highest Soviet political leaders that describes in specific detail the shape of the armed forces and the way they are to be used.

The formulation of Soviet military doctrine is a continuous evolutionary process based on: communist ideology, soviet foreign policy, economic and military strengths of adversaries,soviet resources and geography, history, science and technology.

Soviet military doctrine is based on an elaborate, integrated system of thought. The doctrinal concepts are precisely defined, and each has its place in a hierarchy of importance that corresponds to its military decision-making level. The system deals with all military issues, ranging from national defense policy down to platoon tactics. Soviet military officers are quite familiar with the entire system of thought and routinely express themselves in these terms. They think and formulate decisions using these concepts.

## Military Science

Military science is the study and analysis of the diverse psychological and material phenomena relevant to armed combat for developing practical recommendations for the achievement of victory in war. Unlike doctrine, military science is characterized by controversy and debate. In military science, there may be several points of view, diverse "scientific" concepts, and original hypotheses that are not selected as doctrine and therefore are not accepted as official state views on military issues. Military science encompasses virtually all things military.

## Military Art

Military art is the most important and primary field within military science and is the basis for strategy, operational art, and tactics. It is the theory and practice of conducting armed conflict. The principles of military art are the basic ideas and the most important recommendations for the organization and conduct of battles, operations, and warfare.

The concept of military art and its role in military science are not just empty exercises in the Marxist-Leninist theory. Many Soviet military officers hold advanced degrees in military science and are serious and intense in their study. They are convinced of the superiority of this methodology for preparing the Soviet armed forces to achieve success in modern warfare. The structure of ideas, terminology, and concepts associated with this system of thought constitutes the very vocabulary through which Soviet officers express their perceptions of military problems and the measures they develop to resolve them.

Military art applies to three separate but interdependent levels of combat activity:

- Strategic - national and theater level.
- Operational - fronts and armies.
- Tactical - division and below.

Soviet perspectives on and prescriptions for armed conflict require that tactical success leads to operational success. Similarly, operational gains lead to strategic success.

It is often difficult to separate Soviet tactics from what the Soviets call "operational art" because the maneuver divisions that are the subject of tactics are the maneuver elements that achieve the operational" objectives of armies and fronts. Moreover, the two concepts are closely interrelated in Soviet military thinking and planning. A recurring theme in Soviet military writing is the need for the commander to keep the "operational" goal in mind. The overriding objective of the combined arms offensive is to rapidly turn tactical success into operational success by a well-orchestrated combination of massive fire, maneuver, and deep, violent strikes.

# III. Principles of Military Art (& Laws of War)

*Ref: FM 100-2-1 The Soviet Army: Operations and Tactics (Jul '84), p. 2-2.*

Soviet military theorists consider the following points to be the general principles of military art. They do not represent any special revelation of truth or radical departure from traditional military thought. However, by their emphasis on these particular points, Soviet military leaders reveal the character of their military thinking and predict the basic characteristics of future Soviet military operations.

According to the Soviets, their armed forces must:

- Be fully prepared to accomplish the mission regardless of the conditions under which war begins or must be conducted.
- Achieve surprise whenever possible. Military operations must be characterized by decisiveness and aggressiveness. Forces must strive continuously to seize and to hold the initiative.
- Make full use of all available military assets and capabilities to achieve victory.
- Insure that major formations and units of all services, branches, and arms effect thorough and continuous coordination.
- Select the principal enemy objective to be seized and the best routes for attacking it. Make a decisive concentration of combat power at the correct time.
- Maintain continuous and reliable command and control.
- Be determined and decisive in achieving the assigned mission.
- Maintain complete security of combat operations.
- Reconstitute reserves and restore combat effectiveness as quickly as possible.

These are general principles that apply to all three levels of military art: strategy, operations, and tactics. At each of these levels, there are more specific, detailed principles.

## Laws of War

Soviet military thought subscribes to certain "laws of war" at the strategic level, and "principles of operational art and tactics" which apply to the actual conduct of combat.

In simple terms, these laws mean the following:

- **First Law: Be prepared.** Prepare in peacetime for the next war. Forces-in-being are the decisive factors. The side with the most and best troops and equipment at the start of war will win the war.
- **Second Law:** The side which can best sustain a protracted war will win the war.
- **Third Law:** The higher the political stakes of a war, the longer and more violent it will be.
- **Fourth Law:** War aims must be seen as just. Modern war cannot be waged without public support.

Soviet planning and preparation for war reflect a dominant feeling that war is inevitable. This is not to say that the USSR wants war, but that it is preparing for it continuously.

The Soviet state is autocratic, militarized, and centralized. Its political and economic systems give priority to military requirements. The state allocates resources and directs production for preparation and maintenance of a war footing.

The Soviet Union is prepared to exert itself at great expense to achieve its goals. It is a nation which through civil war, collectivization, attendant famine, and purges inflicted more than 20 trillion deaths on its own citizens from the Russian Revolution to the start of World War II. It is a nation that endured the loss of 20 million people during World War II. Its tolerance for sacrifice is high.

# IV. Soviet Military Principles

*Ref: FM 100-2-1 The Soviet Army: Operations and Tactics (Jul '84), pp. 2-3 to 2-4.*

## Classic Russian Military Principles

- Extreme exertion of force at the very beginning of a war.
- Simultaneity of actions.
- Economy of forces.
- Concentration.
- Chief objective - the enemy's army.
- Surprise.
- Unity of action.
- Preparation.
- Energetic pursuit.
- Security.
- Initiative and dominance over the enemy's will.
- Strength where the enemy is weak.

The most significant points of this list are:

- He who gets to the initial battle with the "most" wins.
- The enemy must be confronted with more than one situation to deal with.
- One should not be diverted by geographical objectives, but should concentrate on the destruction of the enemy's military forces.
- Detailed, exacting preparation must precede an attack.
- Design actions to preempt the opponent and keep him reacting to situations that you control.
- Concentrate on the enemy's weak points rather than his strengths.

Contemporary Soviet military theorists hold that nuclear weaponry and other means of modem warfare have modified the basic principles. By the early 1970's, the following principles dominated Soviet operational art and tactics:

## Russian Military Principles of the 1970s

- Mobility and high rates of combat operations.
- Concentration of main efforts and creation of superiority in forces and means over the enemy at the decisive place and at the decisive time.
- Surprise and security.
- Combat activeness.
- Preservation of the combat effectiveness of friendly forces.
- Conformity of the goal to the actual situation.
- Coordination.

A melding of contemporary writings and those of the recent past, plus the influence of significant classical Russian principles, results in the following specific Soviet principles of operational art and tactics:

# Modern Operational and Tactical Principles

- The offensive is the basic form of combat action. Only by a resolute offense conducted at a high tempo and to great depth is total destruction of the enemy achieved.
- Combat maneuver units must be mobile and capable of rapid movement.
- Fire support, command and control, and logistics must be as mobile as maneuver units.
- Conduct thorough and continuous reconnaissance. Find the enemy's weak points.
- Perform a thorough estimate of the situation and make timely, analytical decisions. Be realistic. Consider the mission, enemy, your own combat power, terrain. weather and light conditions, and time.
- Prepare and plan extensively and in detail.
- The planning and conduct of an operation must involve the full coordination and cooperation of all commanders involved.
- There must be unity of command, a single commander for any operation.
- Fully orchestrate all available combat means in a coordinated, cooperative, combined arms effort.
- Deceive the enemy. Attack from an unexpected direction at an unexpected time. Use terrain and weather to your advantage.
- Strike early with great force. Constantly strive to preempt and dominate the enemy.
- Attack the enemy violently and simultaneously throughout his depth. Carry the battle to the enemy rear with swift penetrations by maneuver units, fires, aviation, airborne and heliborne assaults and by unconventional warfare means.
- Be bold and decisive. Seize and hold the initiative.
- Prosecute an operation relentlessly, without pause, under all conditions of visibility or NBC contamination.
- Keep the enemy under constant pressure and off balance. Do not allow him to react effectively.
- Fully exploit the effects of nuclear or chemical strikes with deep attacks by all available forces.
- Whenever possible achieve mass by concentrated, massed nuclear or nonnuclear fires rather than by massing maneuver forces.
- If maneuver forces must be massed, do so rapidly. Disperse them as soon as possible after the task has been achieved.
- Maneuver first with firepower. Firepower is maneuver.
- Maneuver forces should attack the weakest points in enemy defenses. If necessary, create weak points or holes with nuclear or nonnuclear fires. Bypass enemy strongpoints to strike deeply into his rear.
- Avoid frontal attacks. Whenever possible strike the enemy in the flanks or rear.
- Maintain security of your own flanks and rear.
- Maintain sufficient follow-on force to assure achievement of the mission and to deal with contingencies.
- Maintain uninterrupted combat support.
- Maintain effective, continuous command, control, and communications. Loss of communications leads to loss of control and defeat. Maintain redundant communications at higher levels. Rely on audio and visual signals and well-rehearsed battle drills at lower levels.

# Norms, Initiative, and Flexibility

*Ref: FM 100-2-1 The Soviet Army: Operations and Tactics (Jul '84), pp. 2-11 to 2-12.*

## Norms

Soviet military doctrine includes a system of performance standards, expressed in numerical form, called "norms." Norms define the ideal performance in a multitude of tasks and conditions. They are used to determine things such as interval, rates of march, frontages, logistics requirements, fire support, and training drills.

Norms provide a mathematical prescription for proper action. They are formulated by historical analysis, training exercises, requirements, and gaming models. Based on norms, a given situation has an approved response.

The advantage of this system is that it provides a high degree of combat readiness, at least in the initial stages. Drills at the subunit level (battalion and lower) are well-rehearsed.

The obvious disadvantage to strict adherence to norms is less provision for the unexpected. If a situation arises for which there is no established normative response, a lower-level commander might find himself in peril.

## Initiative

The topic of initiative receives much attention in Soviet military writings. When a plan fails, commanders are strongly urged to use initiative as a cure-all.

Soviet operations and tactics are not as thoroughly rigid as is perceived by many Western analysts. The amount of flexibility exhibited increases with the rank of the commander and the size of force commanded. There is probably little tactical flexibility at subunit level (battalion and lower). The first level where any real tactical flexibility might be found is at regiment, which is the smallest fully combined arms unit. Flexibility in battlefield thought and action increase by degree, upward through division, army, and front.

Soviet officers today are well-educated and well-trained in their military specialties. Most of them are graduates of branch academies where they receive the equivalent of a college education plus a thorough grounding in their branch skills. Though their world outlook is biased by a lifetime of political dogma, they are not ignorant nor incapable of professional, purely military judgment.

## Flexibility

Flexibility in Soviet operations has been evident since the final years of World War II. Since the mid-1960s, Soviet military writers and theorists have emphasized:

- The need for rapid concentration and dispersal of combat power on the modem battlefield.
- The rejection of the classic "breakthrough" achieved by massed forces.
- The need to attack on multiple axes.
- The lack of a continuous front.
- The exploitation of weak points in an enemy defense.
- Swift transfer of combat power from one point to another on the battlefield.
- The achievement of surpise.
- Speed in the attack.
- Independent action by commanders.
- The need to carry the battle deep into the enemy rear.

These concepts are not descriptive of a rigid offensive doctrine, but of one that is both mobile and flexible.

# (Red Team Armies) II. Operational Concept



*Ref: FM 100-2-1 The Soviet Army: Operations and Tactics (Jul '84), chapter 3.*

## Categories of Soviet Combat Action

**Offense** *(chap. 2)*

- Attack Against a Defending Enemy
- Attack from the March
- Attack from a Position in Direct Contact
- Meeting Engagement (enemy is also on offense)
- Pursuit (enemy is withdrawing)

**Defense** *chap. 3)*

- Prepared Defense
- Hasty Defense
- Withdrawal

# I. The Soviet Categorization of Combat Actions

An important consideration in understanding Soviet military thought is their categorization of types of combat actions. It is important to adhere to their categorization and terminology to fully understand the essence of Soviet operations and tactics. The 1966 Soviet book *Taktika* (Tactics) was written at a time when it was assumed that all major combat activity would take place under nuclear conditions. The book described four major categories of combat action: offense, meeting engagement, defense, and withdrawal.

The listing of the meeting engagement as a separate major category of combat reflects the view held at that time that it would be the most prevalent form of combat under nuclear conditions. More recent writings, to include the *Soviet Military Encyclopedia*, indicate that the meeting engagement is looked upon as one element of the broad category of offense, rather than a separate major category. This probably reflects the contemporary Soviet view that both nuclear and nonnuclear warfare are possible and that the attack against a defending enemy may be just as prevalent as the meeting engagement.

Contemporary Soviet writings describe only two basic, diametrically opposed forms of combat action: offense and defense.

## A. Offensive Actions

Offensive actions are divided into three subcategories which key on enemy actions and disposition. When the enemy is stationary, in a defensive posture, the Soviets conduct an attack against a defending enemy. When both the Soviets and the enemy are on the offense and their forces collide, the action that occurs is the meeting engagement. When the enemy is withdrawing, action performed against him is called pursuit.

*See chap. 2.*

## B. Defensive Actions

Defensive actions are not as clearly delineated. Though the Soviets recognize a hasty and a prepared defense, the distinction between them is not absolute. With time and preparation, a hasty defense becomes a prepared defense. Withdrawal is a topic given very little attention in Soviet writings. If not categorically, then at least in perception, it is probably viewed within the larger context of defense.

Adhering to the Soviet terminology is particularly crucial when examining Soviet offensive actions. Too many US analysts have used US tactical terms such as "deliberate attack," "hasty attack," or "movement to contact" to describe Soviet offensive actions. The use of these terms results in a distorted image of Soviet actions. Their tactics are not a "mirror image" of US tactics. To fully understand the Soviet military thought process and the options available to the Soviet commander, the Soviet categorization must be adhered to.

According to the Soviet categorization, there is no such thing as a "breakthrough attack." This is another term used incorrectly and too freely by US analysts. The misuse of this term has resulted in incorrect perceptions of Soviet tactics.

*See chap. 3.*

# II. Combined Arms Offensive Warfare

Although some aspects of the Soviet concept of combined arms are similar to the US military practice of combined arms and joint (interservice) operations, the Soviet concept has a different meaning than does the US term. For example, within the Soviet Army, units of different branches do not normally cross attach among themselves to obtain the optimum mix of combat elements for a given mission. Instead, a unit of one arm will attach its subunits to support or reinforce units of another arm without receiving attachments in return.

The major difference, however, goes beyond variances in methods of attachment and reinforcement The concept of combined arms is far more comprehensive and formalized in Soviet doctrine. It is the cumulative expression of the principles of military art. Combined arms combat is the primary vehicle for their implementation in operations and tactics.

Over the past 60 years, the development of the Soviet combined arms concept has been essentially a doctrinal response to increases in the lethality and mobility of weapons and armies.

Their initial combined arms problem arose from the need to coordinate artillery and infantry during World War I and the Russian Civil War. During the 1930s, as the range and speed of weapon systems began to increase, the Soviets developed the theory and practice of operations in depth. This theory included a number of tactical prescriptions: the primacy of offensive operations, surprise, "shock power," and the combination of several arms and services to attain decisive operational success to a considerable depth within the enemy's defense.

# III. Nuclear Warfare

*Ref: FM 100-2-1 The Soviet Army: Operations and Tactics (Jul '84), pp. 2-7 to 2-9.*

The advent of nuclear weapons caused Soviet planners to go through a long period of rethinking and revising their combined arms doctrine. Modern, totally mechanized armed forces- supported and threatened by weapons that can change the face of the battlefield in a matter of minutes gave a whole new meaning to the high-speed, combined arms operation in depth.

Possible nuclear or chemical attacks by the enemy make concentration inadmissable in its World War II sense. At the same time, the availability of friendly nuclear strikes and the longer ranges of conventional artillery reduce the requirement for massed artillery formations. Improved troop mobility permits both the rapid concentration and quick dispersal essential to the survival of tank and motorized rifle formations as they maneuver on a nuclear-threatened battlefield. In this context, the Soviets now stress that the "quality" of mass must compensate for the reduced quantity formerly provided by concentrations of troops and equipment. This quality takes the form of intense strikes with conventional air, artillery, and weapons of mass destruction.

## Limited Nuclear War Considerations

In the past decade, the Soviet political and military leaders have discussed the possibility of a limited nuclear war. They accept that a war could be limited to a given theater of military operations (TVD) and would not necessarily escalate to an intercontinental exchange of nuclear strikes. Attempting to limit nuclear war to a TVD would place even greater pressure on Soviet forces to achieve theater objectives quickly to present enemy decision makers with a fait accompli that would make escalation clearly unattractive. In this context, the principles of tempo, decisiveness, and mission take on added importance.

The Soviets would prefer to avoid nuclear warfare. They would probably do so as long as their objectives were being achieved and there were no indications that the enemy was "going nuclear." However, the Soviets would attempt to preempt enemy nuclear use by a massive, initial, in-depth, theater nuclear strike.

# IV. The Attack in Depth

*Ref: FM 100-2-1 The Soviet Army: Operations and Tactics (Jul '84), pp. 2-6 to 2-7.*

The principle of attacking in depth was the Soviets' response to the increased capability and mobility of fire support systems (artillery and aviation) and the appearance of mechanized infantry, tank, and airborne forces. Enemy weapons and formations located several kilometers from the FEBA became an immediate threat to forces opposing them and had to be engaged with the same urgency and decisiveness as closer targets. On the other hand, Soviet fire support systems could reach farther, and their tank and infantry formations had increased in mobility. Soviet military theorists concluded that the deeper threat and the potential for deeper fire and maneuver by Soviet forces necessitated a combined arms effort. They decided that simultaneous artilley attack and airstrikes through the entire depth of enemy defenses combined with tank and infantry formations to break through his tactical defensive and to drive rapidly and forcefully into the depth of his operational rear would best attain success in combat. The enemy's lines of communication, command and control would then be destroyed or disrupted and the remainder of the forward edge of his tactical defensive system would begin to fragment and collapse. Disorganized, demoralized, and isolated, enemy commanders would be unable to reestablish an effective and coordinated defense.

The successful execution of this high-speed, deep operation required closely coordinated aggressive action by tank, infantry, artillery, and aviation. The separate arms and services were required to combine their efforts under a single control element to implement a unified plan. As a consequence, the requirement for thorough and continuous coordination among all combat elements throughout the planning and execution phases of every operation increased markedly. Maintenance of reliable and continuous command and control became at once more difficult and more critical. The roles of the combined arms commander and combined arms staff were expanded and refined. The combined arms commander, advised by his staffs has the overall responsibility for the planning and execution of the operation as well as the authority to carry it out

To execute the operation in depth successfully, the combined arms force had to maintain a rapid tempo of advance. By tempo, the Soviets mean not only speed but also the flexibility and aggressiveness to create and develop opportunities and to build advantage upon advantage. To accomplish this, the Soviet armed forces adopted the practice of echeloning their formations.

## The First Echelon

Typically, the first (assault) echelon attacked and penetrated the enemy's tactical defenses, and the second (exploitation) echelon drove through the penetration deep into the enemy's operational rear. Both echelons were controlled by the same combined arms commander. He assigned missions to the commanders of the first and second echelons in support of his overall mission and controlled the entire force until the operation's ultimate objective had been accomplished.

While the putpose of echeloning has changed little over the years, the circumstances under which echeloning is applied and the manner in which it is applied have varied considerably-depending on the relative strength and defensive tactics of the Soviets' enemies. During World War II, Soviet commanders usually employed a heavy second echelon (one third to one half of the entire formation) at the tactical level only when the enemy defensive formations were strong and deeply echeloned and the enemy had large reserves. When enemy defenses were thin and the defender did not possess significant reserves, the Soviets often attacked in a single large echelon (maintaining a relatively small combined arms reserve) to overwhelm the enemy along his entire front. Use of a single-echelon formation simplified command and control problems for the Soviet commander and denied the weaker defender the opportunity to reinforce laterally and to deal with the attacking force as it presented itself in several "waves."

## The Second Echelon

Even when they did not echelon their divisions (tactical echeloning), the Soviets would form an operational second echelon (within armies and fronts). The composition, size, and specific employment of the second echelon force was again determined largely by the enemy's strength, tactics, and disposition. When the enemy was able to establish a strong tactical defensive system of several echelons (reinforced by tactical reserves) and had sizable operational reserves available as well, the attacking Soviet second echelon comprised as much as half of the attacking formation (e.g., two divisions of a four-division army). The missions of this standard second echelon included reduction of bypassed enemy forces, exploitation through the penetration achieved by the first echelon, or an attack in a new direction, and possible replacement or reinforcement of the first echelon if the first echelon suffered heavy losses.

## The Mobile Group

When the enemy was relatively understrength and lacked credible operational reserves, the army second echelon would take the form of a mobile group made up of a tank or mechanized corps (normally one to three divisions reinforced with highly mobile combat and combat service support elements). This group, essentially a large, mobile, operational raiding force, either replaced or supplemented the standard second echelon. The mobile group differed from the standard second echelon in that it was expected to drive to deeper objectives and be able to sustain itself longer without major additional support. It also differed in that while the standard operational-level second echelon usually was primarily nonmotorized infantry, the mobile group was composed of tank or motorized infantry forces. When the mobile group was the only follow-on element, part of its force would usually assist the first echelon to make the initial penetration. When a mobile group and a second echelon were formed to conduct an operation in anticipation of heavier resistance in the tactical defense zone, the mobile group could be committed before or after the second echelon, depending on the actual level of resistance encountered by first echelon units.

The mobile group of the front typically consisted of a tank army. The front mobile group's missions were similar to the army level group except that the objectives were larger and deeper.

In the post World War II era, the Soviets completely motorized all infantry units and increased the number of tanks in divisions. This full mechanization along with the advent of nuclear weapons resulted in dropping the different roles of a second echelon and a mobile group. The second echelon was thought capable of both building up the offensive or exploiting success of the first echelon.

## The Operational Maneuver Group (OMG)

The concept of the mobile group and its role in combined arms combat received renewed Soviet interest as the basis for refining their contemporary operational offensive methods. The modern version of the mobile group, the operational maneuver group (OMG), can move faster, go deeper, and has better combat and combat service support than its World War II counterpart. The OMG concept significantly contributes to fulfilling the existing requirement for the deep theater offensive operation in keeping with the evolving nature of modern war.

The concentration of the necessary amount of force at the right time and place was critical to the maintenance of the tempo required for successful execution of the deep combined arms operation. During World War II, the Soviet Army concentrated tremendous force against a narrow sector of the enemy's defenses to achieve a rapid breakthrough.

# V. Force Ratios

After World War II, but before the introduction of tactical nuclear weapons and the complete mechanization of Soviet ground forces, Soviet military planners routinely weighted a main attack with ratios of 3-5:1 in tanks, 6-8:1 in artillery, and 4-5:1 in personnel. Contemporary Soviet writings indicate that an aggregate ratio of combat power of approximately 3:1 is sufficient in conducting an offensive operation or an attack against a defending enemy.

This 3:1 ratio refers to more than just cumulative numbers of first echelon troops and weapons relative to enemy troops and weapons in a given sector. It is, instead, a more sophisticated calculation of the total force, to include all maneuver units and combat support that a commander can bring to bear relative to the total force with which the enemy can oppose him.

# VI. Echelons

A Soviet tactical commander develops his concept for an attack much the same as a US commander does. The Soviet commander considers the same factors which we know as METT-T (mission, enemy, terrain, troops, and time available). He assesses his objectives, the terrain, enemy forces, and avenues of approach. Then he assigns forces necessary to insure completion of the task. One tool that he uses in allocating forces is echelonment.

Forces may be allocated to a first echelon, a second echelon, a combined arms reserve, or special reserves. If enemy defenses are well prepared in depth, the Soviet commander will normally organize his forces into two echelons, special reserves, and, possibly, a small combined arms reserve. If the enemy defends with most of his forces forward, the Soviets normally will attack in a strong, single echelon, followed by a combined arms reserve and special reserves. Combat organization is variable and adaptable to the situation.

## A. First Echelon

A first echelon is a main attack force. It will contain the majority of the combat power of the formation or unit. Missions of first echelon forces are:

- Penetrate or defeat enemy forward defenses
- Continue the attack
- Under nuclear conditions, exploit nuclear strikes on enemy defenses

## B. Second Echelon

Second echelon forces are assigned missions at the same time as first echelon forces. Possible missions for second echelon forces include:

- Exploit the success of first echelon forces
- Conduct a pursuit
- Destroy bypassed enemy forces
- Replace or reinforce first echelon forces

Regardless of a previously assigned mission, second echelon forces are used to reinforce success, not failure. The main goal at all levels is to carry the battle swiftly and violently into the enemy rear. The commander commits second echelon forces in a manner to best achieve this goal.

Second echelon forces are likely to be dispersed laterally, following behind first echelon forces. Dispersal provides both security and flexibility in commitment.

# VII. Chemical Warfare

*Ref: FM 100-2-1 The Soviet Army: Operations and Tactics (Jul '84), pp. 2-9 to 2-10.*

The Soviets do not perceive clear delineations between conventional, chemical, and nuclear warfare. It is possible that chemical weapons would be used early in an operation or from its onset. Chemical attacks would be directed principally against enemy positions in the forward battle area. Soviet military writings indicate that non-persistent agents would be used across the front of a Soviet attack, while persistent agents would be used to protect their flanks.

Simultaneously with strikes across the front, chemical strikes also could be expected throughout the depth of enemy defenses. These chemical strikes would be combined with other forms of conventional attack to neutralize enemy nuclear capability, command and control, and aviation. Subsequent chemical attacks might be conducted against logistic facilities.

*Besides offensive chemical capability, Soviet forces are equipped with the best chemical protective and decontamination equipment in the world. They know that their chemical capability greatly exceeds that of any other nation. Not to use this capability would deprive them of a decisive advantage.*

The vulnerability of densely concentrated formations to nuclear weapons caused the Soviets to alter their method of achieving mass. The "breakthrough" concept of World War II, with its massed troops and weapons, narrow frontages, and fixed echelons, is maladapted to the nuclear-threatened battlefield. Under nuclear-threatened conditions, the Soviet offensive concept would have the following features:

- Avoid concentrating forces
- Concentrate fires, but not firing weapons
- Attack across broader frontages, on multiple axes
- Avoid enemy strong points
- Probe for enemy weak points
- Penetrate where possible
- Commit follow-on forces when and where they can best contribute to success
- Drive rapidly and deeply into the enemy rear to destroy nuclear weapons and enemy defenses

The distance between echelons is not fixed. It is decided by the commander based on the situation. The second echelon is located close enough to the first echelon to insure timely commitment, but far enough back to provide protection and room for maneuver. Second echelon forces normally advance in march or prebattle formation.

The preferred method of committing second echelon forces is through gaps or around flanks offirst echelon forces. For example, a second echelon regiment normally would pass between first echelon regiments or around the flank of its parent division.

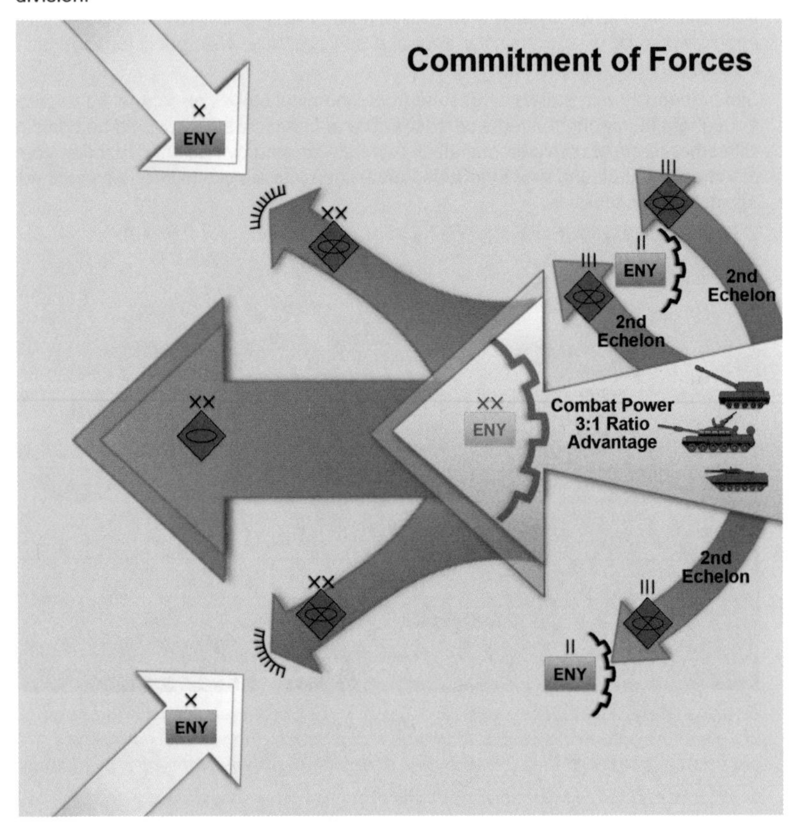


However, the second echelon could be committed on an axis of a first echelon unit. Whenever possible, the Soviets will avoid a passage of lines and intermingling of forces of two echelons, such as would happen if the second echelon unit were passed through the first echelon unit.

## C. Reserve Forces

Combined arms reserves are made up of tank, motorized rifle, and artillery subunits. When a large single echelon is employed in an attack, a combined arms reserve will be used to exploit success. It will advance in a manner similar to a second echelon, but will not have a pre-assigned mission. It is committed when and where the Soviet commander believes it can best lead to deeper penetration and success.

A small combined arms reserve, approximately one-ninth the size of the parent unit, may be formed when two echelons are employed. Such a reserve is used primarily for security and reaction to enemy counterattack.

# (Red Team Armies) III. Personnel & Training



*Ref: FM 100-2-3 The Soviet Army: Troops, Organization and Equipment, chap. 2 and 3.*

## I. Historical Lineage

Red Team Armies (RTA) trace their historical lineage to the Soviet Union, which in turn was greatly influenced and shaped by German Blitzkrieg tactics of the Second World War and the linear tactics of the French and British prior to modern, mechanized warfare.

Because of these influences, RTA place enormous emphasis on the offense. So much so that if an RTA unit slows its momentum or stops to defend, resources of combat power are intentionally stripped from the stalled unit and diverted to other units still pushing the offense. Defense is not rewarded in RTA and may even be punished.

Incorporating much of the Blitzkrieg concepts of combined arms, RTA efficiently employs infantry and armor formations intermixed. Indirect fires from artillery units and also Close Air Support (CAS) from supporting helicopter gunship and fixed-wing aircraft support these formations.

# II. Personnel

*Ref: FM 100-2-3 The Soviet Army: Troops, Organization, and Equipment (Jun '91), chap. 2.*

At the height of the Soviet Union, there were more than 60 million males between the ages of 15 and 49. About 80 percent of these men are fit for military service. Each year, some 2 to 21/2 million young men reach the military registration age of 17. The government will induct at least one-half of them when they become 18 years old. These conscripts constituted approximately 75 percent of Soviet ground force personnel. The remainder, who were deferred for various reasons, serve at a later time on active duty unless they are declared physically unfit for military service. If deferred beyond their twenty-seventh birthday, they remained in the reserves, subject to periodic refresher training. All qualified male citizens remained in the armed forces reserve until their 15th birthday.

The quality of military manpower, particularly of the Great Russian element, was generally good. The Great Russians comprised about 53 percent of the total population. Soviet youths were physically hardy as a result of participation in active sports programs. They were also better educated, more sophisticated, and substantially better trained than their World War II predecessors. Although the conscript received stern discipline and intensive political indoctrination, works hard, and had few comforts or luxuries and little time to himself, his morale was relatively high. He had a genuine love of his native land. His hatred was easily aroused against an invading enemy, of which there have been many in Russia's and the Soviet Union's history. Moreover, Soviet soldiers and sailors have the capacity to withstand deprivations. The Soviet officer was a well-regarded professional who occupies a high social and economic position in society. The officer corps, with its prestige and privileges, stood apart from the troops. In summary, the Soviet armed forces, loyal to the regime, constituted a serious adversary; they were on a par with their counterparts in the West.

## Officers

Officers for the Soviet armed forces entered the service from several sources. The largest number were commissioned upon graduation from military colleges. There were at least 143 military colleges, with average enrollments of 1,000, serving all branches of the armed forces. Besides commissions, graduates receive technical degrees from three-year schools and engineering degrees from schools whose programs can last up to five years.

The Soviets also conducted programs similar to the US ROTC in their universities. These programs gave training in subjects of military value and provide the Soviets with a large number of reserve officers. Military training for the duration of the civilian curriculum leads to a reserve commission, but only infrequently does it lead to active duty. Reserve officer graduates of this program remain liable for active duty call-up until age 30; they may face up to three years of service.

A third source of officer recruitment was the rank and file of soldiers and sailors. Upon completion of their active duty service, conscripts who had a secondary or higher education could earn a lieutenant's commission in the reserves by passing a commissioning examination. Warrant officers, too, could use the commissioning examination as a route to active duty officer rank; they can also receive a direct commission after ten years of active service

Approximately 500,000 officers were on active duty in the Soviet armed forces at any given time. Three to five thousand of these officers were generals and admirals. Nearly 90 percent of Soviet officers belonged to the Communist Party or to the Komsomal. Seven percent of the members of the Communist Party of the Soviet Union (CPSU) Central Committee were military officers.

### Warrant Officers

In January 1972, the Soviets created the warrant officer ranks of praporshchik (army) and michman (navy). This action was an attempt to give the career NCO more incentive, to eliminate the extended service conscript (though this action was later rescinded), and to improve the quality of small unit leadership. Conscripts completing their service obligations and desiring to remain on active duty may apply for these positions if they possess the required education, demonstrated ability, and political reliability. The initial term of service for a warrant officer is five years.

These warrant officers served in close contact with the soldiers and occupy positions as first sergeants, sergeants major, and technical specialists. Although the Soviet press publicizes them as the closest assistants to the officers, the warrant officer ranks are apparently less popular than anticipated. To date, this new program has received too few qualified applicants. The Law of Military Service permits a warrant officer to take an examination to become a lieutenant after five years; after ten years, he may be certified as an officer if he is serving in an officer's position.

### Noncommissioned Officers

The majority of NCOs in the armed forces were conscripts. During registration and induction, authorities identify outstanding conscripts as potential NCOs. Immediately after entering active service, these individuals attended NCO schools for six months of training before they report to units for their remaining active duty. Other outstanding individuals missed during this initial screening receive on-the-job NCO training in their units.

Noncommissioned officers also filled the extended service personnel category. To qualify for this category, a candidate for reenlistment must have completed high school or the equivalent; he cannot he over 35 years of age. He may apply (or reapply) for extensions of two, four, or six years. His branch of service then prolongs his tour of duty according to the branch personnel requirements. As with warrant officer selection, acceptance depends on the candidate's political reliability and military record. Recruiting takes place three months before discharge, with screening conducted by a permanent committee. This committee includes the political officer and secretaries of the Communist Party and Komsomol organizations. Final approval rests with the individual's commander. Former service personnel can return to active duty under this program.

## Conditions of Service

Service in the Soviet armed forces offers potential rewards such as promotion, pay, in-service benefits, and a pension. Conversely, it requires vigorous training, strict discipline, thorough political indoctrination, and adherence to Communist Party policies.

# III. Process-driven Tactics, Techniques, & Procedures (TTPs)

To ensure success in this complex synchronized form of mechanized maneuver warfare, RTA depends wholly on established and prescriptive processes. Such conventional processes make up the doctrine. Doctrine is studied in depth and is adhered to faithfully, unquestionably.

The Soviet military tradition is far from the only military to rely on process-driven tactics. Indeed, British Commonwealth armies only began to wean away from linear process-driven tactics in the Second World War.

Today numerous nations around the world still employ the process-driven tactics of RTA – Russia, China, North Korea, Iran, and numerous armies throughout the Middle East, North Africa, plus Central and South America. Rightfully so.

To understand why, one has to grasp the composite nature of the RTA. Nations who build RTA often have either a strict autocratic leadership that refuses to share power, or diverse ethnic groups who do not speak a common language, or both.

*RTA prescriptive drill is a viable solution for language barriers between diverse ethnicities.. (Courtesy of Hae-jung Larsen and OP EASTWIND.)*

*RTA sergeants are responsible for enforcing fire and march discipline in battle, as well enforcing unit regulations in day-to-day routine. Yet sergeants are not viewed as professional leaders in RTA forces. Instead they are trusted warriors. (Courtesy of Hae-jung Larsen and OP EASTWIND.)*

If the six artillery troops working on a gun cannot speak to each other except through the most rudimentary battle drill, that very prescriptive process becomes critically important for success.

Likewise, if an infantry platoon commander lacks the decision-making authority to vary from any plan, the prescriptive process of the battle order must be adhered to faithfully and without question.

It's easy to be critical of this overly prescriptive, process-driven tactical tradition from a Western military perspective. The battlespace is incredibly and inexplicably dynamic. Strict adherence to any single set of orders would seem to be doomed to failure.

To offset this probability, RTA officers are highly educated men who develop a simple plan, but a complex series of branches and sequences. For every contingency the RTA leader creates a new plan. It is an exhaustive but workable solution, placing enormous emphasis on the commander's capability and shares none of the authority or decision-making with subordinates.

Additionally, subordinate teams, crews and individuals understand the system. As such they know they must rehearse their drill until it becomes second nature. After all, battle drills are not tactics, but they are the micro-tactics that make up the larger scheme of fire and maneuver. In this manner, through exhaustively rehearsed battle drills, subordinate teams, crews and individuals learn to quickly adjust to the commander's new battle order for contingencies, branches and sequels.

Decision-making authority is not shared in the RTA. It belongs to the commander alone. Subordinate leaders and sergeants enforce the commander's authority, but do not share in it.

Because of this, RTA doctrine values prescriptive, process-driven tactics and battle drill. And again, this approach has been found to alleviate language and educational barriers between diverse ethnic groups when working closely together. But the plan must be simple, and it must be redundant.

# IV. Training the RTA Force

*Ref: FM-100-2-3 The Soviet Army, chap 3.*

The officer corps makes up the professional nucleus of RTA forces. Scholars receive at least the equivalent of a bachelor degree prior to their commission as an officer, and many branches such as engineering require a master degree at the minimum. Officers must undergo further training and education in doctrine and junior officers serve in a variety of staff and service support roles prior to being assigned a coveted command position. In this manner, the junior officer's leadership competencies are mentored carefully before being offered a leadership post.

RTA forces most commonly recruit through compulsory conscription. Conscript troops serve on average two years of service and then return to civilian life, though some annual training may be required in the national reserve forces.

A small percentage of senior enlisted troops and junior sergeants who demonstrate adept competency in their craft are offered the opportunity to remain in service on a multiple-year contract. Such contracts are the path to a military career and retirement benefits. Contracted troops make up the backbone of the junior leadership and technical specialists of RTA forces.

Conscript troops receive initial and advanced individual training over a three to six month period. These troops are then sent forward as replacements to regimental units. There they will receive further specialized training unique to the regiment's mission.

*Conscript troops make up the bulk of RTA forces. They typically serve two years. (Courtesy of* Hae-jung Larsen *and OP EASTWIND.)*

Compensation, salary and vacation time are meager for enlisted troops and junior sergeants, but often enough the military is the only means for these men to work outside of their villages and tribes. A life in the military is hard, but it offers adventure and travel that would otherwise be exclusive to the upper caste of society. Too, contractual military service as a career may be the only upward mobility afforded to the son of a farmer or livestock herder. The military uniform brings a measure of respect.

# (Red Team Armies) IV. Force Structure

*Ref: FM 100-2-1 The Soviet Army: Operations and Tactics (Jul '84), chap 1 and FM 100-2-3 The Soviet Army: Troops, Organization, and Equipment (Jun '91), chap 1.*

The Soviet armed forces include five separate components: the strategic rocket forces, the ground forces, the air forces, the air defense forces, and the naval forces. The generic term "Soviet Army" normally includes all but the naval forces.

## I. Troop Categories

For administrative purposes, the Soviet ground forces comprise three categories: combat arms branches (troops), special troops, and services. These are administrative categories pertaining to personnel, not organization categories pertaining to units. Thus, troops of one combat arms branch, such as artillery, may organizationally be in support units subordinate to a unit made up of troops of another combat arms branch (for example, motorized rifle or tank). These support units may also include special troops and services.

### A. Combat Arms Branches

The firing elements of the ground forces comprise combat arms branches (troops). They differ from one another in organization, armament, tactics, and role in combat. Directorates of Ground Forces Headquarters administer the troop branches peculiar to the ground forces.

#### Motorized Rifle

Motorized rifle troops generally parallel the infantry and mechanized infantry of other armies. These troops constitute the basic arm of the ground forces; therefore, various agencies under the Ground Forces CINC, rather than one special organization, administer their affairs. These agencies prescribe motorized rifle and combined arms tactics and organization. They prepare training schedules for motorized rifle and combined arms units. They also administer motorized rifle schools and manage motorized rifle officer person-nel. Other arms and services provide them with logistic support.

#### Tank

The Chief of Tank Troops in Ground Forces Headquarters heads this branch. A Main Directorate of Tank Troops supports him. The Main Directorate is an intricate organization which acts as an administrative headquarters. Tank troop officers command tank units at all levels. Combined arms formations feature a special staff officer as chief of tank troops. He commands subordinate tank elements and reports to the combined arms commander.

#### Missile Troops and Artillery

This is one of the most prestigious branches of the ground forces or the MOD. Artillery troops have long held an honorable position in Russian military annals. In recent decades, technological advances in missile weaponry have enhanced that position. Since missile armaments have also become important to other components, the MOD generally oversees missile equipment development.

### Air Defense Troops (Voyska PVO)

This branch recentlv became a separate component combining air defense elements formerly under the National Air Defense Troops (PVO Strany) and the Air Defense Troops of the Ground Forces (PVO Sukhoputnykh Voysk). Although MOD headquarters now administers them, the troops may serve under combined arms command in the field during wartime. They coordinate closely with aviation and radiotechnical elements in operational matters. Air defense schools previously under the ground forces now belong to the Air Defense Troops.

### Airborne

Airborne troops form a reserve force of the Supreme High Command (VGK) or the wartime Stauka VGK, although operational control of them specifically belongs to the Chief of the General Staff.

The troops are not subordinate to a ground forces field command until the VGK commits them. This definite separation suggests that they have the status of a sixth distinct component of the armed forces, even though they are nominally subordinate to the CINC, Ground Forces, because of this special status.

## B. Special Troops

The special troops provide combat support to the combined arms field forces of the ground forces. They also support the other components of the armed forces. For this reason, they are administered centrally from directorates in the MOD. Ground Forces Headquarters, however, contains specialized directorates or departments in each of the combat support areas to deal with specific ground forces problems. These directorates act as a ground forces administrative echelon for the superior MOD directorates.

- Engineer
- Signal
- Chemical
- Motor Transport
- Railroad
- Road

## C. Services

The Soviet concept of services includes all troops, installations, and duty positions which perform rear area support for the combat arms branches and special troops. Such services are not specific to the ground forces, but support the other armed forces components as well; therefore, various agencies in the MOD administer them. These services differ from the special troops because they apparently have no intermediate administrative directorates at Ground Forces Headquarters.

- Medical
- Veterinary
- Military Topographic
- Finance
- Justice
- Military Band
- Intendance (Quartemaster)
- Administrative

# II. Groupings of Forces

## Front

The front is the largest field formation in war-time. It is an operational and administrative unit whose size and composition are subject to wide variation depending on its mission and situation. Roughly equivalent to a US/NATO army group, a front can include three to five armies. Other forces organic or attached to a front can include artillery, missile, air defense, engineer, chemical, signal, reconnaissance, and rear service units. They can also include aviation, airborne, air assault, airmobile, and special purpose forces.

## Army

The Army is the highest peacetime combined arms formation. The Soviet ground forces designate two types of armies: the combined arms army (CAA) and the tank army (TA). By altering the mix of MRDs, TDs, and artillery and missile support in the army organizations, the Soviets gain flexibility in either offensive or defensive roles.

### Combined Arms Army (CAA)

The combined arms army is an operational and administrative organization; it is the basic Soviet field army. A typical combined arms army includes two to four motorized rifle divisions and one or two tank divisions, plus artillery, missile, air defense, engineer, chemical defense, signal, intelligence, reconnaissance, and rear support units.

### Tank Army (TA)

The Tank Army. The tank army is an operational and administrative unit, and, like the combined arms army, is a basic component of a front. The size and composition of the army will depend on the mission, the situa tion, and the area of operations. A typical tank army includes two to four tank divisions and one or two motorized rifle divisions, plus artillery, missile, air defense, engineer, chemical defense, signal, intelligence, reconnaissance, and rear service units. A typical role of a tank army is to exploit penetrations deep into the enemy's rear areas.

## Manuever Divisions

There are three basic types of maneuver divisions in the Soviet ground forces: motorized rifle, tank, and airborne. They have a combined arms structure as well as a comprehensive array of combat support (CS) and combat service support (CSS) elements.

| MOTORIZED RIFLE DIVISION | TANK DIVISION | AIRBORNE DIVISION |
|---|---|---|
| Division Headquarters | Division Headquarters | Division Headquarters |
| Motorized Rifle Regiment (BMP) | Motorized Rifle Regiment (BMP) | Airborne Regiment (BMD) |
| Motorized Rifle Regiment (BTR) | Tank Regiment | Airborne Regiment (BMD) |
| Motorized Rifle Regiment (BTR) | Tank Regiment | Airborne Regiment (BMD) |
| Tank Regiment | Tank Regiment | Assault Gun Battalion |
| Artillery Regiment | Artillery Regiment | Artillery Regiment |
| SAM Regiment | SAM Regiment | AA Battalion |
| SSM Battalion | SSM Battalion | |
| Antitank Battalion | | |
| Reconnaissance Battalion | Reconnaissance Battalion | Reconnaissance Company |
| Engineer Battalion | Engineer Battalion | Engineer Battalion |
| Signal Battalion | Signal Battalion | Signal Battalion |
| Materiel Support Battalion | Materiel Support Battalion | Transportation and Maintenance Battalion |
| Maintenance Battalion | Maintenance Battalion | |
| Chemical Protection Company | Chemical Protection Company | Chemical Protection Company |
| Medical Battalion | Medical Battalion | Medical Battalion |
| Artillery Command Battery | Artillery Command Battery | |
| Helicopter Squadron | Helicopter Squadron | |
| Other Support Elements | Other Support Elements | Other Support Elements |

# III. Force Structure

The Soviets have organized and equipped their ground forces to support their defensive doctrine. Moreover, they are constantly strengthening and modernizing their organization and equipment to improve their capabilities to fight either nuclear or nonnuclear war. A nuclear exchange in Europe could easily cause tremendous damage to the Soviet Union. Therefore, the Soviets clearly want to be able to fight and win a war in Europe quickly, before either side employs nuclear weapons.

The Soviets have determined that the only way to win such a war is by offensive operations. The Soviet concept of the offensive emphasizes surprise and high rates of advance combined with over-whelming firepower. The concept of combined arms is at the heart of Soviet combat doctrine.

## Major Geographical Groupings

The Soviets organize ground forces by geo-graphical boundaries into theaters of war (TVs), theaters of military operation (TVDs), and military districts and groups of forces. They can organize forces into large field formations called fronts and armies.

### TV

The Soviets envision that hostilities might occur in any of three TVs: the Western, the Southern, and the Far Eastern. A TV is a broad, geo-graphically oriented designation within which Soviet armed forces would function in wartime. A continental TV can include land, air space, and assorted internal and coastal waterways. The Western TV, for example, includes the European land mass and associated islands, the associated air space, the Baltic and Mediterranean Seas, and portions of the Arctic and Atlantic Oceans. The TVs have political and economic significance in shaping Soviet military goals. They contain one or more TVDs.

### TVD

The TVD geographical concept is the focus of planning and control for employment of Soviet armed forces in major theater strategic actions. The Soviet planners divide the world into 14 TVDs: 10 continental TVDs and 4 oceanic TVDs. The continental TVDs include not onlv the land masses, but also the air space, inland waterways, and a segment of the surrounding oceans and seas. The Western TVD of the Western TV, for example, includes NATO's Central Region plus Denmark and the Danish Straits.

In wartime, the Soviets would employ intermediate High Commands of Forces (HCF) that would be responsible to the VGK. In keeping with the Soviet concept of centralized control and com-bined arms operations, the TVD HCF not only controls the assets available in the ground forces, but also the naval and air assets. Some, if not all, of the non-Soviet Warsaw Pact forces might also be subordinate to a TVD HCF. The TVD's most important function in wartime would be to orchestrate and control TVD-wide strategic operations as directed by the HCF in support of VGK campaign plans.

Forces within a TVD can consist of as few as one front or as many as five or six. Other forces allocated to a TVD can include fleets, airborne divisions, tactical aviation, strategic aviation, military transport aviation, air defense forces, and strategic rocket forces.

# V. The Motorized Rifle Regiment (MRR)



*Ref: FM-100-2-3 The Soviet Army: Troops, Organization and Equipment, chap. 4 and 5, and FM 100-63 Infantry-Based Opposing Force, chap 3.*

## I. The Motorized Rifle Regiment (MRR)

At the heart of the RTA is the Motorized Rifle Regiment (MRR). The MRR is the default maneuver organization. The MRR offers far greater mobility and logistical capacity over light infantry units, which are employed only within a very narrow scope of missions and therefore are not favored.

Motorized infantry formations employ costly armored vehicles; air assault infantry units require much more expensive helicopter formations. Even the relatively cheap paratroop infantry units require expensive fixed-wing transport aircraft, plus the airfields and instillations necessary to store and repair these vehicles.

Whether the MRR is equipped with heavy tracked or lighter wheeled armored vehicles, or heavy, medium, or light all-wheel drive trucks, the MRR retains mobility as its primary asset. Whereas a light infantry formation may cover 20 miles in a day's march, the MRR can cover 200 miles just as quickly. It arrives with rested troops, ready to fight. And the MRR arrives with greater capacity in terms of small arms capability and logistical supplies to keep it in the fight longer than any light infantry formation.

Yet again, the MRR costs just a fraction of the cost of expensive airmobile formations. So the MRR just makes good sense from a cost to benefit ratio.

# II. Organizational Structure of the MRR

*Ref: FM-100-2-3 The Soviet Army: Troops, Organization and Equipment, chap. 4.*

There is no single solution for the MRR organization of combat power, though all regiments at least nominally follow the Soviet model.

## A. Motorized Rifle Regiment

Major units within the MRR include usually three rifle battalions, a tank battalion, an artillery battalion, and several specialized companies including headquarters, logistics and air defense. The MRR totals roughly 2,300 troops.

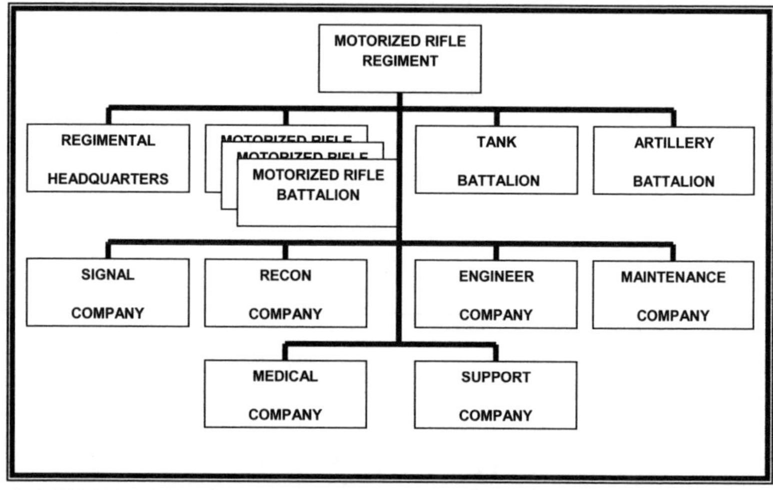


*Ref: FM 100-2-3 The Soviet Army: Troops, Organization and Equipment, p. 4-2.*

## B. Motorized Rifle Battalion

The motorized rifle battalion includes typically three rifle companies, a heavy weapons company including a mortar platoon and anti-armor platoon, plus a separate headquarters platoon. Each battalion totals roughly 475 troops.

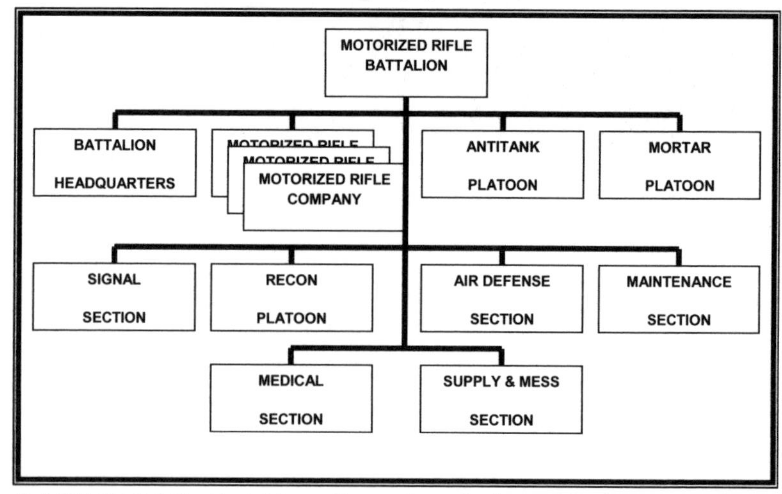


*Ref: FM 100-2-3 The Soviet Army: Troops, Organization and Equipment, p. 4-8.*

## C. Motorized Rifle Company

The motorized rifle company includes three rifle platoons and one headquarters section. The company totals 110 troops.

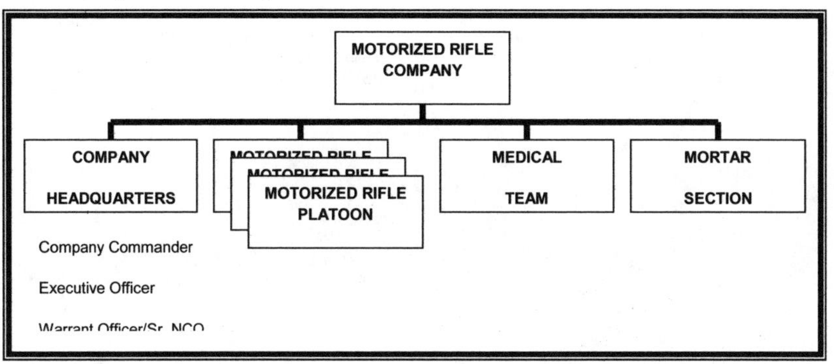


*Ref: FM 100-2-3 The Soviet Army: Troops, Organization and Equipment, p. 4-4.*

## D. Motorized Rifle Platoon

The rifle platoon consists of three squads and one platoon commander and radioman. The platoon totals 32 troops.

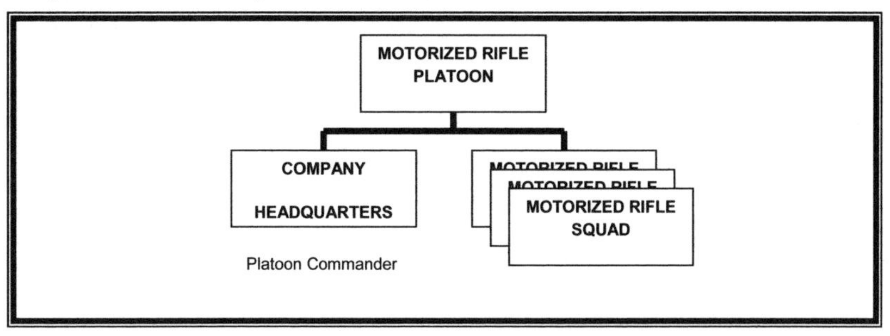


*Ref: FM 100-2-3 The Soviet Army: Troops, Organization and Equipment, p. 4-3.*

## E. Motorized Rifle Squad

The rifle squad consists of a leader, deputy leader, machine gunner and assistant, rocket/ grenadier and assistant, two riflemen, and armor crew. The squad totals 10 troops.

The Soviet 9-man squad was used for decades, being coupled with the BTR series armored vehicles and the venerable BMP-1. However, with the introduction of the BMP-2 and BMP-3 series vehicles, the squad was decreased by one position. The modern RTA squad has eight troops to dismount, including a squad leader and deputy leader. The bronegruppa has an additional 2 or 3-man team, depending on the type of vehicle.

*See following page for an overview of a motorized rifle squad.*

Continued on next page

Continued on next page

Continued from previous page

# Organizational Structure of the MRR (Cont.)

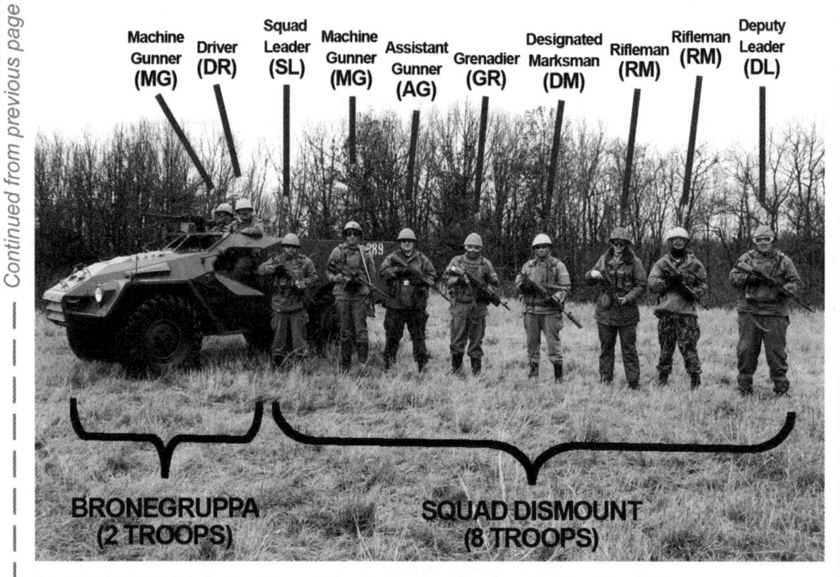


*Ref: FM 100-63 Infantry-Based Opposing Force, chap 3. The Soviet 9-man squad was used for decades, being coupled with the BTR series armored vehicles and the venerable BMP-1. However, with the introduction of the BMP-2 and BMP-3 series vehicles, the squad was decreased by one position. The modern RTA squad has eight troops to dismount, including a squad leader and deputy leader. The bronegruppa has an additional 2 or 3-man team, depending on the type of vehicle. (Courtesy of Hae-jung Larsen and OP EASTWIND.)*

## F. Motorized Bronegruppa

The armor crew (bronegruppa, pronounced "BROAN-group-ah") consists of the vehicle heavy machine gunner, plus the driver. The bronegruppa-armor crew is typically 2 troops. However the term bronegruppa refers to any collection of armored vehicles and their crew when operating independently or temporarily separated from the assigned infantry troops. In such cases the larger element is usually applied, such as platoon bronegruppa or company bronegruppa.

Continued from previous page

Note that the RTA does not break down its maneuver force below the squad, unlike Western armies that further break the squad into fireteams. Of course the squad includes various crews such as the bronegruppa, and machine gunners, and rocket/grenadiers that may certainly be attached to another unit. But the squad is the smallest element of maneuver in the RTA.

This plays further importance due to the ad hoc nature of RTA, which favors task-based organization. This means for each task or mission, the RTA will form into a new battalion, company, or even platoon based on the task at hand. But the RTA will almost never adjust the squad because they have trained and rehearsed the battle drill so exhaustively. Trying to reorganize the squad will almost invariably result in failure.

Now of course the platoon may elect to attach special crews to the squad, such as an extra machinegun or rocket/grenadier crew. But again, they rarely ever break apart or mix together the squad.

# III. MRR Equipment

*Ref: FM-100-2-3 The Soviet Army, chap. 5.*



## A. Tracked IFVs (Infantry Fighting Vehicles)

The most formidable MRR employ tracked infantry fighting vehicles such as the venerable Russian BMP armored vehicle. In some cases RTA nations purchase French AMX-10 series, or Chinese ZBD series armored vehicles.

BMP-1

AMX-10

ZBD-05

*The more formidable MRR (often referred to as "tier-one" regiments) include heavy tracked armored infantry carriers such as the prolific Russian-made BMP series. However RTA forces may also employ the French-made AMX-10 or the more recent Chinese-made ZBD-05 armored fighting vehicles. (Courtesy US Army & OP EASTWIND.)*

Continued on next page

Continued on next page

Continued from previous page

# III. MRR Equipment (Cont.)

## B. Light Armored Vehicles

MRR units most commonly employ wheeled armored vehicles such as the Russian BTR series, Swiss-made Piranha series, or South African Ratel series. Lighter armor vehicles would include armored trucks such as the Russian Tigr, or French Renault Sherpa, or even the Canadian Titan series.

*In contrast to heavy, tracked armored vehicles, lighter armored wheeled vehicles are more affordable when considering the purchase, maintenance and operation of such vehicles. Wheeled armored vehicles also travel faster and cause less damaged to developed roads. Such vehicles are ideal for small RTA nations with good interior roads for reinforcing forces. Most commonly the Russian-made BTR-60, 70, or 80 series are employed. But again, RTA forces may also employ the French-made AMX and South African Ratel vehicle. The French Sherpa, Russian Tigr and Canadian Titan are all recently introduced vehicles that very feasibly could round out RTA forces. (Courtesy US Army & OP EASTWIND.)*

Continued from previous page

## C. Wheeled Transports

At the very minimum, MRR units employ thin-skinned troop transports such as heavy 6x6 wheel drive Russian Ural, Polish Raba H-18, or even American M35 series trucks. Alternatively they may use medium 4x4 vehicles such as the Russian GAZ-66 and its newer variant the GAZ Sadko, or Swiss/German Unimog. Lastly MRR may employ light 4x4 wheel drive vehicles such as the popular Toyota or Ford F150 series pickup trucks.

*Tier-three or reserve regiments are commonly outfitted with wheeled transport vehicles. The idea is that these troops need to move to blocking positions, rear guard service, or will be used to fill personnel losses in tier-one and tier-two units. Large, three axel vehicles such as the Russian-made Ural and Polish-made Raba H-18 can move entire platoons at a time. The prolific Russian GAZ-66 and versatile Swiss Unimog are ideal for moving supplies and a squad or more at a time. East German UAZ and Russian GAZ scout cars, plus the highly mobile Toyota pickup truck are common for reconnaissance roles and even crew-served weapon platforms. (Courtesy US Army & OP EASTWIND.)*

# D. Small Arm Weapons

Squads are equipped with rifle or carbine, most commonly the Kalashnikov weapons in 7.62x39mm (AKM and side-folding AKMS variant) or in 5.45x39mm (AK-74 also available in the folding "S" configuration). Additionally the 8-man dismounted squad most often carries one PKM medium machinegun in 7.62x51mm, one RPK light machinegun and six Kalashnikov weapons, the last of which is commonly fitted with either a 40mm or 30mm grenade launcher tube.

*The machinegun team includes the primary gunner plus an assistant gunner who assists with carrying ammunition, identifying targets, and function of the gun. Often a grenadier is included in the MG team to cover the dead space of defilades. (Courtesy of Hae-jung Larsen and OP EASTWIND.)*

*One of the riflemen is designated the antitank gunner and carries an RPG-7 rocket launcher. This combination of weapons systems permits a squad engagement range out to 800 meters. When used in conjunction with direct fire support from the bronegruppa, the squad has excellent firepower out to 2,000 meters. (Courtesy of Hae-jung Larsen and OP EASTWIND.)*

*It is still the individual rifleman, working in teams who must close with and destroy the enemy. This rifleman carries an AKM and a disposable RPG-26, both of which have a practical range of 200m. Note the tourniquet wrapped around the stock. He also carries two fragmentation hand grenades in pouches on his right back. (Courtesy of Hae-jung Larsen and OP EASTWIND.)*

The MRR squad divides into dismounted infantry and the bronegruppa who stays with the vehicle. In addition to the heavy machinegun or automatic grenade launcher, the bronegruppa driver and vehicle gunner typically carry a pistol such as the Markov PK 9mm, but they may also be issued an AKM.

Vehicle platforms carry various heavy weapons such as the 14.5mm DShKM machinegun, or 12.7mm DShK machinegun, or AGS-30 automatic grenade launcher. At minimum vehicles are armed with a 7.62mm PKM medium machinegun.

| Team/Position | Weapon | Caliber | Rate of Fire | Effective Range |
|---|---|---|---|---|
| ***Bronegruppa*** | | | | |
| Vehicle Gunner | DShK Heavy MG | 12.7mm | 500 RpM | **2,000m** |
| Driver | AKM | 7.62x39mm | 700 RpM | 200m |
| ***Squad*** | | | | |
| Squad Leader | AKM | 7.62x39mm | 700 RpM | 200m |
| Deputy Leader | AKM | 7.62x39mm | 700 RpM | 200m |
| Machine Gunner | PKM Medium MG | 7.62.54mm | 600 RpM | **800m** |
| Assist. Gunner | AKM | 7.62x39mm | 700 RpM | 200m |
| Rocket Grenadier | RPG AT Rocket | Various Warheads | 4 RpM | **400m** |
| Assist. Grenadier | AKM | 7.62x39mm | 700 RpM | 200m |
| Machine Gunner | RPK Light MG | 7.62x39mm | 700 RpM | **400m** |
| Rifleman | AKM | 7.62x39mm | 700 RpM | 200m |

## E. Communication Systems

Because RTA forces have begun to operate as dismounted platoons and squads, independent of the bronegruppa, portable communications have become all the more necessary. And as these critical communication systems become more robust and more reliable, in turn they enhance the distance from which a dismounted patrol can operate away from the bronegruppa and company command. This technology has had a dynamic impact on small unit capabilities for RTA forces in recent decades.

*The larger Russian-made R-159 radio mirrors closely the US-made A/N PRC-77 in terms of size, weight, and capability. It is excellent for battalion, company and platoon radio networks. Smaller radios with more limited ranges such as the R-126 and R-392 are very capable and suitable for platoon and inter-squad communication networks. (Courtesy of Hae-jung Larsen and OP EASTWIND.)*

## F. Navigation Systems

Though still rarely distributed below the officer ranks, RTA forces do have in their inventories dismounted troop compasses suitable for field navigation. But perhaps most impressive is the GLONASS GPS system developed by Russia for internal agency use, and now available to even the civilian market. GPS technology did not pass by China and Russia, and so advanced, rugged, and portable GPS systems are available to RTA forces at the company, platoon and squad level.

## G. Targeting Systems

Night vision devices in RTA forces are much less prolific, and in some cases are almost impossible to come by. Nonetheless, some RTA forces employ advanced night vision capabilities in terms of active light, passive light, and thermal imaging devices.

For navigation and vehicle operation the Russian-made ON-3 passive light goggles are robust and capable, if a bit uncomfortable for any lengthy period of use. The dated but still very much in service 1PN-58 active/passive night vision scope is impressive in its own right, and is also fairly common among RTA forces. More recent additions to RTA capabilities include the hand-held X100 series thermal imaging devices.

If night vision devices are considered sub-standard by Western military standards, RTA daytime optics will stand up to the best any other military can offer. The perennial favorite through the past several decades has been the SVD riflescope – called the POSP 4x26mm with illuminated retical. More recent additions to daytime optics include the Russian Pancreatic 2x10x52mm riflescope, and the Russian Baigish BPO 7x30mm binocular.

# IV. On Point: Deep Battle & the Kalashnikov

In theory the RTA can arm itself with any small arms weapon. In practice, however, the perennial favorite is the Kalashnikov (AKM) series weapon due in part to the vast quantities produced and distributed globally over the past 60 years. It is available, and the AKM has become the icon of RTA small arms.

Strategically speaking the AKM is still a viable choice due to its relative affordability. At an operational level of warfare the AKM is simple to maintain and requires very little logistical support beyond ammunition. And at a tactical level, the AKM is easy to learn and robust enough to maintain the fight.

Certainly there are far better performing small arms rifle and carbine. Yet the AKM is further bolstered by a combination of small arms within the company, platoon and squad.

Even when operating without the direct fires of the bronegruppa or indirect fires from company and battalion mortars, the dismounted squad has the integral firepower to effectively disrupt enemy formations at 800 meters; adequately suppress an enemy force at 400 meters; and at 200 meters the squad can destroy an enemy force quite readily in an equal match.

There is much dispute over the effective range of the AKM. AKM aficionados insist the weapon has an effective range of 400 meters, and AKM detractors insist the weapon has a maximum effective range of just 200 meters.

The AKM series weapon was created for the MRR in "deep battle" concept. Deep battle prescribes a model of find, disrupt, fix, and destroy. To find the enemy is understood. To disrupt means to interrupt the opponents attempt to link with other enemy units and coordinate a response. To fix the enemy means to isolate the target through suppressive fires and therefore commit the enemy to battle. To destroy an enemy force is the desired effect or outcome of deep battle.

Once an enemy force is found, regimental artillery and battalion mortars provide indirect fires to disrupt the enemy. The enemy force is then fixed from company and platoon bronegruppa at distances of 500 meters out to 2000 meters depending on terrain. When the small arms of the dismounted platoon and squad are brought to bear, PKM machinegun and SVD sniper rifles further break up and isolate enemy positions with precision fires out to 800 meters, allowing the dismounted troops to maneuver within a striking distance of 200 meters or less. Finally the enemy is destroyed as the platoon and squad sweep across the objective at point blank range.

*An AK-74 in 5.45x39mm and its predecessor the AKM in 7.62x39mm rest in a bivouac rifle rack with Soviet and East German flags in the background. The Kalashnikov has become the iconoclast symbol of RTA forces. (Courtesy of Hae-jung Larsen and OP EASTWIND.)*

For all the impressive capabilities of advanced rifles of Western armies – M16, Steyr, Sig, FAL, G3, these weapons offer little advantage when on the receiving end of a properly executed deep battle attack.

Chap 2

# Offensive Operations



*Ref: FM 100-2-1 The Soviet Army: Operations and Tactics (Jul '84), chapters 4 & 5.*

The Soviets emphasize swift, efficient movement, or transfer, of combat power from one point on the battlefield to another. This is accomplished by rapid column movement in march formation and successive deployment into prebattle formation and attack formation. Commanders insure that their unit is constantly ready to perform a march, with minimum warning and preparation. Units frequently rehearse the march, and its conduct is strictly controlled. They practice deployment from march column into prebattle and attack formation in standard battle drills. These formations and drills are designed for a rapid transition into combat while maintaining maximum security, speed, and firepower.

## Offensive Operations

**Attack** *(pp. 2-13 to 2-32)*

- Attack Against a Defending Enemy
- Attack from the March
- Attack from a Position in Direct Contact

**Meeting Engagement** *(pp. 2-33 to 2-35)*

**Pursuit** *(p. 2-36)*

Offensive actions are combat operations conducted to defeat and destroy enemy forces and seize terrain, resources, and population centers. They impose the commander's will on the enemy. A commander may also conduct offensive actions to deprive the enemy of resources, seize decisive terrain, deceive or divert the enemy, develop intelligence, or hold an enemy in position. This chapter discusses the basics of the offense. The basics discussed in this chapter apply to all offensive tasks.

The commander seizes, retains, and exploits the initiative when conducting offensive actions. Specific operations may orient on a specific enemy force or terrain feature as a means of affecting the enemy. Even when conducting primarily defensive actions, wresting the initiative from the enemy requires offensive actions.

Effective offensive operations capitalize on accurate intelligence regarding the enemy, terrain and weather, and civil considerations. Commanders maneuver their forces to advantageous positions before making contact. However, commanders may shape conditions by deliberately making contact to develop the situation and mislead the enemy. In the offense, the decisive operation is a sudden, shattering

# Tasks of Decisive Action (U.S. Military Doctrine Perspective)

*Ref: The Army Operations & Doctrine SMARTbook (5th Rev. Ed.), The Lightning Press, pp. 1-28 to 1-29 (ADRP 3-0 Operations, pp. 2-4 to 2-8).*

In U.S.military doctrine "decisive action" requires simultaneous combinations of offense, defense, and stability or defense support of civil authorities tasks.

## A. Offensive Tasks

An offensive task is a task conducted to defeat and destroy enemy forces and seize terrain, resources, and population centers. Offensive tasks impose the commander's will on the enemy. In combined arms maneuver, the offense is a task of decisive action. Against a capable, adaptive enemy, the offense is the most direct and a sure means of seizing, retaining, and exploiting the initiative to gain physical and psychological advantages and achieve definitive results. In the offense, the decisive operation is a sudden, shattering action against an enemy weakness that capitalizes on speed, surprise, and shock. If that operation does not destroy the enemy, operations continue until enemy forces disintegrate or retreat to where they no longer pose a threat.

### Offensive Tasks

**Primary Tasks**

- Movement to contact
- Attack
- Exploitation
- Pursuit

**Purposes**

- Dislocate, isolate, disrupt and destroy enemy forces
- Seize key terrain
- Deprive the enemy of resources
- Develop intelligence
- Deceive and divert the enemy
- Create a secure environment for stability operations

### Defensive Tasks

**Primary Tasks**

- Mobile defense
- Area defense
- Retrograde

**Purposes**

- Deter or defeat enemy offensive operations
- Gain time
- Achieve economy of force
- Retain key terrain
- Protect the populace, critical assets and infrastructure
- Develop intelligence

## B. Defensive Tasks

A defensive task is a task conducted to defeat an enemy attack, gain time, economize forces, and develop conditions favorable for offensive or stability tasks. Normally the defense alone cannot achieve a decision. However, it can set conditions for a counteroffensive or counterattack that enables Army forces to regain the initiative. Defensive tasks can also establish a shield behind which wide area security can progress. Defensive tasks are a counter to the enemy offense. They defeat attacks, destroying as much of the attacking enemy as possible. They also preserve and maintain control over land, resources, and populations. The purpose of defensive tasks is to retain terrain, guard populations, and protect critical capabilities against enemy attacks. Commanders can conduct defensive tasks to gain time and economize forces so offensive tasks can be executed elsewhere.

## C. Stability Tasks

Stability is an overarching term encompassing various military missions, tasks, and activities conducted outside the United States in coordination with other instruments of national power to maintain or reestablish a safe and secure environment, provide essential governmental services, emergency infrastructure reconstruction, and humanitarian relief. (See JP 3-0.) Army forces conduct stability tasks during both combined arms maneuver and wide area security. These tasks support a host-nation or an interim government or part of a transitional military authority when no government exists. Stability tasks involve both coercive and constructive actions. They help to establish or maintain a safe and secure environment and facilitate reconciliation among local or regional adversaries. Stability tasks can also help establish political, legal, social, and economic institutions while supporting the transition to legitimate host-nation governance. Stability tasks cannot succeed if they only react to enemy initiatives.

### Stability Tasks

**Primary Tasks**

- Establish civil security (including security force asst)
- Establish civil control
- Restore essential services
- Support to governance
- Support to economic and infrastructure development

**Purposes**

- Provide a secure environment
- Secure land areas
- Meet the critical needs of the populace
- Gain support for host-nation government
- Shape the environment for interagency and host-nation success

## D. Defense Support of Civil Authority Tasks

DSCA is support provided by U.S. Federal military forces, Department of Defense civilians, Department of Defense contract personnel, Department of Defense component assets, and National Guard forces (when the Secretary of Defense, in coordination with the Governors of the affected States, elects and requests to use those forces in Title 32, U.S. Code, status). This support is in response to requests for assistance from civil authorities for domestic emergencies, law enforcement support, and other domestic activities, or from qualifying entities for special events. Defense support of civil authorities is always conducted in support of another primary or lead federal agency.

### Defense Support of Civil Authorities Tasks

**Primary Tasks**

- Provide support for domestic disasters
- Provide support for domestic CBRN incidents
- Provide support for domestic civilian law enforcement agencies
- Provide other designated support

**Purposes**

- Save lives
- Restore essential services
- Maintain or restore law and order
- Protect infrastructure and property
- Maintain or restore local government
- Shape the environment for interagency success

*Refer to The Army Operations & Doctrine SMARTbook (Guide to Unified Land Operations and the Six Warfighting Functions) for discussion of the fundamentals, principles and tenets of Army operations, plus chapters on each of the six warfighting functions: mission command, movement and maneuver, intelligence, fires, sustainment, and protection.*

action against enemy weakness that capitalizes on speed, surprise, and shock. If that operation does not destroy the enemy, operations continue until enemy forces disintegrate or retreat to where they are no longer a threat.

The offense is the default mode of operations for the RTA. It is the means by which the RTA imposes its will upon an enemy. Considerable resources are given to units that are conducting offensive actions, all the more true if that unit is appreciating significant gain within the battlespace.

RTA offensive operations may be directed against an enemy force, terrain, or enemy resources such as facilities or materiel supplies as the main objective.

Furthermore, RTA offensive action may come in the form of a detailed and deliberate attack against fortified enemy positions, or it may come in the form of a movement to contact against a dispersed enemy force that is conducting a mobile defense or retrograde.

Whichever the case, the RTA almost invariably employs classic “hammer and anvil” tactics to trap the enemy objective between two or more RTA forces.

Chap 2

# (Offensive Operations) I. Front & Army Operations

Offensive Operations

*Ref: FM 100-2-1 The Soviet Army: Operations and Tactics (Jul '84), chapter 4.*

## I. TVD Offensive

Front and army operations normally take place within a theater of military operations (Russian: TVD), encompassing a considerable part of the territory of a continent and comprising a level of command. A TVD offensive has a strategic mission to defeat and destroy enemy field forces, to capture vital territory, and to bring about the political destruction of the enemy.

Offensive operations within a IVD could be supported by-

- Strategic aviation
- Strategic rocket forces
- Airborne forces
- Transport aviation
- Naval and naval infantry furces

Within the TVD, the operational formations are fronts and armies. Afront is a wartime formation comprised of several armies or separate divisions. Its size varies with the mission it is given within the overall strategic operation. An army is the largest peacetime ground maneuver formation at the operational level. In wartime, the composition and size of an army also varies dependent upon mission. An army may be either tank or combined arms. Its structure provides adequate control and ground-based support for the divisions assigned to it during the army's participation in a front operation.

Divisions and smaller organizations are found at the tactical level. The division has a fixed organization and serves as the "building block" and maneuver element of armies. The motorized rifle and tank divisions are balanced, powerful, and mobile organizations capable of operations in a nonnuclear as well as a nuclear environment. At this level, the Soviets emphasize both sustainability and mobility. Organic logistic assets can sustain the division for several days of high-intensity, high-speed combat and are as mobile as the maneuver units.



# II. Front Offensive

The mission of a front offensive is to seize key political and economic centers and concurrently to destroy enemy military forces defending them.

A front offensive involves much more than attacks against enemy forward defensive positions. It involves coordinated, repetitive, intensive strikes throughout the entire depth of enemy field forces. These strikes are accomplished by an initial, massive, nonnuclear air operation, heliborne and airborne assault, possibly coordinated with deep attacks by an operational maneuver group, all available unconventional warfare means, surface-to-surface rockets and missiles, electronic warfare, possible chemical warfare, and, if deemed necessary, nuclear warfare.

The overriding aim in a Soviet front offensive is to delay or prevent the war from turning nuclear by the swift, early destruction or neutralization of enemy nuclear weapons by nonnuclear means. High rates of advance by attacking ground forces, coupled with strikes throughout the rear, are intended to cripple the enemy's ability to respond effectively to the Soviet offensive and to resort to tactical nuclear warfare. The top priority target for Soviet weapons would be enemy nuclear delivery systems.

## A. Offensive Planning

In planning an offensive operation for the front, consideration is always given to those situations in which either side would employ nuclear weapons. Destruction or neutralization of the enemy's nuclear·capable delivery systems is considered essential. Thus, continuous reconnaissance is planned to target those systems with a nuclear capability accumtely. Planning and nonnuclear operations in objectives, employment of forces, main and supporting attacks, and axes of advance. The similarities end, however, in planning the scheme of maneuver and fire support. Normally, conventional operations require successive intermediate operations with a continuous regrouping of forces. Frontal aviation is given the mission to engage targets deep in the enc!my rear area while the artillery has the mission to neutralize the enemy near the FEBA. In contrast, nuclear operations keep the number of intermediate operations to a minimum. Front objectives are attained by employing high speed operations along multiple axes of advance, exploiting the results of the nuclear fire plan.

Planning at front level must support the conduct of operations in the enemy's rear area. Armies assigned to the front-

- **Attack along one or more axes to split the defenders into separate or isolated groups.** These groups are to be destroyed while the offensive is continued toward the enemy's rear area.
- **Attack along converging axes to envelop enemy forces**. These forces are to be destroyed as the offensive continues to the depths of the enemy's defenses.

The width of a front offensive zone could extend to approximately 350 kilometers. The frontage, organization, rate of advance, and concept of the front offensive are all variable based on missions, enemy defenses, terrain, weather, and time.

# B. Offensive Phasing

*Ref: FM 100-2-1 The Soviet Army: Operations and Tactics (Jul '84), pp. 4-2 to 4-3.*

To assist in phasing offensive operations at the operational level, the Soviets have defined a series of terms outlining various depths of the enemy defenses and the objectives encompassed within those depths. The initial phase of the operation requires the penetration of the enemy's forward defenses and the neutralization or destruction of the enemy in the area defined as the "tactical depth." This depth includes the reserves of the forward enemy divisions. The subsequent phase calls for the neutralization or destruction of those enemy units in the area encompassed by the "immediate operational depth." The enemy corps reserves are found in this area. When the situation permits the introduction of a front's second echelon armies as exploitation forces, the enemy's strategic reserves at Anny Group and Theater level are attacked The final phase of the offensive is the accomplishment of the front final objectives: the capture of logistical, political, and economic centers and the neutralization of remaining enemy forces.

The categories of objective depths which regulate front offensive operations are identified below.

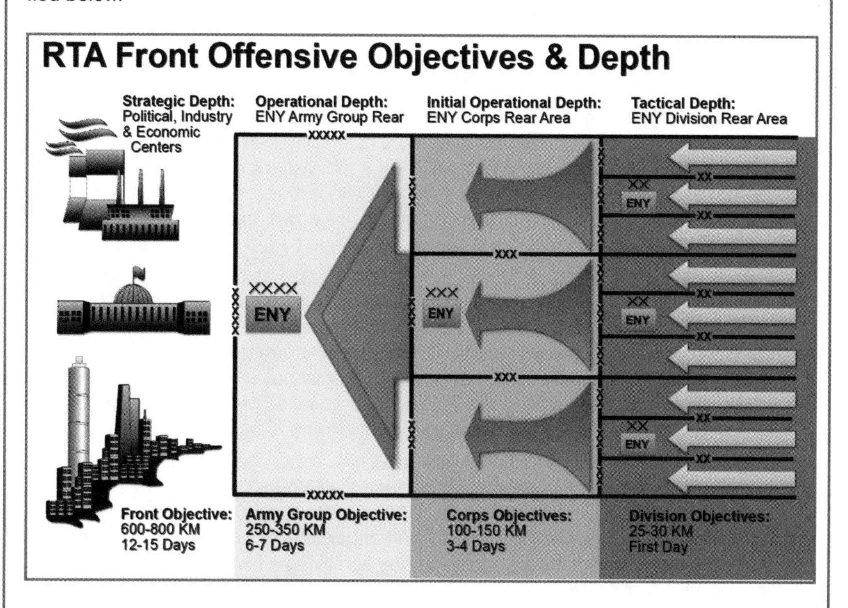


Offensive Operations

Offensive Operations

## C. Rapid Advance

The Soviet offensive is characterized by a high rate of advance. Over a period of several weeks or more, the Soviets anticipate a rate of advance of approximately 50 kilometers per day under nuclear or nonnuclear conditions. Rate of advance is not expected to be uniform. While fighting through enemy defensive positions, the Soviets expect a rate of several kilometers per hour or up to 30 kilometers per day. Once a major penetration has been achieved, the rate would increase considerably.

When confronting an enemy that has taken up defensive positions, the Soviets attempt to strike weak points in the defense and to drive to the enemy's rear whenever possible by bypassing his major force concentrations. They attempt to cripple the enemy quickly by destroying or disrupting his nuclear capability, his command and control facilities, and his logistic system before he could effectively react.

Even if the Soviets are forced to deal with an enemy that is emplaced in defensive positions across their entire frontage, they still attempt to avoid a costly, time-consuming battle of attrition. They would strive to develop penetrations leading to the enemy rear to topple the enemy defensive structure. They anticipate that elements of a front second echelon probably would not have to combat enemy forces in defensive positions. After the first two to five days of the war, they expect prepared positions to have been overrun and combat to be characterized by rapid movement into the enemy rear interrupted by violent, relatively brief, meeting engagements.

## D. Concentration of Forces

A front normally conducts a main attack over one or more axes whose proximity to one another depend upon whether the front is to split or envelop the enemy in its drive towards its objectives. The direction of a main attack would be decisive in the defeat of the enemy and seizure of territory. One or more supporting attacks accompany the main attack. A supporting attack ties down opposing enemy forces to prevent them from reinforcing the sector threatened by the main attack.

Certain sectors of enemy defenses may be designated as breakthrough sectors. These are areas, normally across a main attack axis, that an operational-level commander deems necessary, desirable, or likely for major penetration. Under nuclear conditions, enemy defenses in a breakthrough sector are destroyed by tactical nuclear strikes, followed by rapid exploitation by maneuver units. Under nonnuclear, but nuclear-threatened conditions, the sector is attacked by massed air and artillery fires and numerous attacks on multiple axes by maneuver units.

The benefit gained by the attacker who uses only conventional weapons on the nuclear-threatened battlefield is that the enemy also must avoid concentrating forces. The defender must leave. gaps and/or lightly manned sectors between his units. Whenever possible, the Soviet commander directs his attack against these undefended or lightly defended areas, thereby achieving a favorable force ratio without massing his own forces.

The greater range and increased mobility of modem artillery weapons enable Soviet artillerymen to mass fires against a target without concentrating the weapons themselves. This practice reduces their vulnerability to a nuclear strike and makes it more difficult for the enemy to determine long in advance where a main attack might be made. The fires of combat helicopters and close air support fixed-wing aircraft also are integrated into their overall fire planning. This again enhances the Soviets' ability to focus a great deal of firepower without putting masses of troops at risk to an enemy nuclear strike.

When the Soviets do concentrate forces, they are likely to do so in several locations along the FEBA and in relatively small numbers in anyone sector. By narrowing the width of an attack frontage, they achieve superior force ratios at several points along the FEBA. In such a situation, they probably attack with most forces in the first echelon.

# E. Attack Echelons

*Ref: FM 100-2-1 The Soviet Army: Operations and Tactics (Jul '84), pp. 4-4 to 4-5.*

As a very general rule, combined arms armies would be used in the first echelon of a front. Then tank armies would normally appear in its second echelon, combined arms reserve, or operational maneuver group (OMG).

Tank armies may be piaced in the first echelon for attaining greater speed when terrain and other conditions permit this employment. This variant would be likely if a massive nuclear strike preceded the ground offensive or if enemy defenses were not well prepared.

Most forces of afront are placed in its first echelon. The mission of the front's first echelon would be to overcome enemy defenses and to attack through the immediate operational depth (to enemy corps rear areas).

## *Front* First Echelon

Front first echelon forces are reinforced by artillery, other combat support, and logistic elements from front second echelon forces. The remainder, or follow-on, forces of the front could include-

- A second echelon or a combined arms reserve
- An operational maneuver group (OMG)
- Special reserves

## *Front* Second Echelon

A front second echelon (or a combined arms reserve), normally at least one army, has a mission of exploiting success achieved by first echelon forces by continuing the main thrust of the offensive to reach deeper objectives. Committed follow-on forces then become part of a new first echelon. Then a combined arms reserve normally is constituted from former first echelon forces.

The Soviet commander is more likely to use multiple, narrow penetrations when he has a clear numerical advantage over the enemy across his entire frontage and when the enemy has positioned the bulk of his defending forces forward. When enemy defenses are echeloned in depth, the Soviets tend to use an attack force echeloned in depth to maintain the momentum of the attack after the initial penetration.



## F. The Front Operational Maneuver Group (OMG)

Since the late 1970s, important changes in the operational employment and organization of Soviet ground maneuver formations have been observed. The most significant operational change has been the concept of employing a tailored high-speed exploitation force at army and probably front level. This force, called the operational maneuver group (OMG), is tailored for the situation and is designed to move deep into the enemy rear area and to seize critical objectives, normally before second echelon Soviet formations are committed to combat. Afront OMG could be committed well before the front immediate objective (enemy corps rear) is attained.

The OMG is an updated version of an older concept infused with new technology. It was widely used in the final stages of World War II when the Germans and Japanese were unable to present a deeply echeloned defense and had no large operational reserves. The predecessor of the OMG was the army and front "mobile group" of World War II. Mobile groups were large operational exploitation forces used to move rapidly and decisively deep into the enemy's rear area to destroy his command and control and lines of communication, to defeat his reserves, to encircle and destroy his forces, and to capture or destroy key political and economic centers.

### OMG Mission

The mission of an OMG is to help the first echelon penetrate the enemy defenses, if required, and then to raid deep into the enemy rear as early in the offensive as possible. The OMG is to destroy enemy nuclear weapons, air defenses, communications, command and control, to seize airfields or disrupt lines of communication, and to assist advancing main forces

# III. Army Offensive

An army in the first echelon of ajront offensive normally has a mission to attack through enemy defenses to the immediate operational depth, the enemy corps rear area. The achievement of an army's mission is the culmination of successive attacks conducted by its divisions.

A combined arms army may have two to four motorized rifle divisions and one or two tank divisions. A tank army may have two to four tank divisions and one or two motorized rifle divisions. An army offensive normally has a frontage 60 to 100 kilometers wide. The first echelon of an army normally contains most of the army's combat power. Army follow-on forces could include-

- A second echelon or a combined arms reserve
- An operational maneuver group
- Special reserves

## A. Echelonment of Forces

When an OMG is formed at army level, the bulk of the forces available to the army commander probably is distributed between the first echelon and the OMG. This may cause the second echelon or reserve to be smaller in those armies where OMGs are employed.

If enemy defenses are not well prepared in depth and not backed up by operational-level reserves, the army probably attacks in a single strong echelon followed by a combined arms reserve and, possibly, an OMG. If the enemy is well prepared in

# G. Nonnuclear Front Offensive

*Ref: FM 100-2-1 The Soviet Army: Operations and Tactics (Jul '84), p. 4-6.*

A nonnuclear Soviet front offensive probably would begin with a massive air operation, conducted continuously for several days, using massed assets from frontal, strategic, and naval aviation The two main goals of the air operation are to neutralize enemy theater nuclear capability and to gain tactical air superiority for the remainder of the operation. Targets of the air operation are nuclear delivery systems, airfields and aircraft, air defense systems, and command and control facilities.

The Soviets are willing to accept great losses in their own air assets to achieve their goals. They believe that they could conduct the remainder of the offensive with older, possibly obsolescent, aircraft provided they succeeded in crippling enemy tactical air power.

Ground attacks by front ground forces are preceded by a massive artillery preparation conducted by first echelon armies. If nuclear weapons are used from the onset, they are used in a massive, in-depth strike before the nonnuclear preparation. Whether they are used or not, nuclear strikes always are included in fire planning.

An airborne operation conducted by a front could be launched either at the start of an offensive, or at a later time, possibly after completion of the air operation. It could be of airborne-regiment or possibly division size. linkup may be planned with advancing ground forces, probably an OMG. Possible objectives include nuclear weapons, command and control centers, enemy airfields, major bridges, and logistic facilities.

Soviet airborne forces are equipped with BMD airborne assault vehicles. On the ground, in the enemy rear, they fight as motorized infantry. A front may also employ small, foot-mobile, special-purpose airborne forces to conduct reconnaissance and sabotage in the enemy rear.

depth and does have operational reserves,the army probably attacks in two echelons. In other words, if the enemy defense has an operational second echelon ( or reserve) the Soviets employ an operational second echelon to sustain the momentum of the offensive.

First and second echelon forces operate in concert to destroy defending enemy forces before them, up to assigned mission (objective) depths. Second echelon forces of an army normally are committed after the army's immediate objective is attained. An army OMG, if employed, could be committed as early as the first day of an operation

One or more divisions in the first echelon probably attack on a predetermined army main attack axis. Other first echelon divisions conduct supporting attacks. Achievement of a "breakthrough" of enemy prepared defensive positions is a probable mission of forces conducting the main attack of an army.

### *Army* First Echelon

First echelon regiments of the army's first echelon divisions attack from the march at top speed to achieve deeper penetration of the enemy's main defenses, and to exploit surprise and enemy disorganization. Second echelon regiments of the army's first echelon divisions would exploit the best penetrations into the deep tactical rear of the enemy.

### *Army* Second Echelon

The army's second echelon or combined arms reserve, normally about division size, advances behind army first echelon forces. It is dispersed laterally on multiple routes to minimize vulnerability to enemy detection and attacks. Based on the development of the battle and on his assigned mission, the army commander commits his follow-on forces at the most opportune time and place. He does this to achieve a "breakthrough," deeper exploitation, and dissolution of enemy tactical and immediate-operational defenses.

### Use of Forward Detachments

The offensive is characterized by surprise, speed, and a striving to preempt or forestall the enemy. Some subunits of first echelon forces may attempt to strike deep into the enemy forward defensive area before enemy defenses are fully organized and solidified. Such missions are likely given to forward detachments of an anny's first echelon divisions, fully supported by artillery and close air support. It is also possible that an army could employ a tank-heavy regimental-sized "operational" forward detachment to achieve similar but deeper results in the enemy main defensive area.

## B. The Army OMG

Army OMGs likely are formed from resources that are normally part of or supporting the army. OMGs may be established before an operation as part of the initial plan or during an operation to exploit an unforeseen opportunity. At army level, the OMG probably would be as large as a reinforced division. An OMG could operate 100 kilometers or more beyond other army forces.

The relationship between the OMG and the second echelon in an operation varies depending on the concept of operation. If the OMG is operating away from the main axis of advance, its activities and those of the second echelon may not be directly related. If the OMG is operating on the main axis of advance, the second echelon may be required to destroy forces bypassed by the OMG or to secure the OMG's lines of communications.

Unlike the second echelon, the OMG acts as a large operational raiding force. Typically, it is assigned an ultimate objective or objectives (perhaps located on the main axis) but is expected to disrupt, capture, or seize other objectives along the way, while attempting to avoid a decisive engagement with large enemy forces.

# (Offensive Operations) II. Division & Lower Tactics



*Ref: FM 100-2-1 The Soviet Army: Operations and Tactics (Jul '84), chapter 5.*

The Soviets emphasize swift, efficient movement, or transfer, of combat power from one point on the battlefield to another. This is accomplished by rapid column movement in march formation and successive deployment into prebattle formation and attack formation. Commanders insure that their unit is constantly ready to perform a march, with minimum warning and preparation. Units frequently rehearse the march, and its conduct is strictly controlled. They practice deployment from march column into prebattle and attack formation in standard battle drills. These formations and drills are designed for a rapid transition into combat while maintaining maximum security, speed, and firepower.

## I. The March

A march is an organized troop movement conducted in column formation on roads or cross country. It may be simply an administrative move from one point to another. In wartime, however, the march often will be governed by the possibility of enemy contact. It is planned and conducted with the expectation of contact.

A march may be conducted-

- When moving from a rear assembly area to a forward assembly area or attack position.
- When leaving an assembly area to launch an attack from the march.
- When moving forward in anticipation of a meeting engagement.
- During a pursuit.
- When conducting a passage of lines.

In any march, the challenge facing the commander is the proper disposition of combat and support elements within the column, to insure efficient transition into combat. The column organization, established before starting the march, should minimize or preclude any reorganizing before commitment in battle.

Having received an order to conduct a march, the Soviet commander issues a warning order to his subordinate commanders. He then conducts an estimate of the situation to include-

- Mission of the march.
- Time available.
- Locations of possible or anticipated enemy contact.
- Enemy strength and disposition.
- Disposition of friendly forces and missions of adjacent units.
- Attachments and supporting units.
- Terrain, weather, and light conditions.
- Possible march routes.
- Nuclear, biological, and chemical (NBC) conditions.
- Control measures.
- Reconnaissance and security.

Based on this estimate, he selects routes, if they have not been specified by his commander. The following norms apply:

- A division is assigned either a march zone or march routes. As many as four routes are possible.
- A regiment is normally assigned one or two routes.
- A battalion marches on one route.
- Distance between routes should be at least 3 kilometers to reduce vulnerability to nuclear strikes.

Planning the march is carried out in as much detail as time and information will permit. If possible, a route reconnaissance is conducted to determine route conditions; to locate contaminated areas, choke points, or obstacles; and to determine requirements for engineer or decontamination support.

Considering the total length of the march and the time available, the commander determines the average rate of march for the entire march. He then divides the march route into segments. Based on the terrain, he determines the permissible rate of march over each segment and the time to complete each segment. He then determines control measures for conduct of the march and the times associated with each control measure.

Prescribed times for units to pass from assembly areas to march column are indicated below.

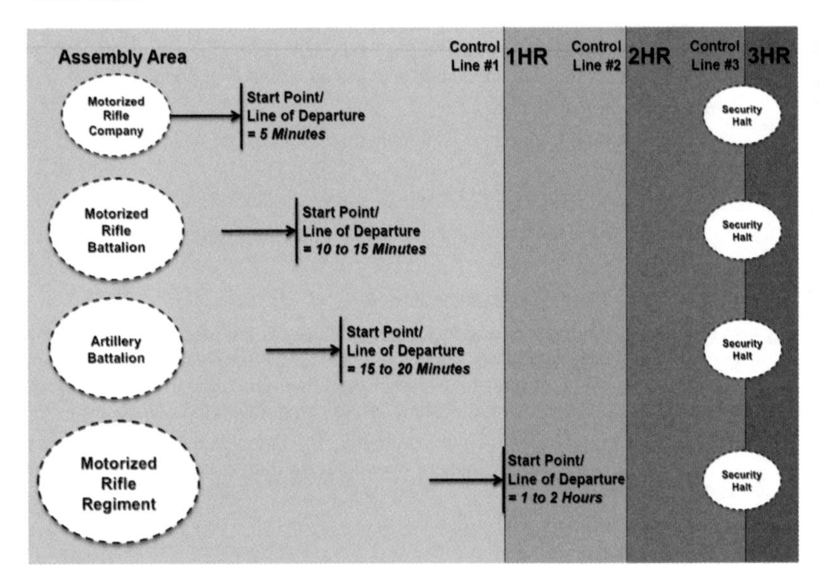


A start line or start point is designated for the beginnng of the march. It must be far enough from assembly areas to allow columns to form and reach the required speed as they pass the start point.

Control lines (points) are established to insure timely and orderly movement. Their number will be a function of the distance to be covered, the terrain, weather, time of day or night, and state of the roads. Usually they are designated for every 2 to 3 hours of movement. Elements of the force must cross these control lines or points at the designated time.

Halts and rests are specified to preserve the strength of personnel and to maintain equipment. Short halts are 20 to 30 minutes duration every 2 to 3 hours of movement. The column formation is not disturbed, and unit intervals are maintained.

# Principles of Attack Doctrine

*Ref: FM 100-2-1 The Soviet Army: Operations and Tactics (Jul '84), p. 5-13.*

Principles of attack doctrine include:

- Conduct aggressive reconnaissance.
- Breach enemy defense at weak points or gaps. Maneuver against enemy flanks and rear.
- Bypass strongpoints.
- Rapidly maneuver forces and fires in decisive direction.
- Mass fires.
- Give priority to destruction of enemy nuclear weapon systems.
- Strike rapidly and deeply into enemy rear.
- Maintain momentum under all conditions.
- Employ radioelectronic combat.

The two methods of conducting an attack against a defending enemy are to attack from the march and to attack from a position in direct contact.

## Attack from the March

An attack from the march, the preferred method of attack, is launched from march formation out of assembly areas in the rear. Subunits deploy laterally at designated control lines and assume attack formation within approximately 1,000 meters of enemy defenses.

The Soviets perceive the advantages of the attack from the march to be as follows: The unit is not committed before attack. The attack increases chance of surprise, allows greater flexibility, decreases vulnerability to enemy artillery, and enhances momentum. Preparation for combat is performed out of enemy contact.

Disadvantages of the attack from the march are:

- Commanders may not be familiar with terrain and enemy dispositions.
- It is more difficult to coordinate fire and maneuver and simultaneous combined arms efforts.

## Attack from a Position in Direct Contact

An attack from a position in direct contact, the less preferred method, is launched from a position which may be part of, or immediately behind, a defensive position. It is most often used when changing over to the offense from the defense.

The advantages of an attack from a position in direct contact are as follows:

- It allows more thorough study of terrain and enemy disposition.
- It permits more refined organization of battle.
- It is easier to coordinate fire and maneuver.

The disadvantages of an attack from a position in direct contact are as follows:

- Unit may be already committed.
- Unit is under threat of attack during preparation.
- There is less chance of surprise.
- There is less chance to build up momentum and to overcome inertia.

# Planning for the Attack

*Ref: FM 100-2-1 The Soviet Army: Operations and Tactics (Jul '84), p. 5-14 to 5-17.*

Division-level planning and preparation for the attack are based on the objectives and missions assigned by the army commander. The division commander assesses the situation, outlines his concept and intentions, specifies preliminary actions and missions, and directs the preparation of required information and planning. Warning orders are then passed to subordinate and attached units, specifying where, when, and by what means the attack will be conducted.

Preliminary actions are regulated by a strict timetable. The less time available, the more rigidly the work is regulated. Concurrent planning and action at all levels is emphasized.

Soviet attack plans are worked out in great detail. Despite the demands such planning may impose, in favorable circumstances the average reaction times to mounting an attack when already in contact, from receipt of orders or contact report to an H-Hour, are indicated below.

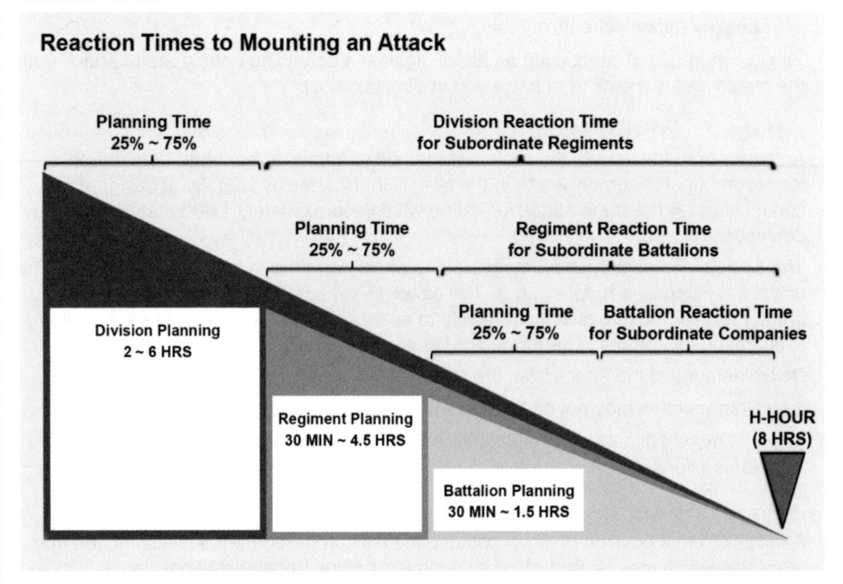


On receipt of a mission, the division commander and his chief of staff immediately assess the assigned mission, calculate available and required time, and establish what information about the situation they need, what they already have, and what is lacking. Analysis of the assigned mission centers on the role of the divisions in the attack; where, unless told, its main effort should be concentrated; what attack formation should be used; and what rates of advance are possible during the attack.

The division commander reviews the army's offensive plan, the allocation and procedures for employment of nuclear and chemical weapons, and the role of the division in the army's scheme. He notes the axes, objectives, and groupings of flanking division(s).

The basis for his attack planning stems from consideration of-

- Objective(s).
- Enemy dispositions.
- The army's fire plan, particularly the provision for nuclear/chemical fires, and the allocation of artillery.

- The terrain in the assigned attack zone, the weather and light conditions, and time of the attack.
- Combat effectiveness and supply situation of all elements of the division.

The balance of forces directly influences the alignment of Soviet troops for the attack. The calculation of the relative balance of forces is made across the entire zone of the planned action and to the full depth of the assigned mission. When nuclear weapons are employed, the commander assesses the balance of forces after expected nuclear strikes. In calculating the balance of forces, the Soviets attempt to determine the quantity and quality of the opposing forces. Besides a precise count of battalions and companies, tanks, artillery, mortars and antitank weapons, this estimate also assesses morale, actual strength in personnel and equipment, and the combat experience and readiness of each side.

The assessment of the balance of forces derives from intelligence estimates that primarily pertain to-

- Grouping of forces and the structure of enemy defenses in the attack zone to the depth of the attack mission.
- Presence and location of enemy weapons of mass destruction and their possible employment.
- Distribution of strongpoints in the defense and location of antitank weapons.
- Existence of gaps, breaks, and boundaries in the defense.
- Location of reserves, especially armor, and the possible nature of their commitment.
- Location and organization of enemy artillery and mortars.
- Positions critical to the stability of the defense.
- Perimeters of strongpoints & defensive areas on the FEBA and in the depth of the defense.
- Obstacles.
- Probable areas of nuclear or chemical strikes.

In planning an attack from the march and the required movements of troops to the line of attack, critical attention is given to timing. Usually the next higher commander specifies the routes, start lines or points, lines of deployment, and the line and time of attack. The length of the routes and distances from a start line to other control lines are measured and broken down by 5 kilometer segments. Permissible speeds are determined for different sectors based on the condition of the routes, the time of year and day, the weather, the composition of the columns, and possible enemy action during movement. Average speeds are calculated, and schedules for troop movements are developed. In calculating troop movements, planners reduce the speed of movement from successive lines of deployment to the line of attack by 25 to 50 percent from the march speed.

An attack against a defending enemy may be staged from an assembly area. If an assembly area is occupied, the stay is limited to the time necessary to assign missions to subordinate units, to check preparations, and to organize combat formations. The assembly area is located far enough forward for first echelon regiments to move to their lines of deployment, normally during the hours of darkness, and to reach their attack lines during the artillery preparation.

Troops are dispersed in assembly areas with their attached reinforcements and are grouped by battalions. Their movement routes, with prescribed control and deployment lines, permit rapid, effective movement to the attack line. The attack line is designated in the combat order. It is planned to be as near as possible to the forward positions of the enemy defense.

If a division assembly area is used, it would probably be located about 60 to 75 kilometers from the forward edge of the battle area (FEBA) and cover an area of 300 to 600 square kilometers. First echelon regiments could occupy assembly areas as close as 20 to 30 kilometers from the FEBA.

Within units, vehicles pull over to the right side of the road with spacings of not less than 10 meters between them. Refueling, minor maintenance, and if necessary, partial decontamination are accomplished. Long halts are used on marches of over 24 hours duration. They are not normally scheduled at night to allow maximum time for night movement. If used, they are 2 to 4 hours duration, usually at the beginning of the second half of a day's movement. Units disperse offroad in camouflaged positions. Maintenance, resupply, and decontamination (if required) are accomplished and troops are fed a hot meal.



Day rest is scheduled after a night march and night rest after a day march. Troops are dispersed and concealed in such manner to facilitate rapid continuation of the march. Necessary logistical functions are accomplished.

March formation normally consists of the following elements:

- Reconnaissance.
- Advance guard (or forward security element of a battalion).
- Flank security elements.
- Main force.
- Rear security element.

The focus for march planning is security of the main force and creation of conditions for its successful commitment into battle.

The organic reconnaissance battalion precedes its division on the march. Scout elements of the reconnaissance battalion may operate 50 kilometers forward of the division. A regiment is preceded by its organic reconnaissance company, whose scouts may operate 25 kilometers forward. Reconnaissance forces are trained to obtain as quickly as possible the following information about enemy forces:

- Nature and location of enemy nuclear delivery systems.
- Movement axes of enemy columns.
- Strength and composition of enemy forces.
- Deployment lines and routes.
- Location of contaminated areas.

The advance guard precedes the main force on the same route and provides movement security and warning. It normally consists of about one third of the total combat power of the main force. The advance guard of a motorized rifle regiment is normally a motorized rifle battalion reinforced with tank, artillery, antitank, antiaircraft, engineer, and chemical elements. The advance guard of a tank regiment is normally a similarly-reinforced tank battalion. In a division marching on multiple routes, the lead regiment on each route forms its own advance guard. There is no "divisional advance guard," as such.

The advance guard, in its turn, will dispatch to its front a forward security element (FSE) consisting of about one third of its combat power. A forward security element of a regiment's advance guard will normally be a reinforced company. (The FSE is known as an "advance party" in some texts.)

The FSE is preceded by a combat reconnaissance patrol (CRP). The CRP is normally a platoon reinforced with engineer and NBC reconnaissance elements. It reports intelligence information and makes the initial contact with any enemy forces encountered.

Flank and rear security elements for a regiment are normally of platoon size. (More detailed information on the organization and function of march elements is found under The Meeting Engagement later in this chapter.)

March considerations include dispersion, rate of march, and march order. Particularly under nuclear conditions, march formations must maintain dispersion both laterally

# Fire Planning

*Ref: FM 100-2-1 The Soviet Army: Operations and Tactics (Jul '84), pp. 5-17 to 5-18.*



Fire planning, being highly centralized, integrates conventional artillery and air strikes as well as missile strikes and possible nuclear or chemical fires. The fire plan includes details which specify the time of assignments, groupings, and displacement of artillery. Fragmentary orders provide specifics concerning the missions of designated artillery units and identify the location of observation posts and firing positions. Deadlines for units to be ready to fire are specified. Artillery units are among the first combat forces to deploy.

For the attack, fire planning is conducted in the first echelon regiments and divisions based on the scheme of maneuver and fire plan of the division and higher headquarters. The chief of rocket troops and artillery at division level receives instructions from and advises the division commander on-

- Nuclear fires allotted to the division and plans for integrating nuclear, chemical, and conventional fires and available air strikes.
- Fires to create passages through obstacles and obstructions.
- Priorities of sectors of the enemy defense which are to be neutralized.
- Starting time, duration, and phases of the fire preparation.
- Methods of firing in support of the attack.
- Plans for partial decentralization of artillery control during the accompaniment phase in the enemy depths.
- Plan of support for commitment of second echelon forces and reserves.

The CRTA incorporates the planned fires of the RAGs and DAGs into a division fire plan. The completed division plan is forwarded to army level for approval and incorporation into the army plan. Adjustments in the organization for combat and planned fires are made as the planned attack develops. These changes are also forwarded to the army CRTA.

A possible fire plan outlining the timing for an artillery fire preparation is shown below.

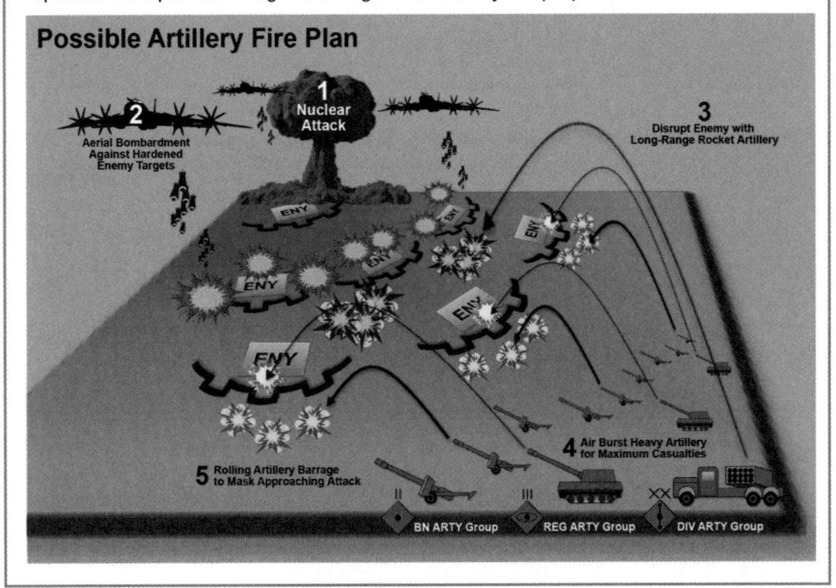

and in depth. A division attains lateral dispersion by marching in a zone up to 25 kilometers wide on as many as four routes, each separated by 3 to 4 kilometers.

The average rate of march is based on the total route distance and the time allowed for the march.

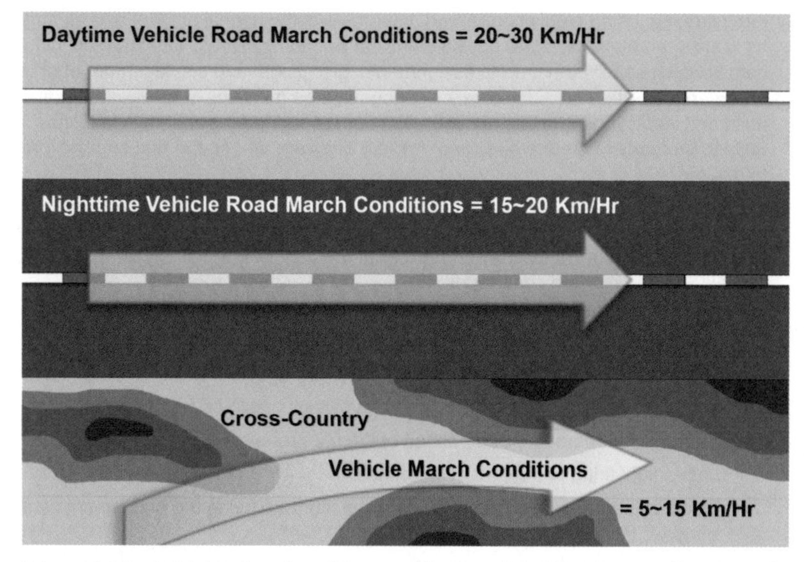


Dispersion in depth is a function of the organization of the forces on each route and the intervals between units and vehicles. The commander balances the requirement for dispersion in depth with the requirement for timely commitment of his forces in case of enemy contact.

The depth of a march formation depends on the number of march routes, the interval between units, and the interval between vehicles and between subunits in each column.

The average movement intervals and vehicle speeds shown in the tables below apply to marches of some duration. If enemy contact is made, units may move at maximum speeds.

| UNIT | LOW VISIBILITY INTERVAL | SPEED (LOW VISIBILITY ~ HIGH VISIBILITY) | HIGH VISIBILITY INTERVAL |
|---|---|---|---|
| Between Vehicles in CO Formation | 25m | 15Km/Hr ~ 40Km/Hr | 50m |
| Between CO in BN Formation | 25m | 15Km/Hr ~ 40Km/Hr | 50m |
| Between BN in REG Formation | 3Km | 10Km/Hr ~ 30Km/Hr | 5Km |
| CSS Behind REG Formation | 3Km | 10Km/Hr ~ 30Km/Hr | 5Km |
| Between REG in DIV Formation | 5Km | 5Km/Hr ~ 20Km/Hr | 10Km |
| CSS Behind DIV Formation | 15Km | 5Km/Hr ~ 20Km/Hr | 20Km |

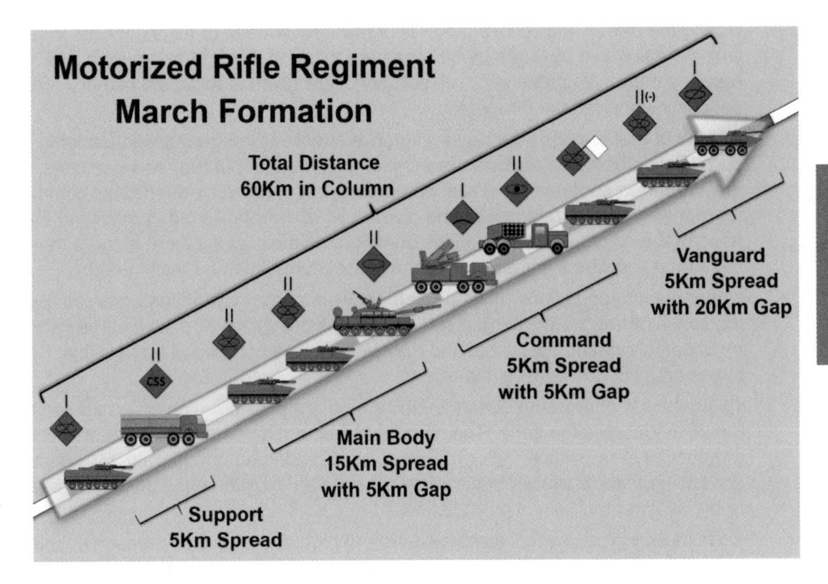




To assist movement and enforce march control, each regiment employs a traffic control platoon and each division employs a traffic control company. Traffic regulators wear distinctive black uniforms with white belts and, helmets. Before the march, they normally are placed at critical points such as turns, intersections, choke points, and control points. Use of traffic regulators permits less reliance on maps and radio communications.

Use of radios is restricted to minimize risk of radioelectronic detection, jamming, and enemy attack. Subunits normally march under radio listening silence. The Soviets are well drilled in and rely heavily on hand and arm signals, flags, and light signaling devices. During long halts, wire communications may be used, extensive use is also made of motorcycle-mounted couriers.

Air defense for the march normally is planned in advance and includes organic and supporting antiaircraft weapons and aviation. Air defense weapons can be located in the column or in stationary positions occupied in advance. Normally, the weapons are distributed throughout the column.

When enemy aircraft appear, the commander gives the signal to open fire. Simultaneously the column speeds up and vehicle spacings are increased to a distance of up to 100 meters between vehicles. If a large group of aircraft attack, the column may be forced to disperse or seek concealment off the road.

Engineer support for the march allows the force to overcome or bypass those areas which would disrupt the march. Engineer subunits may be formed into-

- A movement support detachment (MSD) which performs route reconnaissance, removes obstacles, organizes bypasses, marks the route, and does limited road repair.
- A mobile obstacle detachment (MOD) which provides protection for advancing columns by mechanically laying minefields and creating expedient obstacles on likely enemy approaches.

Logistic support of the march can be divided into two phases: before the march and during the march. Before the march, rear services elements are brought forward to replenish supplies, to perform maintenance, and to evacuate the wounded and sick. Refueling and maintenance elements are sent forward to halt or rest areas. Every attempt is made to replenish fuel reserves on the vehicles before combat.

During the march, logistical support is performed in areas of halts or rests. Vehicles which break down between these areas are taken to the right of the road and repaired there. Wounded and sick personnel are given medical aid in place. The seriously wounded are evacuated.

Control of rear services during the march is affected through detailed planning and coordination between rear services chiefs, commanders of rear services units, and the supported commander. A rear command post, headed by the deputy commander for rear services (at regimental and division level) is established. It moves at the head of the column of rear services units (on the main axis if there is more than one column) but will be situated wherever the best control can be maintained.

Under nuclear conditions, units probably will encounter contaminated areas. Bypassing zones of radioactive contamination reduces casualties and saves time spent on decontaminating personnel and materiel but may not always be possible. Some zones could be too large to bypass.

Two methods of crossing contaminated zones are possible. The first is immediate movement across the zone. The other is movement across the zone after waiting for a reduction in radiation levels. The crossing is made on primary routes to insure high speed and control, unless better axes are selected to reduce the distance traveled or to bypass areas of very high radiation.

Units move across the contaminated area at high speeds with increased spacings between vehicles, especially in dusty conditions. Personnel wear protective equipment and use the protective systems of combat vehicles.

When a decision is made to wait for a reduction of radiation levels, forces disperse and camouflage. After radiation levels have fallen, the crossing is made without significant change in deployment.

The Soviets use their best available fire suppression means to preclude an enemy attack during their movement across the contaminated area. This fire suppression mission is an ideal role for self-propelled artillery.

Throughout the march, order, speed, and interval are enforced vigorously. The Soviet penchant for detailed planning and execution dominates such activity.

Platoon leaders normally ride in the lead vehicle of a platoon column. Company and battalion commanders ride near the front of their march formations. Regimental commanders normally are located near the front of the regimental main force.

The march is completed when the last control measure is crossed and the unit enters a new assembly area, or when it enters prebattle formation or combat.

# II. Prebattle Formation

For the sake of speed, the Soviets prefer to remain in column or march formation whenever possible. They normally resort to lateral deployment only by necessity, such as when combat is imminent. The next, successive lateral deployment out of march formation is into prebattle formation (known incorrectly as “approach march formation” in some Western publications). In prebattle formation, a unit advances dispersed laterally and in depth. This formation is used when approaching the battlefield, moving in the depths of a defending enemy’s rear area, and attacking enemy defenses when preparatory fires have significantly reduced enemy resistance. Prebattle formation also may be used to rapidly cross nuclear-contaminated zones and areas that are burning or obstructed.

Prebattle formation minimizes troop vulnerability to enemy tactical nuclear strikes and conventional artillery and air strikes. It facilitates rapid maneuver as well as quick deployment into attack formation. Units in prebattle formation either deploy into attack formation or return to march formation, depending on the tactical situation. A unit might remain in this formation for a lengthy period of time. It normally would pass through some form of prebattle formation when moving from the march into full deployment for an attack.

In prebattle formation, a battalion advances with its companies deployed on line, deployed in a forward or reverse wedge, or echeloned left or right. Each company moves in march column within the formation. Deployment into and out of prebattle formation is rehearsed often by set battle drill.

A company in prebattle formation advances with platoon columns in one of the formations described. In prebattle formation a unit does not laterally deploy beyond platoon columns. The intervals between company or platoon columns in prebattle formation will be large enough to allow full deployment of the subunit into attack formation without additional lateral expansion of the entire formation. Prebattle formation provides a combination of speed, dispersion, flexibility, and firepower in an anticipated direction.



# III. Attack Formation

Normally, the attack formation is assumed immediately before combat. In prebattle formation, platoons, and possibly companies remain in column. Attack formation is assumed when platoons disperse laterally into line formation. Within their company, however, platoons need not be formed on line but may be also arrayed in wedge or echelon formations, based on the situation. However, an array of platoons on line is most common. Tanks on line normally precede BTRs or BMPs. If troops dismount, they normally follow closely behind the tanks. BTRs or BMPs normally follow between 100 to 400 meters behind the tanks. Attack formation normally is assumed within about 1000 meters of enemy positions.

Platoon leaders normally are located centrally.

Company commanders normally are located centrally and slightly to the rear of lead elements. Attack formation is sometimes referred to as "combat formation" or "battle formation" in Western publications. It is called attack formation in this manual to distinguish it.

The attack against a defending enemy is employed when the enemy is in a defensive position, and the Soviets know his location. It normally follows a plan, based on intelligence on enemy disposition and the factors of mission, terrain, troops, and time available.

The attack against a defending enemy is the tactic which has been incorrectly described as a "breakthrough" or "deliberate attack." These terms are incorrect because they do not fully describe all options available to the Soviet commander conducting what he calls attack against a defending enemy.

## Tactical Objectives

Soviet tactical objectives are expressed as dashed lines on a terrain map, arrayed at various depths, based on enemy dispositions and terrain. Assignment of an objective to a maneuver unit requires that unit to attack to the limit of the objective line and to destroy or neutralize enemy troops, weapons, equipment, and support systems.

The objective lines, all normally assigned by the next higher commander, are based on his knowledge of the enemy and his concept of attack. Divisions and regiments normally are assigned an immediate objective and a subsequent objective. Battalions and companies normally receive an immediate objective and a subsequent direction of attack. A battalion may sometimes be assigned a subsequent objective.

At the tactical level, objectives form a progressively higher and deeper hierarchy. The depths of objectives are not fixed dimensions, but vary with each situation.

In the initial phase of an attack, when configuration of enemy defenses may be evident, commanders may assign objectives to subordinate commanders to create, at each level, a minimum 3 to 1 advantage in combat power.

An idealized, but representative, hierachy of tactical objectives for an attack in which a 3 to 1 ratio is created at all levels is portrayed in the illustration below. This illustration shows a hierarchy of objectives for a division attacking in an army first echelon at the beginning of an offensive operation If the division attack is successful, it will reach an enemy brigade rear area or, possibly, the enemy division rear area.

As the offensive continues and enemy resistance decreases, objective depths would increase based again on the situation. If enemy resistance were light (during a later phase of an offensive), a division final objective could be as deep as 80 kilometers.



## Hierarchy of Tactical Objectives

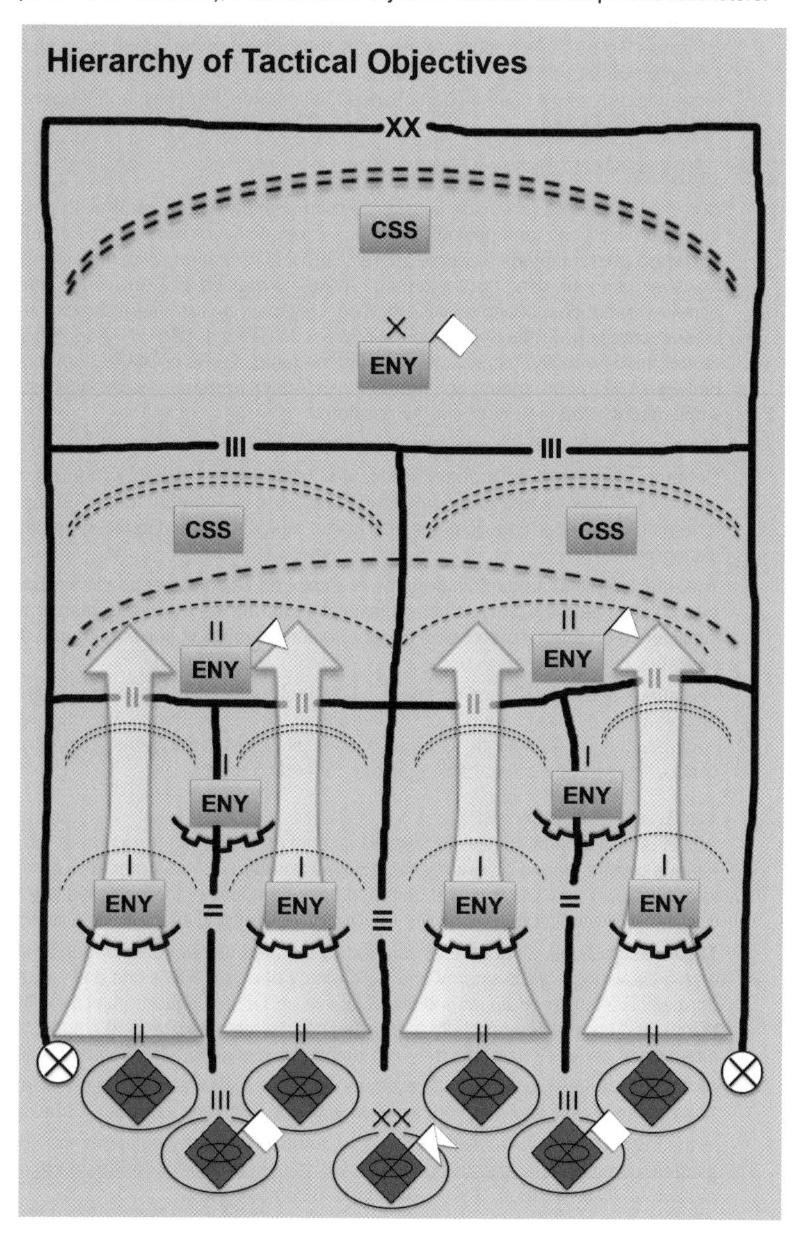

# Forms of Maneuver

*Ref: FM 100-2-1 The Soviet Army: Operations and Tactics (Jul '84), pp. 5-13 to 5-14.*

The three basic forms of maneuver in the attack are the frontal attack, the flank attack, and the envelopment.

## Frontal Attack

The frontal attack is directed against the enemy's frontline forces to penetrate his defenses along single or multiple axes. A unit conducting a frontal attack attempts to create openings for subsequent exploitation. The frontal attack was previously one of the most frequently employed forms of offensive maneuver. Its success depends on superiority of forces and firepower, the presence of sufficient reserves, and thorough planning. The frontal attack, by itself, is the least preferred form of maneuver. Normally, it is used in combination with a flank attack or an envelopment.

## Flank Atttack

The flank attack is conducted to strike enemy forces in their flank or rear at a relatively shallow depth. It normally is initiated through gaps or breaches in enemy formations. Forces conducting the flank attack and those conducting a simultaneous frontal attack coordinate fire support.

## Envelopment

The envelopment is a deeper attack that causes the enemy to turn and fight in a new direction. It is launched against enemy open flanks or through gaps or breaches. There is no requirement for mutual fire support with forces conducting a frontal attack.

The Soviets seek to exploit massive suppressive fires through the vigorous, sustained, forward movement of attacking units. Attacking forces attempt to bypass strongpoints and to envelop defensive positions. The maneuvers used vary with the situation. Units attempt to exploit gaps in a defense and to maneuver against its flanks and rear. The objective is a strike into the key points and to the full depth of an enemy defense.

# A. Division Attack

*Ref: FM 100-2-1 The Soviet Army: Operations and Tactics (Jul '84), pp. 5-18 to 5-22.*

A division normally conducts an attack as part of its parent army offensive, having missions that contribute to the accomplishment of the army's missions. The manner by which the Red Team Army (RTA) division achieves its mission is the culmination of fires and attacks by its maneuver regiments. The basic concept for an attack is to strike enemy defenses with intensive fires, find or create a gap, then slip through and drive deep at top speed.

A likely mission for a division attacking in the first echelon of its parent army would be to penetrate enemy forward defenses, attack through the enemy brigade's rear, and to continue the attack to the full tactical depth of the enemy division's rear area.

A division normally attacks with most of its combat power in a first echelon with remaining forces organized into a second echelon, a combined arms reserve, or special reserves including as engineer, chemical, or antitank subunits.

The main difference between a second-echelon force and a combined arms reserve is that the former has an assigned mission while the latter does not. A combined arms reserve is used to exploit success or to react to contingencies.

The division commander may designate a main attack axis based on terrain, disposition of enemy defenses, or the order received from higher command. Two of its first echelon regiments would probably attack along the main attack axis. A third regiment might conduct a supporting attack or come abreast the main attack.

A fourth regiment normally has a mission to continue the attack against a deeper objective along the main attack axis as a second echelon. Normal commitment of a second-echelon regiment takes place after the division's immediate objective has been achieved. However, the time of commitment depends on the success of first-echelon forces and the manner in which the enemy uses his reserves. The commander commits the second echelon when and where it can best contribute to overall success. The division commander could commit the second echelon on an alternate axis, based on his evaluation of the developing situation.

A fifth regiment may be designated as a combined arms reserve. It would not have an assigned objective at the beginning of an attack. It would be held in readiness to attack along the most opportune axis at a time determined by the division commander.

Before being committed, second echelon or combined arms reserve subunits advance approximately 15 kilometers to the rear of the first echelon. This distance varies with the situation. The commander keeps second echelon or reserve forces far enough forward to influence the battle in a timely manner, but far enough to the rear to protect them from the bulk of enemy direct fire and direct support weapons prior to commitment to battle.

When attacking with three regiments in a single echelon, a division zone of attack is normally 12 to 18 kilometers wide. This width could vary considerably with the situation. Within the zone of attack there probably would be no distinct, continuous division "attack frontage." Each of the three first echelon regiments attacks on its own axis, with situation-variable spaces between regiments.

If enemy defenses are not well prepared and most of the enemy force is deployed forward, a RTA division may attack on multiple axes with no *obvious* main attack.

The leading regiments attack and probe for weak points in enemy defenses, penetrate wherever they can, develop penetrations, and carry the attack as deeply as possible. The division commander allows the battle to develop to a stage where he can determine which penetration promises the best opportunity to drive into the enemy rear. He then commits his combined arms reserve through this penetration.

The challenge facing the opposing commander under such an attack is to maintain the integrity of his main battle area. Otherwise, he may be forced to commit his reserve before the direction of the RTA main attack becomes obvious.

The organization, concept, and conduct of a division attack vary with the division's mission and the commander's estimate of the situation.

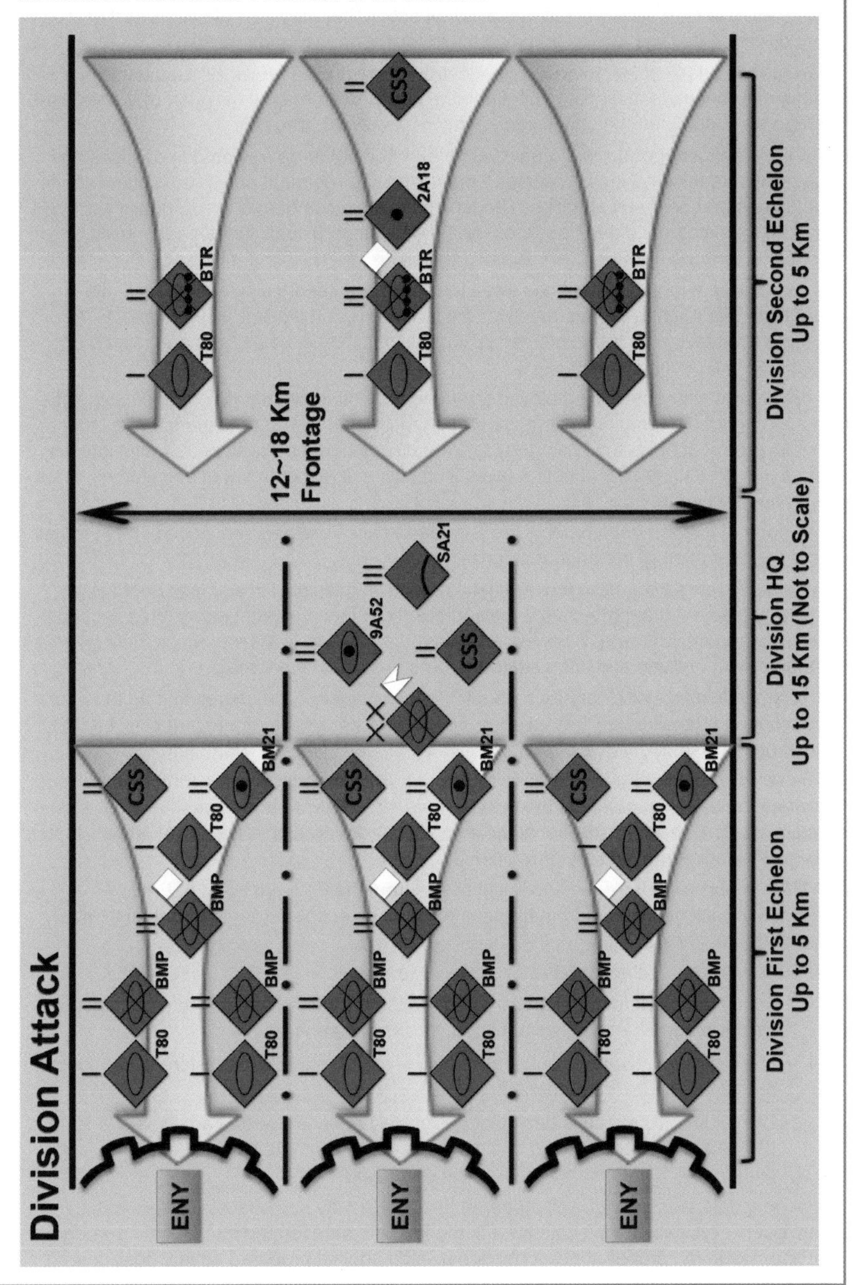

# B. Regimental Attack

*Ref: FM 100-2-1 The Soviet Army: Operations and Tactics (Jul '84), pp. 5-22 to 5-23.*

The Red Team Army (RTA) regiment is the smallest fully combined arms ground force element. It is capable of limited independent action, but may also attack as part of a parent division. This section will focus on the independent regiment attack.

A regiment attack seeks to penetrate, destroy, or neutralize forward strongpoints of defending enemy battalions, to continue the attack to an enemy battalion rear area, and prepares to continue the attack into enemy brigade rear areas.

An RTA regiment normally is organized for combat into three reinforced battalions and possibly a tank company in reserve. A motorized rifle regiment has three motorized rifle battalions and one tank battalion. The tank battalion's companies are normally assigned to the three motorized rifle battalions. An RTA regiment also includes a reconnaissance battalion, divided between the three rifle battalions.

Alternatively, a tank regiment has three tank battalions and a single motorized rifle battalion that may be divided amongst the three tank battalions. In either case, RTA regiments attack with two reinforced battalions in its first echelon, and one reinforced battalion in a second echelon.

Forward detachments are employed throughout an offensive operation, particularly after penetrating the enemy main defense area. A regiment forward detachment of a tank-reinforced reconnaissance company may be dispatched for a swift penetration into the enemy depths to seize and hold a tactical objective until the arrival of main forces. It may also be used for tactical raids.

Missions of forward detachments are intended to accelerate the advance of main forces and the disruption of the enemy defense.

Advance guards differ from forward detachments in mission. An advance guard is a security element that protects the main attack force by engaging enemy forces encountered on the march route. Whereas a forward detachment is a deep attack force with an independent mission and often alternate route than the main force.

A regiment's attack can vary from about 3 to 8 kilometers wide, depending on the attack concept and the situation. Yet the most typical attack frontage of a regiment is 4 to 6 kilometers. Distance between echelons varies but is typically 5 kilometers.

The motorized rifle regiment or tank regiment has an organic howitzer battalion that subdivides the batteries amongst the three maneuver battalions to augment their mortars. A regiment often receives additional rocket artillery from division. The rocket artillery then forms the regimental artillery group (RAG).

A RAG is normally deployed 1 to 4 kilometers from the Forward Edge of Battle Area (FEBA). Attack helicopters from division, or close air support from the front might also support a regiment.

The RTA regiment attack follows a routine sequence:

- Aerial bombardment and artillery preparation is planned and executed to end just before maneuver units assault enemy forward defenses.
- The regiment advances out of assembly areas at least 20 kilometers away, concurrent with artillery fire preparation.
- The regiment's subunits deploy at designated release points: battalions at 8 to 12 kilometers from the enemy; companies at 4 to 6 kilometers from the enemy; and platoons at 1 to 3 kilometers from the enemy position.

If enemy defenses are not well prepared, the attack may be conducted in pre-battle formation – typically a long column with the lead element formed into a fighting wedge or online. However, proper attack formation is used against prepared enemy positions.

In general, RTA doctrine does not prescribe lateral deployment into attack formations except when absolutely necessary. Units will remain in pre-battle formation whenever possible, for sake of speed. Even after a lateral deployment, subunits may revert back to the march formation if enemy resistance is weak.

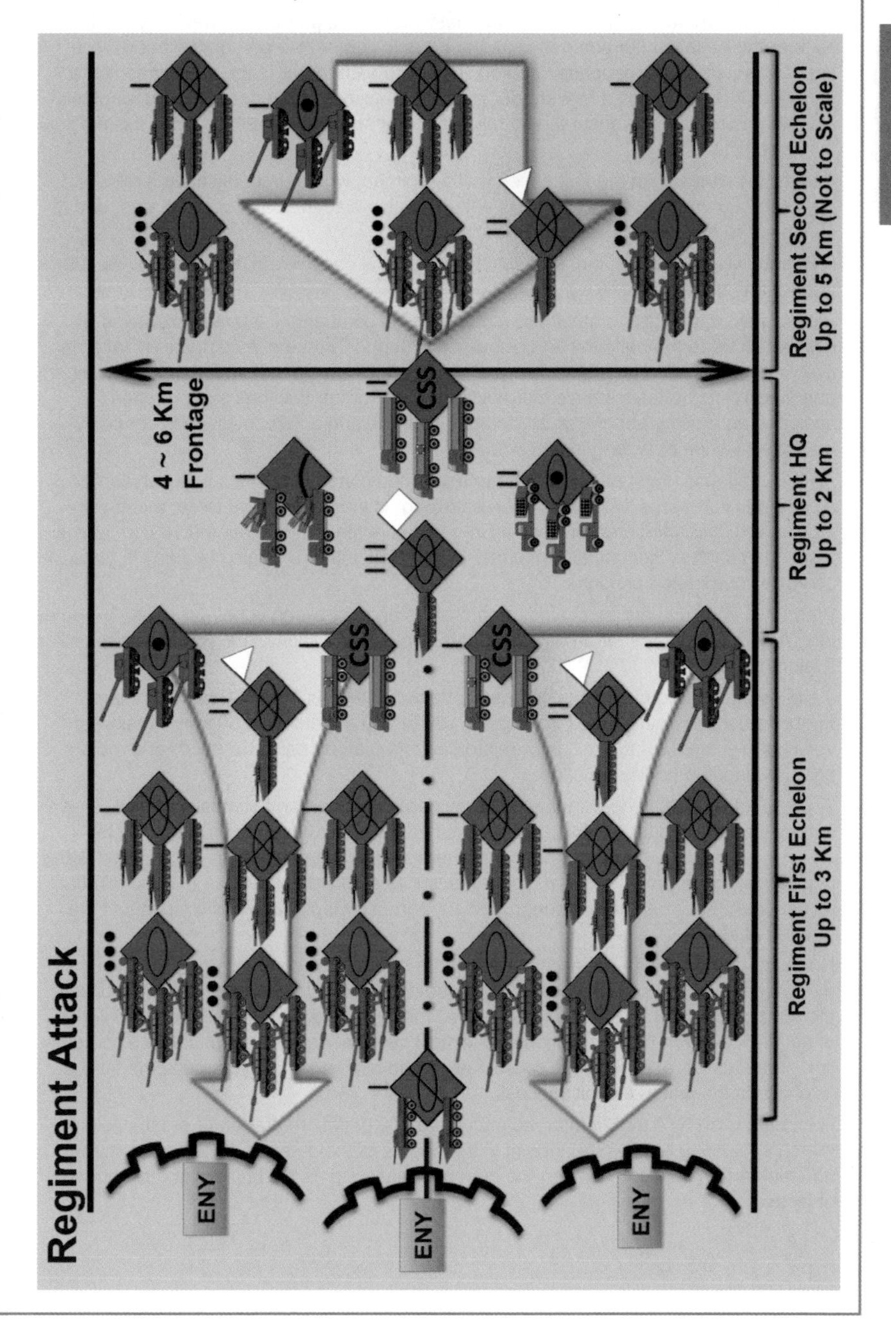

# C. Battalion Attack

*Ref: FM 100-2-1 The Soviet Army: Operations and Tactics (Jul '84), pp. 5-24 to 5-26.*

The Red Team Army (RTA) battalion normally attacks as part of its parent regiment. Neither the battalion nor company has the organic combat support or combat service support required for independent action. The exception to this is the employment of a battalion or company as a forward detachment to accomplish a deep, independent mission. In such a circumstance, the battalion or company may be reinforced to sustain itself for some time.

A battalion attacking in the first echelon of a regiment would probably have a mission to attack through strongpoints of enemy battalions, to seize the battalion rear area, and to continue the attack in an assigned direction.

RTA subunits normally do not stop on objectives and consolidate, but continue the attack deeper into the enemy rear.

A motorized rifle battalion has three motorized rifle companies. A tank company is typically attached to the battalion and dispersed is support of the rifle companies. (Alternatively a tank battalion has three tank companies and may have a motorized rifle company attached.) Rifle battalions have integral supporting mortar sections and are often assigned an artillery battery, an air defense platoon, and a reconnaissance company – particularly when operating independently.

An RTA battalion might attack with three reinforced companies in a single echelon, plus a company in reserve. However, when attacking as an independent force, a battalion attacks with two reinforced companies in a first echelon and one reinforced company in a second echelon. Reconnaissance then deploys as either a single company in force, or as three coordinated platoons.

When two echelons are employed, a normal distance between echelons is 1 to 3 kilometers. A normal frontage for an attacking battalion is 1 to 2 kilometers, within a zone of 2 to 3 kilometers.

A typical tank or motorized rifle company attack frontage is from 500 to 800 meters. Platoons normally attack on a frontage of 100 to 200 meters, with 50 meters between vehicles. Yet the frontage of a tank-reinforced rifle platoon could extend to 400 meters, again depending on the situation.

There would probably be little maneuver evident in platoon and company tactics. These subunits normally attack online and in unison. However, maneuver probably will be evident in the way a battalion commander moves his companies. One such option is the deployment of dismounted troops to maneuver as an enveloping force to conduct attack by fire, while the remaining Bronegruppa supported by tanks and artillery conduct the forward assault.

Normally, company and battalion commanders are located centrally and slightly to the rear of lead elements in command and control vehicles. If the commander were killed, the attack would not halt. It would be carried forward on its own momentum of violence of action. However, the elimination of a tactical commander would diminish the coordination of the attack, especially fire coordination, and almost certainly damage the tactical flexibility of the unit to exploit success.

Illustrated is an RTA tank-reinforced motorized rifle battalion attacking from the column march against an enemy strongpoint in the depths of the defense. Note the company and platoon release points along the march formation, plus the primary and secondary objectives.

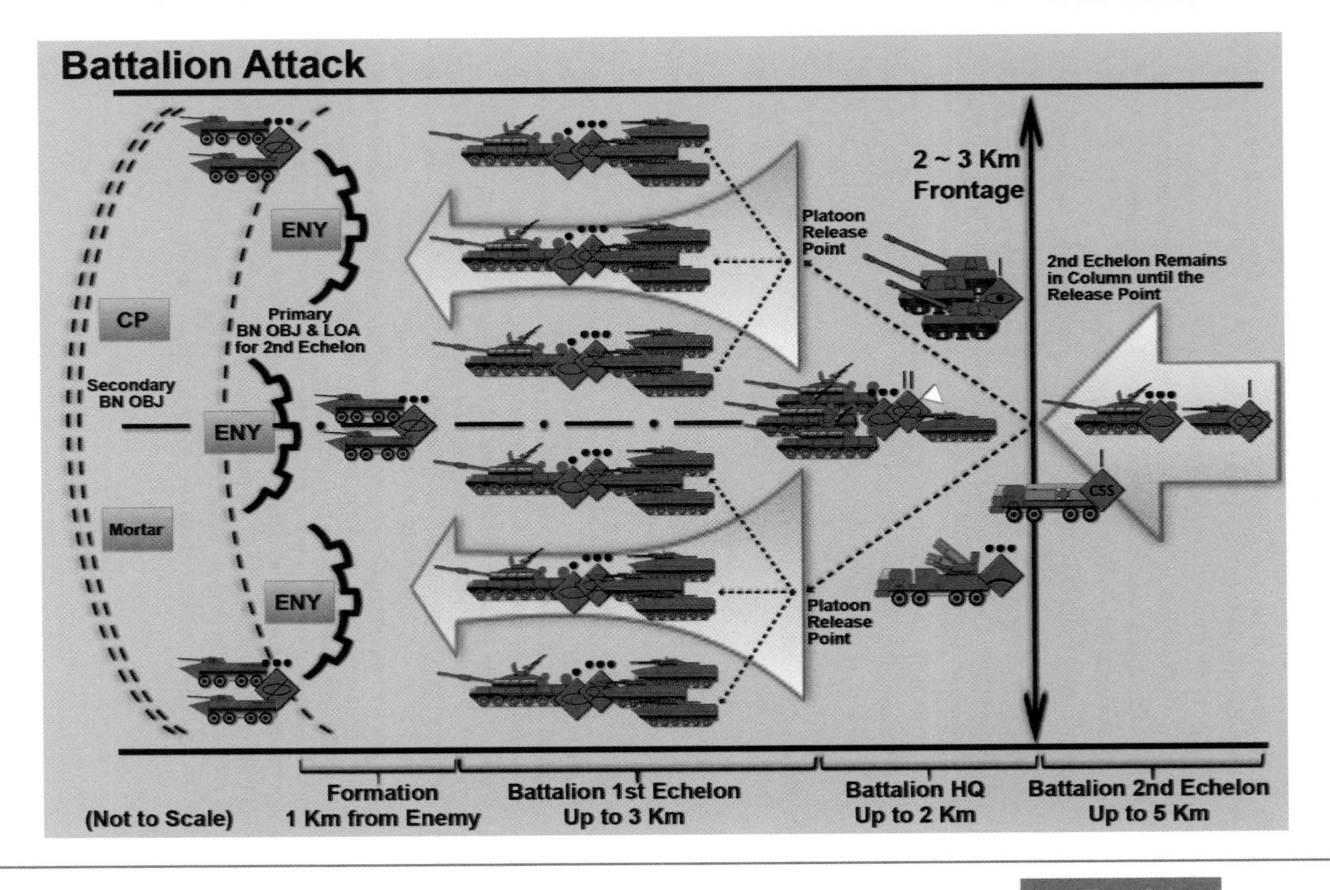
Battalion Attack
2 ~ 3 Km Frontage
Platoon Release Point
2nd Echelon Remains in Column until the Release Point
ENY
CP
Primary BN OBJ & LOA for 2nd Echelon
Secondary BN OBJ
ENY
CSS
Mortar
ENY
Platoon Release Point
(Not to Scale)
Formation 1 Km from Enemy
Battalion 1st Echelon Up to 3 Km
Battalion HQ Up to 2 Km
Battalion 2nd Echelon Up to 5 Km

# IV. Conduct of the Attack

The mounted assault for the Red Team Army (RTA) is conducted at speeds of approximately 12 to 20 kilometers per hour (8-12mph). This speed allows tanks to fire on the move to reduce vulnerability to antitank weapons. Dismounted assault speed is approximately 5 kilometers per hour, or less.

RTA units prefer mounted assault. The benefits include:

- Vehicle protection of troops from chemical or radiation contamination.
- Vehicle speed reduces the effect of enemy antitank capabilities.
- Violence of action defeats weak enemy defenses.

If a dismounted attack is planned, a dismount line is designated within about 100 to 200 meters from the FEBA – the practical range of Kalashnikov rifle. RTA troops dismount with armored vehicles in defilade to protect the infantry from enemy fire.

RTA units employ dismounted assault only when:

- Maximum firepower is required against well-entrenched enemy.
- The enemy has significant antitank capability.
- Securing river fords or bridges.
- Clearing obstacles or minefields.
- Over rough terrain with no high-speed avenues of attack.

The most probable array of mounted assault with combined tank and motorized infantry includes a line of tanks followed by a line of infantry armored vehicles (BMP or BTR).

If dismounted assault is employed, the most probable array of combined tank and motorized infantry mounted assault includes a line of tanks followed by dismounted infantry. A third subsequent line of supporting infantry armored vehicles (BMP or BTR) follows behind.

Dismounted riflemen follow closely behind tanks to destroy enemy antitank positions. The BTRs or BMPs normally remain within 100 to 400 meters behind tanks, engaging fortified positions as coordinated. If the terrain is rugged or heavily wooded, motorized rifle vehicles might lead the assault instead of tanks.

Engineer assets defeat minefieldsS with minesweeper or plow tanks, and line charges. Sappers or artillery fire may also be employed to defeat enemy minefields. Smoke and suppressive fires cover minefield and obstacle clearing. RTA forces create a single lane through enemy forward obstacles, per platoon.

The artillery fires suppress the enemy position until the first echelon elements reach the FEBA. Maneuver commanders shift artillery fires about 200 meters ahead of lead elements, depending upon weapon caliber with no pause between the preparatory fires and the start of fires in support of the attack. While fighting through enemy defenses, fires on successive concentrations or lines will be provided.

Fixed-wing air strikes normally are used for targets beyond artillery range. Attack helicopters provide close air support on the FEBA in direct support of ground units.

RTA units go into the final assault moving at maximum possible speed.

# V. The Meeting Engagement

The Red Team Army (RTA) doctrine describes meeting engagements as an encounter between two or more opponents when both forces are conducting offensive action. This is most often the result of obscured situational awareness.

## A. Objectives and Characteristics

The objectives of the meeting engagement include the destruction of the enemy's forces, seizure of key terrain to insure favorable conditions for future operations, and continuation of the advance.

An offensive generally develops unevenly over a wide front. The meeting engagement is characterized as:

- An unclear and fluid situation.
- Continuous effort to seize and maintain the initiative.
- Deployment into combat from the march at high speed.
- Violent battles over a wide front with considerable room to maneuver.
- Extremely limited planning time and heavy reliance on battle drills.

RTA forces do not look upon the meeting engagement as a purely chance occurrence. Commanders are trained to anticipate the likely point of a meeting engagement, to choose terrain, and to take the initiative. Aggressively initiative combined with fire and maneuver will win the meeting engagement.

The meeting engagement requires:

- Continuous reconnaissance and the correct interpretation of information.
- Speed in decision-making, planning, and issuing of orders.
- Anticipation of the enemy's most likely and dangerous course of action.
- Achieving momentum through immediate maneuver.
- Deployment of flank and rear security.

## B. Organization of the March

The organization of a march formation anticipating a meeting engagement varies with the situation. An organic reconnaissance company precedes a regiment conducting a march, usually out to about 25 kilometers.

The advance guard of a motorized rifle regiment usually consists of a motorized rifle battalion reinforced with artillery, tanks, air defense, engineer, and chemical elements. The forward security element is normally a motorized rifle company reinforced with tanks, artillery, mortars, and engineers.

The advance guard main body constitutes the bulk of the combat power of the advance guard. The advance guard main body has the mission of either eliminating enemy opposition, permitting continuation of the march, or fixing the enemy force to permit a flank attack by the main force. Artillery and tanks are habitually placed forward in the column. If a threat comes from the flank, artillery and tanks may be placed in the middle of the column.

The main force is comprised of about two thirds of the combat power of the regiment. The main force maneuvers to destroy enemy forces that cannot be quickly overcome by the advance guard. The composition of the main force may vary. Elements of the regimental engineer company are dispersed throughout the formation. The signal company and chemical defense company are probably in the middle or rear of the formation. Additional attachments from division may be allocated to the regiment's main force.

Rear security elements of up to company strength are normally positioned up to 3 kilometers from the advance guard and the main force. Depending on the enemy threat, flank security elements of up to platoon strength are dispatched up to 3 kilometers from the column.

*See following pages for discussion of the conduct of the meeting engagement.*

# C. Meeting Engagement (Phases)

*Ref: FM 100-2-1 The Soviet Army: Operations and Tactics (Jul '84), pp. 5-29 to 5-36.*

## Initial Phase

The initial phase of the meeting engagement is that period of combat from the time of enemy encounter by the leading element up to the commitment into battle of the main force. The initial phase is carried out by the elements of the advance guard.

The subsequent employment of the main force depends on the outcome of the initial phase. The use of reconnaissance reporting may permit employment of long-range fires, both artillery and air, to inflict damage on the enemy and to delay his advance.

At the time of initial contact, the advance guard main body is moving in march column 5 to 10 kilometers behind the forward security element. As the forward elements of the advance guard encounter the enemy, the regimental commander is at or near the head of his main force, some 20 to 30 km to the rear of the advance guard. This deliberate spacing is calculated to give the commander about 2 hours for planning and execution of his battle.

## Deployment of Main Force

When the advance guard becomes engaged, the main force continues its forward movement. The deployment of the main force depends on the outcome of advance guard action.

The four possible outcomes of advance guard action are:

- Attack by the advance guard is successful.
- Advance guard achieves no immediate success.
- Advance guard fails but is able to hold ground.
- Advance guard is in retreat, unable to hold the enemy.

When the outcomes of the advance guard action require deployment of the main force, the commander decides what form of maneuver to use – frontal attack, flank attack, envelopment, or a combination of these maneuver options.

The envelopment and the flank attack are the preferred forms of maneuver. However, in some cases the frontal attack is required. The time available to execute a maneuver may be a major factor in the commander's selection of a form of maneuver. If envelopment occurs, terrain must be trafficable and should provide covered or concealed routes for the enveloping force.

The preceding description of the meeting engagement focuses on the actions of a motorized rifle regiment. Unless such a regiment has been assigned an independent mission, such as pursuit or acting as a forward detachment, it is marching as part of a division force. Consequently, the development of battle might require the commitment of the follow-on elements of the division. The procedures are substantially the same as in the example of the lead regiment.

The meeting engagement will not always unfold in the sequence of encounters by reconnaissance elements, advance elements, and main bodies. Neither will it always begin with a head-to-head meeting; it may arise from direct encounter by main bodies, or from oblique encounters.

RTA doctrine for a successful meeting engagement requires surprise, rapid and decisive maneuver, and concentrated preemptive fires against the enemy. RTA commanders recognize that a hastily planned attack is more than offset by the benefits of a quick strike against the enemy before the enemy initiates action.

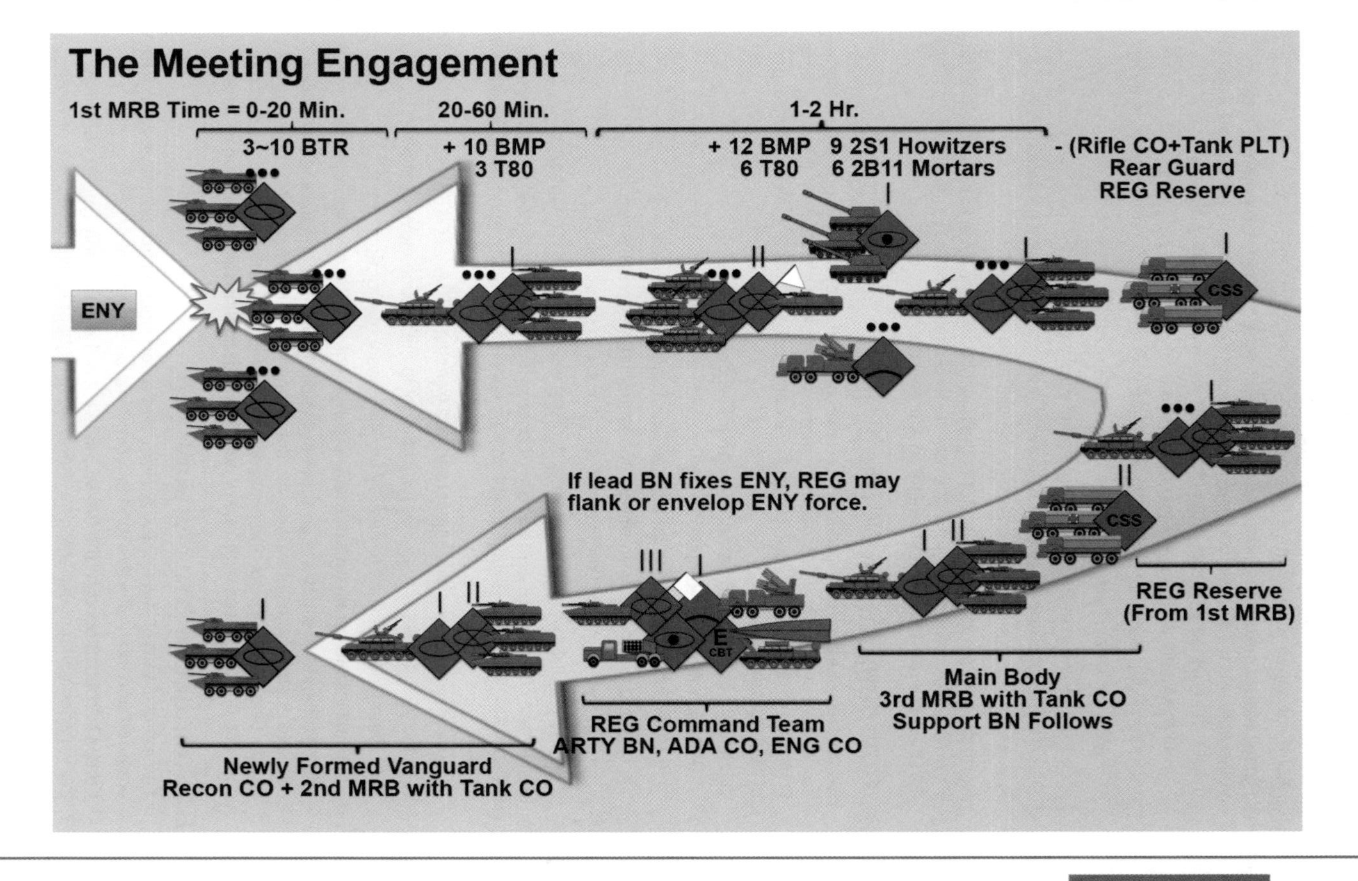


Offensive Operations

Offensive Operations

# VI. Pursuit

Red Team Army (RTA) doctrine describes the pursuit as an attack on a withdrawing enemy force through frontal or parallel maneuver combined with attacks against the enemy's flanks to catch them in their route of egress. The intent of the pursuit is to destroy or capture the enemy force in detail.

Pursuit features swift and deep movements of forces to strike the enemy's most vulnerable areas. By definition, a pursuit occurs when the enemy withdraws. This means the RTA commander must anticipate an enemy withdrawal:

- Immediately after a meeting engagement.
- After deep penetration of enemy defenses.
- When the enemy is threatened by encirclement.
- When the enemy is conducting a relief-in-place.
- Or when the enemy relocates to avoid nuclear or chemical contamination.

*See facing page for an illustration of a tacitcal-level pursuit.*

Normally, a regimental commander is the lowest command level to order the pursuit. However, RTA commanders at all levels are expected to seek the initiative and move into pursuit when indicators of withdrawal are evident.

## A. Planning for the Pursuit

Centralized planning and decentralized execution characterize the pursuit. Preservation of control is a primary concern in such a fast-moving situation. At the same time, RTA forces attempt to disrupt the enemy's command and control, as an integral part of destructive pursuit.

Continuity of the RTA commander's control is achieved by:

- Designating the direction, routes or zones of advance, and objectives.
- Establishing deadlines for completion of specific missions.
- Issuing fragmentary orders, as subsequent developments require.
- Augmenting normal radio communications with aerial relays.
- Coordination of reconnaissance, artillery fires and close air support.

Active reconnaissance, appreciation of enemy tactics, and knowledge of the current tactical situation are essential in obtaining indicators of enemy withdrawal. Indicators include:

- Increased enemy movement rearward from the FEBA.
- Increased artillery fires that may attempt to mask such movement.
- Enemy preparations to destroy facilities, resources or equipment.
- Small-scale counterattack that is incongruent with the situation.

The commander's situational awareness is paramount. Reconnaissance identifies possible enemy routes of egress, the conditions and critical terrain for those egress routes, plus enemy forces and capabilities. Once the pursuit is initiated, its success depends on RTA forces high rate of advance with continuous application of force.

## B. Conduct of the Pursuit

The forms of pursuit are frontal, parallel, and a combination frontal and parallel. The preferred and most effective form is a combination frontal and parallel.

Forces in contact conduct the frontal pursuit. It is the most likely type of pursuit at the very beginning of the enemy withdrawal, at night or in difficult terrain, or when off-road maneuver is limited.

# Tactical Pursuit

*Ref: FM 100-2-1 The Soviet Army: Operations and Tactics (Jul '84), p. 5-36 to 5-40.*

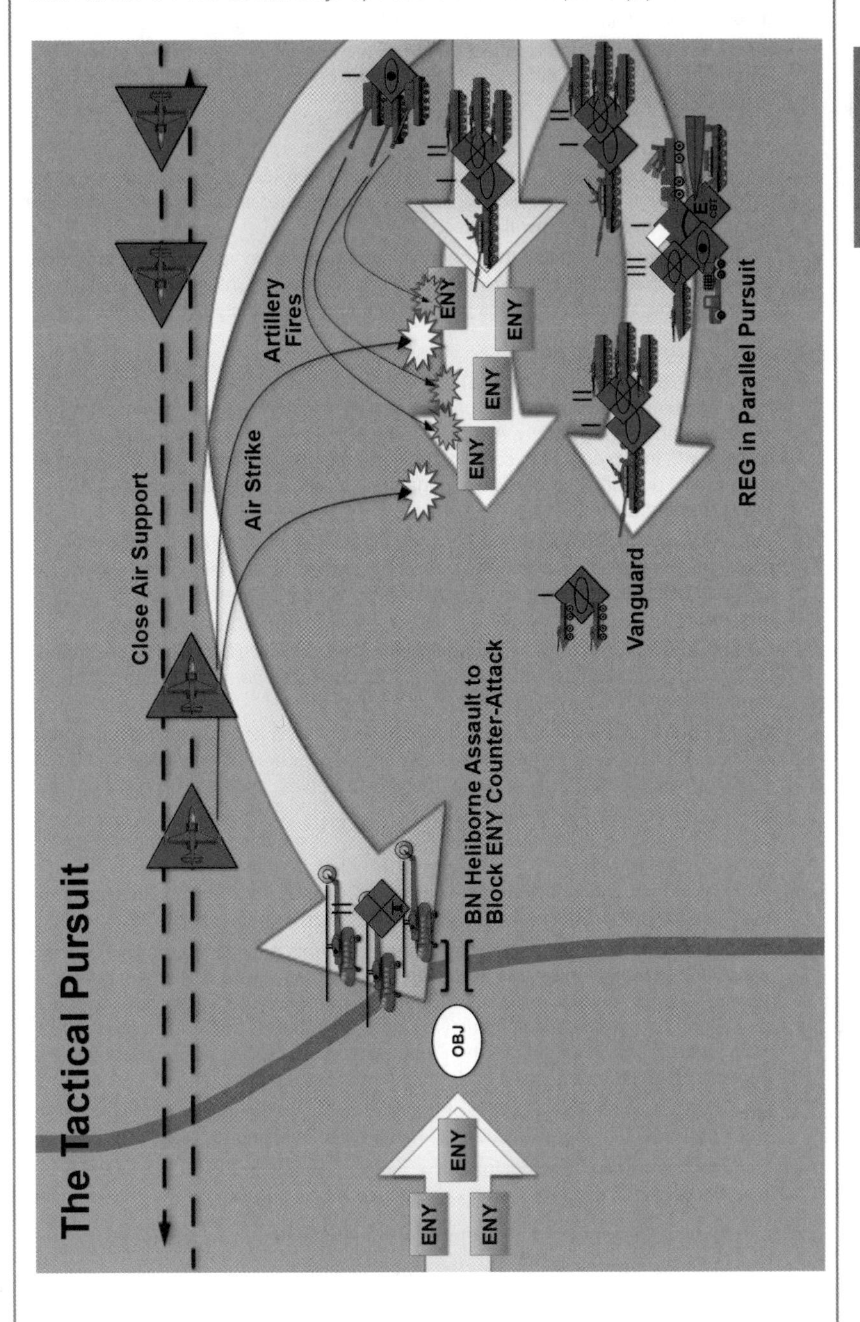


Offensive Operations

## Frontal Pursuit

Frontal pursuit applies constant pressure on the enemy. It limits his freedom of maneuver, his ability to take up defensive positions, and his ability to disengage. The aim of a frontal pursuit is to force the enemy to deploy and to accept combat under unfavorable conditions, and to delay the withdrawal.

Maneuver and flank attacks, though limited, are conducted. The frontal pursuit normally is not decisive since it only pushes the enemy back on his approaching reserves.



## Parallel Pursuit

In the parallel pursuit, the pursuit force advances on routes parallel to the withdrawing enemy. High-speed parallel pursuit may permit either attack on the enemy's flank or cutting his main withdrawal routes.

Under threat of flank attack, the enemy may be required to split his force and delay withdrawal while defending against the pursuer's attacks. Unless accompanied by frontal pursuit, this method gives the enemy some opportunity to maneuver and counterattack.

## Combination Frontal and Parallel Pursuit

In the combination of frontal and parallel pursuit, the main pursuit force moves parallel to the withdrawing enemy. A smaller force pursues directly, maintaining constant contact with the enemy. The combination form has the advantages of both frontal and parallel pursuit. It hinders disengagement, leads to flank attacks, and cuts the enemy's withdrawal routes.

The actions of the frontal pursuit force are aimed at facilitating the commitment of a parallel pursuit force, which is preferably tank heavy. The parallel force, with security elements in the lead, also uses march formations until deployment for the attack is required.

Heliborne or airborne forces may be assigned missions similar to those described for forward detachments. Vertical envelopment permits operations much deeper into enemy territory.

During pursuit, artillery missions include fire on columns and concentrations at road junctions, defiles, bridges, and crossings. They also include the repulse of enemy counterattacks, destruction or delay of enemy reserves, and destruction of enemy means of nuclear or chemical attack.

Close air support complements other fire support in the destruction and disorganization of the retreating enemy, particularly mobile targets. The situation during the course of a pursuit may become obscure. Consequently, reconnaissance is an important factor in insuring the success and coordinating air assets.

As the pursuit is developed, reconnaissance elements provide information on the disposition of retreating enemy formations and on the forward movement of his reserves. Because of the potential depth of the operation, aerial reconnaissance may be the primary means of identifying significant threats to pursuit forces. This intelligence is vital at the stage when a pursuit force faces the risk of becoming overextended. It could be the basis for termination of the pursuit.

The pursuit is terminated on order of the next higher commander. Conditions under which pursuit is terminated include the following culminating factors:

- The enemy has been destroyed.
- The pursuing force has outdistanced its logistic support.
- The pursuing force has become overextended and may be destroyed.
- Victories have diminished for the pursuing force.

Chap 2

# (Offensive Operations) III. Small Unit Tactics

Offensive Operations

*Ref: FM 100-2-1 The Soviet Army: Operations and Tactics (Jul '84), chap. 5, and Sharp, Soviet Infantry Tactic in World War II, chap. 3, 8 and 13.*

## I. Small-Unit Offensive Tactics

The offense is the default mode of operations for the RTA. It is the means by which the RTA imposes its will upon an enemy. Considerable resources are given to units that are conducting offensive actions, all the more true if that unit is appreciating significant gain within the battlespace.

RTA small-unit offensive operations may be directed against an enemy force, terrain, or enemy resources such as facilities or materiel supplies as the main objective.

Furthermore, RTA offensive action may come in the form of a detailed and deliberate attack against fortified enemy positions, or it may come in the form of a movement to contact against a dispersed enemy force that is conducting a mobile defense or retrograde.

Whichever the case, RTA small units almost invariably employ classic "hammer and anvil" tactics to trap the enemy objective between two or more RTA forces.

# II. Hammer & Anvil Attack

*Ref: FM 100-2-1 The Soviet Army: Operations and Tactics, chap. 5.*

The RTA divides its force depending on the nature of the enemy objective. It may maintain both elements as mounted mechanized forces, or it may dismount the infantry as a light force and maintain the armored vehicles as a separate, heavy bronegruppa force.

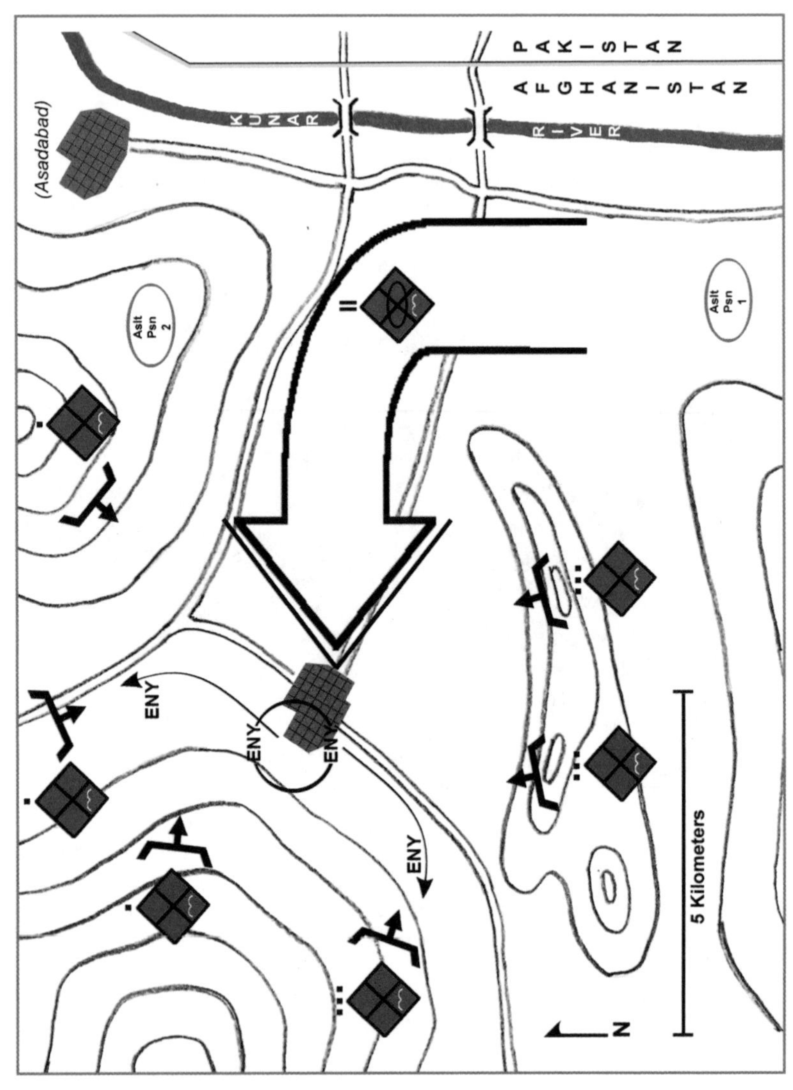


*Ref: Grau, The Bear Went Over the Mountain, p. 11 and FM 100-2-2 The Soviet Army, p. 2-8. The hammer and anvil involves a mobile force that pushes the enemy back against prepared fighting positions conducting attack-by-fire into the engagement area.*

## A. Array Combat Power of the Attack

Which element functions as the attacking "hammer" and which element functions as the blocking "anvil" also depend on the nature of the enemy objective.

The effort is for the attack force to locate, attack, and push the enemy force off the initial objective to send them retreating into the prepared killing zones of the blocking force. That is why the blocking force most often maintains the mass casualty producing weapons integral to the vehicles in the bronegruppa. Too, the bronegruppa moves much faster than a dismounted attack force. In some instances the bronegruppa may wait until the attack force has initiated the engagement before the bronegruppa moves into position.

| ENY OBJ | Attack Force | Blocking Force |
|---|---|---|
| Entrenched Fortifications | Heavy: Armor + INF | Heavy: Armor + INF |
| Urban Fortifications | Heavy: Armor + INF | Heavy: Bronegruppa |
| Light Defenses - Open Terrain | Heavy: Armor + INF | Heavy: Bronegruppa |
| Light Defenses – Restricted Terrain | Heavy: Armor + INF | Light: Dismounted INF |
| Special Purpose Attack | Light: Dismounted INF | Heavy: Bronegruppa |

## B. Considerations for the Attack

The selection of the blocking force location is every bit as critical as the location of the attack itself. If the enemy force can see the blocking force in position, they're very unlikely to fall back into those prepared kill zones. Instead, because the enemy is trapped with few options, they'll almost certainly fight harder from their defensive positions against the attacking force. This can prove disastrous for an RTA attack.

The blocking force location must then be discrete. It should be positioned at a point along the enemy's anticipated egress route, far enough back that the enemy force is unaware of the blocking force presence. Alternatively, the blocking force may be camouflaged carefully so as the enemy cannot observe it – a difficult feat to achieve with vehicles of the bronegruppa, but a possible solution nonetheless. Finally, if the bronegruppa has a cleared route to the blocking position, the commander may opt to dispatch the bronegruppa to its assigned blocking position only after the enemy is pushed off the initial objective. In this manner, the intended location of the blocking force is not disclosed to the enemy.

*Caution: Simplicity dictates that the blocking position is occupied before the engagement. The option to move the bronegruppa after the engagement has initiated must be used only when the route is obviously substantial enough to support the bronegruppa – and it has already been cleared of obstacles such as anti-armor mines.*

# C. Execution of the Attack (Hammer and Anvil)

1. From the assigned Assault Position (AP) the blocking force assumes attack-by-fire positions along the enemy's route of egress. The blocking force makes careful use of noise and light discipline to ensure the enemy is caught unaware. Once in position, the blocking force must indicate this via the designated communication signal.

2. Battlefield deception may be employed against heavier enemy fortifications. Feign attacks, artillery barrage and multiple concentrations of smoke canister may be employed to confuse the enemy as to the true location of the assault/breach team. When appropriate such attacks may take place under conditions of darkness, rain, or other forms of limited visibility to further impair enemy capabilities.

*The platoon bronegruppa is guided into a blocking position by a scout team (Note the UAZ vehicles). From the blocking position the bronegruppa can cutoff the enemy escape or prevent reinforcement. (Courtesy of Hae-jung Larsen and OP EASTWIND.)*

*Feign attacks are commonly employed to confuse the enemy as to the true location or direction of the main attack. At the squad and platoon level, feints are sometimes used to draw enemy fire and then attack those exposed enemy positions. (Courtesy of Hae-jung Larsen and OP EASTWIND.)*

3. With the blocking force in position and battlefield deception techniques underway, the attack force departs its assigned AP. The attack force will break into a heavy weapons support team and an assault/breach team. The support team assumes a support-by-fire position in over-watch. The assault/breach team identifies an appropriate point along the enemy's defense to penetrate.

*With forces in blocking position and battlefield deception in play, the support section quickly assumes overwatch. Supporting fires suppress and disrupt the enemy from an effective response. Virtually any type of crew served weapon is used. (Courtesy of Hae-jung Larsen and OP EASTWIND.)*



*The assault team creates a breach in the enemy's defenses that is immediately exploited for further tactical gain. The assault team seeks the least exposed avenue of attack and often employs smoke to hide individual troops from enemy gunners. (Courtesy of Hae-jungLarsen and OP EASTWIND.)*

4. Once the enemy defenses have been penetrated, the gap is compromised to further exploit enemy vulnerabilities. Synchronized use of supporting direct and indirect fires help to disrupt the enemy attempts to coordinate an effective defense. Often this includes artillery and Close Air Support (CAS) fires.

5. With the enemy unable to muster an effective defense, they will fall back, escaping through their lines of communication – their routes of egress. It is important that the attack force places continued pressure on the enemy as they attempt to escape. This pressure serves to push the enemy into prepared killing zones of the blocking force.

6. The blocking force will conduct attack-by-fire to further disrupt and reduce the enemy numbers in the prepared kill zones. If necessary, the pursuing attack force will continue to defeat the enemy in detail by attacking the smaller, isolated enemy forces suppressed within the kill zones.

# III. Special Purpose Attacks

*Ref: FM 100-2-2 Specialized Warfare and Rear Area Support, chap. 2.*

RTA conduct special purpose attacks in a myriad of forms, though primarily such actions are classified as ambushes or raids. More often than not, such special purpose attacks are employed in tandem, creating a network of coordinated yet independent actions by small tactical units.

## A. The Raid

The fire and maneuver schematics of the raid are conducted very much the same as the RTA attack, as discussed in the previous section. Where there is principled difference between the raid and the attack rests with the intent of both actions.

The attack seeks to destroy an enemy force or occupy terrain/facility, and then stay. The attacking force will remain in the area for a significant period of time. This tactical gain has an immediate and potentially permanent benefit to the operational environment.

*RTA commanders almost exclusively value the offense over defense. And battle drill at the small unit level reflects this preference. (Courtesy of Hae-jung Larsen and OP EASTWIND.)*

By contrast, the raid seeks a far more temporary tactical goal that has the potential to benefit the tactical, operational and even strategic disposition of the RTA purpose. Raids may be conducted to destroy key enemy personnel or materiel resources; to capture high-value enemy personnel for intelligence information; or to rescue and repatriate RTA forces that have been taken prisoner by the enemy. But the key element may boil down to simply that the raiding force will leave immediately after achieving those objectives.

For the sake of clarity, when conducting the raid the blocking force will be renamed "security force". It has the dual purpose of stopping enemy personnel from escaping the raid objective – and keeping any reinforcing enemy patrols away from the raid objective.

Aside from these identified distinctions, raids are otherwise conducted with the same fire and maneuver considerations as the RTA attack. There is little need to rehash that. So instead, this section will explore the other form of special purpose attack – the ambush.

## B. The Parallel Ambush

An ambush is a surprise attack on a moving or otherwise temporarily halted enemy force. Surprise and an overwhelming level of Violence of Action (VOA) are the hallmarks of a successful ambush.

RTA ambushes may employ any combination of support team, assault team, and/or security team. Which teams are employed depends largely on the target and whether or not the enemy has nearby forces that may attempt to reinforce or rescue the enemy target.

*The directional nature of the ambush leaves the RTA unit vulnerable. Ambushes are carefully planned, coordinated and rehearsed. Here a squad leader briefs his deputy leader and two senior enlisted troops attached to his squad. (Courtesy of Hae-jung Larsen and OP EASTWIND.)*

### Special Considerations for Parallel Ambush

The location and formation from which to spring an ambush is most critical. The parallel formation is the preferred RTA ambush as it offers multiple perspectives of the prepared kill zone.

The parallel ambush is formed by two lines of troops who appear to place each other within their assigned sectors of fire – but of course this is not the case at all. Instead the parallel ambush uses either common low ground or common high ground in between the two lines of troops as a safety barrier. In this manner only the enemy target receives the trauma of being fired at from multiple sides, simultaneously. Indeed a third line of troops is often included to join the two parallel lines into a "U" formation when the ambush team is certain of the enemy's approaching direction.

Additionally, RTA commanders must identify ambush positions that are far enough away from the kill zone that their troops will not be readily observed by the enemy force. Yet the ambush position also has to be near enough such that their primary weapons are still effective. This requires a delicate balance.

Too close, and the enemy detects the ambush force. Too far away, and the enemy escapes with relative ease.

*Ref: Parallel ambush is the preference of RTA forces. In this example a third element (near) closes off the enemy's path, trapping them in the low ground below. Teams have set into position and coordinated their sectors of fire. Work priorities include camouflage next. Grau, The Bear Went Over the Mountain, map 39. (Courtesy of of Hae-jung Larsen and OP EASTWIND.)*

As a rule of thumb, RTA daytime ambushes on dismounted enemy personnel are between 50m and 100m, terrain permitting. Nighttime ambushes on dismounted enemy are closer, typically between 10m and 50m, visibility permitting.

RTA daytime ambushes on a light armored enemy force are generally prescribed at 200m. And daytime ambushes on heavily armored enemy forces are common at 300m and farther, again terrain permitting.

Nighttime ambushes on vehicle convoys are rare because few of the appropriate weapon systems have reliable night vision sights. However there are notable exceptions, such as on brightly moonlit nights and in terrain where enemy armored formations are easily canalized.

| Target Type | Effective Weapon | Optimal Range |
|---|---|---|
| Enemy Personnel | Light & Medium Machinegun | 100m – 400m |
| | Rifle & Carbine | 25m – 200m |
| | Anti-Personnel Mine | 10m – 50m |
| Light Armor Vehicles | Medium & Heavy Machinegun | 200m – 800m |
| | Rocket Propelled Grenade | 200m – 400m |
| | Grenade Launcher | 50m – 300m |
| Heavy Armor Vehicles | Guided Missile | 300m – 1500m |
| | Rocket Propelled Grenade | 200m – 400m |
| | Anti-Tank Mine | 0m |

# RTA Ambush Teams

## Security Teams

Security teams are often small in number. For anti-armor ambushes the security team must be able to fend off any enemy attempt to rescue forces caught in the kill zone. Security teams for anti-armor ambushes then require armor-defeat capabilities in the form of command detonated anti-tank mines or rocket propelled missiles/grenades.

Security teams for anti-personnel ambushes carry light weapons, but may also be assigned light machineguns and command detonated anti-personnel mines.

## Support Teams

Support teams often make up half the ambush force, or possibly more in specific instances. The support team carries mass casualty producing weapons for anti-personnel ambushes, such as machineguns, grenade launchers, anti-personnel mines and mortars. For anti-armor ambushes support teams carry heavier missiles that may be wire-guided.

## Assault Teams

Assault teams have the dangerous task of assaulting across the kill zone to finish off or capture enemy forces. Assault teams often carry just small arms and hand grenades. They may also carry specialized weapons and gear for destroying enemy equipment, caring for wounded comrades, or immobilizing enemy prisoners of war.

*As a general rule of thumb all three teams – support, assault, security – are used in the ambush. However, economy of force weighs into such planning. If for example no assault will be made of the ambush kill zone, these troops are used to bolster the security and support sections. Likewise, if there is little threat of enemy reinforcement patrols, security of each team can be handled internally, and the security troops will be used to strengthen the support and assault sections.*

# Execution of the Parallel Ambush

1. A security team is positioned during the reconnaissance phase of the ambush. This security team will observe the ambush kill zone and report any changes back to the commander. The intent is to protect the ambush team from being counter-ambushed or counterattacked by enemy forces. The location of this security team becomes the release point for the ambush.

2. On order from the Objective Rally Point (ORP), the entire ambush teams departs the ORP to link up with the security team at the release point. The order of march is the remainder of the security force, the heavy weapon support team, and the assault team.

*The security team left behind in overwatch once the kill zone has been selected also function as a guide for the rest of the ambush patrol. This is particularly important during nighttime operations. This position becomes the default release point. (Courtesy of Hae-jung Larsen and OP EASTWIND.)*

3. From the release point, the security team moves to the far flanks of both parallel teams. Once the security team is in position, the support team moves into position, and last the assault team moves into position. This may take considerable time. Plan accordingly.

4. Work details are attended to at this point – including the setting of mines or other obstacles to slow the enemy in the kill zone. Also, RTA troops must camouflage themselves so as not to be observed by enemy forces within the kill zone. Noise, light, and movement discipline must be enforced. Yet in the most extreme conditions, it is not reasonable to expect such diligence from troops for more than a couple of hours. Certainly there are exceptions to that rule of thumb, based on the nature of the target, terrain, and relative distance from the kill zone.

5. Once set, the ambush waits for a target. When a suitable target enters the kill zone, the commander will give the order to open fire. This may be done vocally, by pyrotechnic signal, or simply by initiating fire with a weapon.

Caution: If an unsuitable target moves into the kill zone, such as enemy armor when the ambush team has no anti-tank weapons, the "No Fire" rule is in effect. This means that the commander will not give the order to fire. Instead, the enemy target will simply pass through the kill zone unaware that they are being observed.

6. At the instant the commander gives the order to open fire – ALL troops shoot into their assigned sectors of the kill zone. It does not matter that they can clearly see enemy targets or not. They must fire to shock and suppress any enemy countermeasures. The exact number of magazines they shoot, and the amount of time will be predetermined in the Operations Order (OPORD) based on the type of target, the size of the ambush team, and the nature of the terrain and visibility conditions.

*RTA troops fall back through the ambush release point – though in practice there is often more than a single release point for the parallel ambush. (Couresy of Hae-jung Larsen and OP EASTWIND.)*

7. If the commander intends to sweep the objective with the assault team, a prearranged signal will be issued. Whether this signal is a vocal command, whistle, or flare – ALL troops must lift and/or shift their fires off the objective. This avoids fratricide as the assault team sweeps across the kill zone.

8. On order, the assault team sweeps the entire kill zone online. They secure the opposite side of the kill zone, in full view of the support team, and conduct assigned tasks for each specialty team. This may include enemy POW/KIA search, demolition teams, and first aid litter teams. Once these tasks are concluded, the assault team commander gives a prearranged signal to the ambush commander that the objective is complete.

9. The ambush commander then gives the signal to withdraw. Most often the assault team and support team withdraw from the ambush location simultaneously, while the security team provides rear cover. Once the assault and support teams have passed by the commander standing at the release point, the commander will give the next signal, telling the security team to withdraw.

10. All elements of the ambush team meet back at the ORP and form an immediate 360$^0$ defense. The ORP is typically one terrain feature back from the ambush site. At this distance the team can attend wounded comrades, enemy POW, and make ready any damaged equipment. Before the ambush team departs the ORP – all Priority Intelligence Requirements (PIR) are disseminated amongst the entire team! In this manner, even if only one of the ambush team makes it back to friendly forces, the value of the ambush will not have been lost.

*The ambush patrol ends up where it began – back in the Objective Rally Point. Here the commander will disseminate relevant information of the mission and the troops will reconsolidate and reorganize before continuing their patrol. (Courtesy of Hae-jung Larsen and OP EASTWIND.)*

# IV. On Point: Time Discipline in the Ambush

The ambush is a quiet place. Boredom, anxiety and excitement complicate the need to remain diligent in observing the kill zone. Troops begin to fidget and move. This causes not only distracting noises, but the human eye quickly sees such movement.

Of the statistically few ambushes that actually make contact with an enemy target, fully half of those ambushes are visually detected before the enemy even walks into the kill zone. And being discovered by the enemy while set in ambush could be very dangerous for the ambush team.

Just as commanders must strike a balance of optimal weapon range per target and the desire to get as close to the kill zone as possible, so too must the commander balance the amount of time spent sitting in ambush. The closer the troops are to the kill zone, the greater diligence is required in terms of noise, light and movement discipline. The farther back from the kill zone, the more such requirements are somewhat relaxed.

*While RTA doctrine allows significantly greater time than its Western counterparts for the ambush to conduct the business of destroying the enemy in the kill zone, it remains a balancing act. Commanders who stay too long may have their routes of egress cut off. The squad could very well have the ambush turned on it instead. (Courtesy of Hae-jung Larsen and OP EASTWIND.)*

This means that it is difficult to maintain noise, light and movement discipline beyond a two-hour duration at 10 meters from the kill zone – even less in extreme heat or cold. However, at 200 meters from the kill zone, such diligence might be expected for considerably longer periods of time, perhaps even a day or longer in a single ambush.

Lastly commanders must pay attention to their watch once the ambush has been initiated. One of the mistakes RTA commonly make is staying too long in the ambush, treating it as if it were a rolling battle instead of an intense short fight. Ambushes are directional in nature. If the enemy gets into the flanks or rear of the ambush formation, the route of egress can be cut off and all may be lost. Hit hard, hit fast, and then leave quickly.

# Defensive Operations



*Ref: FM 100-2-1 The Soviet Army: Operations and Tactics (Jul '84), chap. 6.*

## I. The Role and Nature of the Defense

Soviets consider the offensive as the only means to achieve decisive victory. However, defensive doctrine has not been totally overlooked. Grounded in the histories of World War II and the great defensive battles of Stalingrad, Moscow, and Kursk, the Soviets have developed a doctrine that is mindful of recent technological developments such as ATGMs and nuclear weapons. Stated reasons for assuming the defense are-

- To consolidate gains
- To await additional resources when temporarily halted by the enemy during the course of an offensive
- To protect the flanks of a formation or a seacoast
- To repulse an enemy counterthrust
- To regroup after severe losses suffered from nuclear weapons
- To free resources for other units that are on the offensive
- To await logistic support

### Defensive Operations

**Prepared Defense** *(pp. 3-7 to 3-10)*

**Hasty Defense** *(pp. 3-11 to 3-12)*

**Withdrawal** *(p. 3-13 to 3-16)*

In most of these cases, the defense is temporary and leads to the resumption of the offense. The two major forms of the defense are the prepared defense and the hasty defense (sometimes called "defense in the course of the offense"). A hasty defense may turn into a prepared defense if conditions and availability of resources do not favor resuming the offense in that sector.

The defense at front and army levels may involve the entire formation during the initial stage of hostility where an enemy attacks across international borders, or in a sector where no offensive action is planned. Usually only part of the formation is on the defense while the rest takes offensive action.

During World War II, entire theaters were on the defense. Extremely dense defenses sometimes were developed, consisting of three or more static defensive belts with the majority of the combat forces deployed in the first defensive belt.

The development of nuclear weapons required modification of this concept and increased the importance of a security echelon and a reserve. Modern defensive doctrine at front and army levels stresses defense in depth; but rather than multiple continuous belts, the defensive area consists of clusters of strongpoints. At both front and army levels, the key is stubborn defense of the forward area by motorized rifle forces deployed in depth and decisive counterattacks by highly mobile, tank-heavy forces of a second echelon and a reserve. The increased fluidity of combat has required an increase in the size of reserves.

The operational reserve and second echelon may make up half of the force. While second echelon divisions of an army will occupy defensive positions, their major tasks will be to counterattack and to destroy enemy forces penetrating the forward defenses.

It is the first echelon divisions that hold the forward edge of the army and front defenses. It is at division level that we find all the principles of defense employed. Therefore, the remainder of this chapter will examine the defense as conducted by a first echelon division.



# II. Conduct of the Defense

At division level, the tactical defense is very important and can be an integral part of a larger offensive operation. A typical Soviet response against a counterattack is to place a division on the defense to halt the attack while other divisions continue the advance.

## A. Division-level Defense

When a division is ordered to assume the defense, the commander issues orders based on a map reconnaissance and personally clarifies missions on the ground. He determines key terrain, enemy avenue; of approach and probable main attack axis, areas for possible nuclear and chemical strikes, organization for combat, maneuver requirements, organization of strongpoints, probable counterattack axes, and locations of command posts and command observation posts. Soviet commanders are expected to make maximum use of the terrain and to avoid establishing patterns that would make enemy targeting easier.

A tank or motorized rifle division typically defends a sector 20 to 30 kilometers in width and 15 to 20 kilometers in depth. The commander normally organizes the main defensive area in two echelons and a reserve. The first echelon's mission is to inflict losses on the enemy, to force him to concentrate, and to canalize him into fire sacks. The second echelon's mission is to stop and destroy enemy penetrations or to reinforce or replace troops of the first echelon.

While there is no rigid requirement for the composition of echelons, normally at least two regiments are placed in the division's first echelon. In a motorized rifle division, the first echelon consists of motorized rifle regiments. A tank regiment usually is employed as a division's main counterattack force.

The division commander issues a combat order which contains information about the enemy, the mission, the concept of the operation, the location of the FEBA, and the position to be occupied. The order further specifies the following details:

- For first echelon regiments: reinforcements, missions, defense sectors, and axes and areas in which main efforts are to be concentrated.
- For second echelon regiments: reinforcements, missions, defense sectors, and axes and deployment lines for counterattacks.
- The time that positions are to be occupied.
- Coordination requirements.

When the defense is established before contact with the enemy, the Soviets establish a security echelon up to 15 kilometers forward of the main defensive area.

# III. Defensive Planning Fundamentals

*Ref: FM 100-2-1 The Soviet Army: Operations and Tactics (Jul '84), pp. 6-4 to 6-5.*

> *A type of combat action conducted for the purpose of repulsing an attack mounted by superior enemy forces, causing heavy casualties, retaining important regions of terrain, and creating favorable conditions for going over to a decisive offensive. Defense is based on strikes by nuclear and all other types of weapons; on extensive maneuver with firepower, forces, and weapons; on counterattacks (or counterstrikes) with simultaneous stubborn retention of important regions which intercept the enemy direction of advance; and also on the extensive use of various obstacles. Defense makes it possible to gain time and to effect an economy in forces and weapons in some sectors, thereby creating conditions for an offensive in others.*
>
> *Soviet Dictionary of Basic Military Terms*

Defensive Operations

In the Soviet view, the prepared defense is distinguished from the hasty defense by the amount of time and engineer support available for preparation of the defense. The types tend to merge as a function of time. The latter stages of a hasty defense may approximate the early stages of a prepared defense. The prepared defense is more detailed than the hasty defense, so this section will deal mainly with it for descriptive purposes. Two fundamental considerations affect the division commander's defensive planning:

## 1. The defense should provide protection against nuclear weapons

First, the defense should provide protection against nuclear weapons. Defense under nuclear conditions demands dispersion, deception, and field fortifications. The advent of small-yield nuclear weapons has complicated the problem of dispersion. When the minimum yield of a warhead was approximately 20 kilotons, dispersion was achieved by maintaining intervals between battalions. The development of warheads of less than I kiloton increased the need for dispersion so that now, according to the Soviets, company and platoon strongpoints are the basis of the defense. Increased dispersion leads to problems in fire support coordination and troop control. Furthermore, a defense that is too dispersed does not offer sufficient resistance to accomplish the defensive missions. As a result, the Soviets caution that dispersion must not be accomplished at the price of effective defense.

## 2. The defense must be organized in sufficient depth to provide effective fire and maneuver

The second fundamental consideration is that the defense must be organized in sufficient depth to provide effective fire and maneuver. The enemy must be engaged at as great a range as possible and must continue to meet an ever-increasing volume of fire as he nears the defensive positions. Fire support weapons must be positioned so that they can shift their fires against threatened axes within the defensive position. To counterattack enemy penetrations, units deployed in the depth of the defense must be in position to maneuver and concentrate rapidly.

A system of fire is constructed to bring all available fires on the enemy as he approaches and to provide for continuous fire at the forward edge, the flanks, and within the defensive position. In addition, it should provide for the rapid concentration of fire against threatened axes.

The elements which make up the security echelon come from the division's second echelon. A security force of up to battalion size may be deployed in front of each first echelon regiment.

A detailed and coordinated fire plan is developed. Weapons are positioned so that the maximum amount of fire can be brought to bear directly in front of the FEBA Enemy penetrations are blunted by shifting artillery fire and by conducting counterattacks.

The commander controls the defense through a series of command posts and command observation posts. At division level, there are normally four command posts: a main command post, a forward command post, an alternate command post, and a rear area command post.

The main command post is located in the rear of the defensive sector and contains the bulk of the staff. The chief of staff directs its operation.



The division commander establishes a forward command post with a small group of selected staff members. The composition of this group varies but usually includes the operations officer and chief of rocket troops and artillery (CRTA). This post may be as close as 3 kilometers from the FEBA.

An alternate command post contains representatives from key staff sections. Displaced from the division main command post, it is ready to take over direction of the division if the main command post is damaged or destroyed.

The rear area command post is established and controlled by the deputy commander for rear services.

Besides the command posts, the commander may establish command observation posts which are controlled from the forward command post. These posts have radio and wire communications and permit the commander and his CRTA to better observe different sectors of the battlefield.

There is no rigid structure for the location of command posts. Command posts are established where the commander orders them established. He makes use of terrain to camouflage command posts and places them according to his mission concept. The Soviets avoid establishing command posts on distinguishing terrain features.

They anticipate radio communications to be difficult and often impossible or undesirable in combat and they train accordingly. During training exercises, the Soviets regularly practice the use of radio, wire, pyrotechnic (visual signals), sound, and courier communications. It is standard procedure for them to employ wire communications in a defensive position or an assembly area. This means of communication -- including the prompt restoration of destroyed lines receives heavy emphasis in Soviet tactical exercises.

## B. Regimental-level Defense

A regiment may be used in the first or second echelon of the division defenses. As part of a division's first echelon, its mission is to prevent penetration of the main defenses by repulsing enemy assaults with intense fire and counterattacks by its reserve. When given the mission to defend in the division's second echelon, a regiment attempts to defeat any enemy penetration of the division's first echelon.

Regimental subunits normally are dispersed so that a single low-yield nuclear strike can destroy no more than one company. Dispersion is also limited to ensure the stability of the defense and to maintain the capability to maneuver.

A division first echelon's mission is to prevent penetration of the main defenses by repulsing enemy assaults with intense fire and counterattacks by its reserve. When given the mission to defend in the division's second echelon, a regiment attempts to defeat any enemy penetration of the division's first echelon.

Regimental subunits normally are dispersed so that a single low-yield nuclear strike can destroy no more than one company. Dispersion is also limited to ensure the stability of the defense and to maintain the attacks capability to mass fires. The defensive frontage for a regiment is normally 10 to 15 kilometers. The depth may vary from 7 to 10 kilometers.

A regimental reserve normally is positioned near the regiment's second echelon. It is usually of company size and tank heavy. Its mission is to conduct counterattacks against an enemy penetration.

A regimental antitank reserve normally is formed from the antitank missile battery (found only in motorized rifle regiments), the engineer company, and either a tank or motorized rifle platoon. The engineer company probably operates as a mobile obstacle detachment to emplace hasty minefields and obstacles. The antitank reserve occupies an assembly area generally near the regimental command post.

A regiment in the division first echelon has its command post centrally located between its first and second echelons. A regimental command observation point may be established in the area of one of the subordinate battalions. Regimental logistic units and the rear area command post are positioned to the rear of the regimental second echelon. Communications are established between the command and observation posts. Wire is the primary mode, supplemented by messengers, pyrotechnic signals, and radio.

The division commander is responsible for security forward of the FEBA. The regiment is responsible for local security in front of the defensive positions of its first echelon battalions. When time and terrain limit establishment of a security echelon by division, regiments in the first echelon organize combat outposts. Each first echelon battalion places a reinforced motorized rifle platoon forward, across the main expected enemy avenue of approach into the battalion defensive area. The reconnaissance company of the first echelon regiment perfomls screening and reconnaissance activity in front of the combat outposts. Each battalion organizes its own observation and listening posts.

## C. Battalion-level Defense

After receiving the mission from his regimental commander, a battalion commander begins organizing his assigned sector. The regimental order is as complete as possible. As a minimum, it contains the battalion's mission, trace of the FEBA, and battalion boundaries.

In a hasty defense, there may be no time for the regimental commander to issue an order with detailed supplementary instructions. Consequently, the motorized rifle battalion commander is allowed more initiative and flexibility in organizing his defensive position in this situation. The battalion initially consolidates on the terrain it occupies or attempts to seize critical terrain favorable for the defense. In contrast, organization of a prepared defense is centrally planned by the regiment.

A typical battalion defensive area is 3 to 5 kilometers wide and up to 2 kilometers deep. A battalion usually defends with companies in a single echelon. Single echelon deployment permits the greatest concentration of firepower but it also reduces defense in depth. When a battalion defends on a narrow frontage and/or greater depth is required, it may deploy in two echelons, with two companies in its first echelon and one in its second echelon. Reserves are located behind the second echelon. The distance between the first and second echelons can be up to 2 kilometers.

A company occupies a strongpoint 500 to 1000 meters in width and up to 500 meters in depth. Normally, all three platoons of a company defend in one echelon.

Artillery, tanks, engineers, and chemical defense troops attached to a battalion may be allocated to the companies. This allocation depends on the number and types of attachments received by the battalion and the importance of the sectors the companies are defending. Although artillery may be assigned to the companies for direct fire support, artillery is usually positioned to provide the best fire support for the entire battalion.

The battalion commander positions a small reserve (normally a platoon) where it can most rapidly and effectively stabilize the defense in the event of an enemy penetration. Key terrain and likely enemy avenues of attack are factors in determining where the battalion reserve will be positioned. Reaction time for a mounted reserve is based on speeds of 20 to 30 kilometers per hour in daytime and 15 to 20 kilometers per hour at night.

The mortar battery of a motorized rifle battalion is deployed in accordance with the overall fire plan and is positioned to provide close-in fires for the company strongpoints.

The battalion's rear service elements are located in covered and concealed positions within the battalion area. Rear service elements are responsible for their own security and should change locations frequently to avoid destruction from enemy air and artillery fire.



Defensive fires are centrally organized and are planned as far forward of the FEBA as possible. Fires are concentrated on avenues of approach using a series of designated fire lines. The distance between theese lines is 400 to 600 meters on high-speed avenues. The distance is less on less-likely avenues of approach because of a probable slower rate of advance. Artillery fire is used to separate attacking infantry from their tanks approximately 200 to 400 meters from the FEBA. Final protective fires are planned within 100 meters of the FEBA, with concentrations to halt the advance of enemy forces that have penetrated the defenses.

Antitank defenses are organized to engage enemy tanks at an effective range up to 3 kilometers forward of the FEBA. Normal distance between tanks and antitank weapons in defensive positions is about 100 meters. On open terrain, there may be up to 200 meters between tanks in defensive positions. The terrain is a dominant factor in positioning tanks and antitank weapons. Each tank and antitank weapon has a primary and secondary sector of fire as well as primary and alternate positions.

Barrier plans and the system of fire complement each other. Both antitank and antipersonnel minefields are laid forward of the FEBA and throughout the depth of defensive positions. Antitank obstacles are covered by direct and indirect fires.

The Soviets constantly emphasize that the defense is a temporary form of combat that makes the transition to the offense easier. This transition can be made, however, only when each level of command is able to counterattack. The Soviets stress that counterattacks should be made when the enemy attack is stalled and he is unable to secure the terrain seized and to bring his reserves forward.

Each level of command is prepared to conduct a counterattack. If the enemy's forces and fires overwhelm the Soviets' first echelon defenses and prevent them from conducting a counterattack, subunits hold their position, strike the enemy with all available fires, and create sufficient resistance for a counterattack by forces of the next higher command. As the enemy advances into the depths of the Soviet defense, he advances on positions that have been better prepared; and he encounters progressively larger, more powerful (primarily tank-heavy) second echelon formations, which act as counterattack forces.

As previously discussed, the Soviets emphasize dispersion into company-sized strongpoints, while maintaining mutual fire support as a defense against tactical nuclear weapons. By forming company strongpoints, adequate maneuver space is created to shift forces and to counterattack once the enemy's main attack is determined. The strongpoint is usually centered on the platoon in the second main trench.

The next higher commander authorizes a counterattack to be launched. In most cases, counterattacks are initiated from the flanks. Counterattacks are preceded by intense air and artillery fires and the fires of adjacent units. The counterattack force attacks from the march. Counterattacks at army or division levels may be the opening phase of a Soviet counteroffensive.

Chap 3

# (Defensive Operations)
# I. Prepared Defense

*Ref: FM 100-2-1 The Soviet Army: Operations and Tactics (Jul '84), chap. 6.*

## I. Concepts of the Prepared Defense

In organizing and establishing a prepared defense, the Soviet commander considers the same factors addressed by a US commander:

- Mission
- Enemy
- Terrain
- Troops
- Time

In analyzing his mission, the commander determines what it is he must accomplish and for how long. The destruction of an amphibious assault along the coast will require different measures than will the protection of an exposed flank.

The enemy and his weapon systems influence the mix of weapons and the type and amount of preparation required. Whether or not he is in contact makes a great difference to the defender. The terrain and vegetation also affect the force composition and deployment. This includes consideration of natural features such as high ground and other key terrain, rivers, and marshes. The troops available for commitment to the defense seriously affect the force dispositions. Finally, the amount of time available to establish the defense will temper all these considerations.

### Requirements for Establishing the Defense

- The deployment and employment of a security echelon
- The location and deployment of forces in a main defensive area
- The location of "fire sacks" (kill zones) and ambush sites
- Construction of minefields and obstacles
- The location, composition, and employment of the reserve

## A. Security Echelon

The security echelon or zone is that portion of the battlefield forward of the main defensive area. It is occupied by a force whose mission is to delay and deceive the enemy as to the location and deployment of the main defensive forces. The security force engages the enemy at the longest possible range and attempts to cause him to deploy prematurely.

The security force's size and composition depend on those factors mentioned earlier. The zone may extend to a depth of 30 kilometers at army level and 15 kilometers at division level. It is at least far enough forward to prevent aimed direct fire from being placed on the main defensive area.

The security force deploys on the best terrain to effect maximum damage to the attacking enemy. Obstacles and barriers are used extensively. When faced with encirclement or decisive engagement, the forces of the security zone attempt to withdraw under cover of artillery fire and to return to the main defensive area.

## B. Main Defensive Area

The main defensive area may appear as bands, belts, or layers, but it is simply a defense in depth. The basic element of the main defensive area is the company or platoon strongpoint. This is established on terrain that is key to the defense and must be retained at all costs. The subunit occupying the strongpoint prepares an allround defense with alternate and supplementary firing positions for all weapons. Fires are planned to be mutually supporting as well as provide for fire sacks. Vehicles are dug in, and a network of communication trenches is constructed linking weapon positions with supply, command and control, and fighting positions. Everything that can be is dug in and given overhead protection. Wire provides the primary means of communication. Minefields, obstacles, and barriers are emplaced and covered by fire. In addition, the Soviets rely heavily on the use of maneuver by fire and fire sacks to damage or destroy the enemy force.

## C. Fire Sacks

Maneuver by fire is the concentration of fires from many guns from dispersed firing positions. Fire is concentrated on an advancing enemy in a sudden and devastating strike or series of strikes. Fire sacks are formed based on key terrain, enemy avenues of approach, defensive strongpoints, obstacles and barriers, and preplanned fires. (The Russian term for this defensive deployment translates to "fire sacks" and is so used here in.) Fire sacks are similar to the US concept of a kill zone. Obstacles and barriers are planned along the edge of the fire sack to contain the enemy force, and reserves are placed where they can counterattack into the "sack" after the fires are lifted to destroy any remaining enemy.

Fires are planned to cover all approaches to the position. Finally the entire position is camouflaged. This may include the use of dummy positions to draw fire and to deceive the enemy as to the true location of the defenses.

Strongpoints are linked with other strongpoints until a defensive area or belt is formed. This occurs at every level, thus multiple belts are formed. Included in and between these belts are headquarters, logistic facilities, reserves, and combat support forces. Each of these elements is responsible for its own security.

## D. Minefields and Obstacles

### Minefields

Minefields are placed forward of the defensive position to slow the enemy and to force him to concentrate. Fires are planned to attack these concentrations and to prevent or delay breaching. Minefields are designed to break up the enemy's assault and to strip away the infantry's supporting armor. They are also designed to force the

# II. Characteristics of the Defense (U.S. Military Doctrine Perspective)

## A. Disruption
Defenders disrupt the attackers' tempo and synchronization with actions designed to prevent them from massing combat power. Commanders employ disruptive actions to unhinge the enemy's preparations and attacks. Disruption methods include misdirecting or destroying enemy reconnaissance forces, breaking up formations, isolating units, and attacking or disrupting systems.

## B. Flexibility
The conduct of the defense requires flexible plans. Commanders focus planning on preparations in depth, use of reserves, and the ability to shift the main effort. Commanders add flexibility by designating supplementary positions, designing counterattack plans, and preparing to counterattack.

## C. Maneuver
Maneuver allows the defender to take full advantage of the area of operations and to mass and concentrate when desirable. Maneuver, through movement in combination with fire, allows the defender to achieve a position of advantage over the enemy to accomplish the mission.

## D. Mass and Concentration
Defenders seek to mass the effects of overwhelming combat power where they choose and shift it to support the decisive operation. Commanders retain and, when necessary, reconstitute a reserve and maneuver to gain local superiority at the point of decision.

## E. Operations in Depth
Simultaneous application of combat power throughout the area of operations improves the chances for success while minimizing friendly casualties. Quick, violent, and simultaneous action throughout the depth of the defender's area of operations can hurt, confuse, and even paralyze an enemy force just as that enemy force is most exposed and vulnerable.

## F. Preparation
The defense has inherent strengths. The defender arrives in the area of operations before the attacker and uses the available time to prepare. Defenders study the ground and select positions that allow the massing of fires on likely approaches. They combine natural and manmade obstacles to canalize attacking forces into engagement areas. Defending forces coordinate and rehearse actions on the ground, gaining intimate familiarity with the terrain. They place security, intelligence, and reconnaissance forces throughout the area of operations. These preparations multiply the effectiveness of the defense. Commanders continue defensive preparations in depth, even as the close engagement begins.

## G. Security
Commanders secure their forces principally through protection, military deception, inform and influence activities, and cyber electromagnetic activities. Security operations prevent enemy intelligence, surveillance, and reconnaissance assets from determining friendly locations, strengths, and weaknesses. Protection efforts preserve combat power. Military deception and cyber electromagnetic activities inaccurately portray friendly forces, mislead enemy commanders, and deny those same enemy commanders the ability to use cyberspace and the electromagnetic spectrum.

*Refer to The Small Unit Tactics SMARTbook (Leader's Reference Guide to Conducting Tactical Operations) for complete discussion of offensive and defensive operations. Related topics include tactical mission fundamentals, stability & counterinsurgency operations, tactical enabling operations, special purpose attacks, urban operations & fortifications, and patrols & patrolling.*

enemy into areas where concentrated fires of all weapons may be brought to bear. Minefields within the main defensive area are placed to confine the enemy within fire sacks and to make the employment of the reserves easier. Besides preplanned minefields, the Soviets also employ hasty antitank minefields laid by engineer mobile obstacle detachments, by mechanical minelayers, or by helicopter. Hastily laid minefields normally are used with an antitank reserve to counter enemy tanks that may have penetrated the depths of the defense.

### Obstacles (including Minefields)

Obstacles (including minefields) are used to slow, disorganize, and canalize the enemy force. They are used alone or with preplanned fire concentrations. The use of natural obstacles is stressed; they include lakes, rivers, marshes, escarpments, and densely forested areas. Artificial obstacles may include antitank ditches, wire entanglements, abatis, and antiheliborne and antiairborne stakes.



## E. Anti-Tank Defense

Antitank defense is essential to any defense and is of great concern to Soviet tacticians. The system of antitank (AT) defense is composed of-

- Subunit strongpoints containing well-sited AT weapons.
- Tank ambushes set up throughout the defense.
- Antitank reserves placed to respond to enemy tank penetrations.
- Tanks within the second echelon to bolster the first echelon or to counterattack.
- Mobile obstacle detachments.
- Artillery in the direct fire role, both in forward positions and from positions in the depths of the defense.
- Antitank obstacles covered by fire and complementing the maneuver of fires and forces.
- Maneuver by antitank forces and weapons.

Antitank guns and ATGMs are concentrated by platoon and battery. They employ multilayered crossfires, long-range fires, and all-around fires. Cooperation between guns and ATGM systems is considered essential to adequate antitank defense. As with all facets of combat, the integration of combined arms is considered paramount.

Attack helicopters mounting rockets and antitank missiles are used as mobile, quick-reaction, antitank reserves. Emphasis is placed on their use to defeat tank penetrations or flanking maneuvers.

The reserve is positioned to undertake multiple missions: blocking, counterattacking, reinforcing, and providing rear area security.

## F. Counterattacks

Counterattacks are planned at every level for use if the enemy succeeds in breaching forward defensive positions. Commitment of this force requires the authority of the next higher commander. With the exception of first echelon battalions, whose reserve companies may have to conduct a frontal counterattack, this force generally is launched from a flank. Regimental and higher counterattacks normally are spearheaded by tanks, preceded by an intense air and artillery preparation, and supported by the fires of adjacent units. A counterattack normally is conducted from the march. While tactical counterattacks usually are planned to restore the defenses, those at operational level may be the opening phase of a counteroffensive.

Chap 3

# (Defensive Operations)
# II. Hasty Defense



*Ref: FM 100-2-1 The Soviet Army: Operations and Tactics (Jul '84), chap. 6.*

## I. Concepts of the Hasty Defense

The writings of Soviet tacticians indicate that the hasty defense will be more prevalent than the prepared defense. They acknowledge that there may be diverse situations in which the hasty defense must be established. The force making the transition to the defense may be in contact with the enemy. If so, a limited attack could be required to gain defensible terrain. Conversely, it may be necessary to establish a defense to the rear and withdraw to it. In any case, the nature of a hasty defense does not provide time for detailed preparation.

The same factors of mission, enemy, terrain, troops available, and time available considered in a prepared defense are the primary considerations in establishing the hasty defense. They may differ in that-

- The mission of hasty defense is more transitory
- The enemy situation is clearer, and attack is imminent
- The terrain may be unfavorable for organization of a defense; it may be better suited for the attacker
- Time will be short

### A. Reverse Slope Defense

Establishing the defense when in contact with the enemy poses particular problems, since forces may have to dig in while under fire and observation of the enemy. For this reason, a reverse slope defense is often chosen. Part of the force is left in contact with the enemy on the forward slope(s), while the remainder of the force prepares the position on the reverse slope(s). The Soviets recognize the following advantages of a reverse slope defense:

- It hinders or prevents enemy observation of the defensive position
- Attacking forces will not be able to receive direct fire support from following forces
- Enemy long-range antitank fires will be degraded
- Attacking enemy forces will be silhouetted on the crest of the hill
- Engineer work can be conducted out of direct fire and observation from the enemy

A disadvantage is that the maximum range of all weapon systems cannot be exploited. When possible, both forward and reverse slope defense are used to take maximum advantage of the terrain.



When the force going over to the defensive is in contact with the enemy, it is extremely difficult to establish a security echelon. If established, its depth is not nearly as great as in the prepared defense. Additionally, long-range fires do not play the part they do in the prepared defense because the opposing forces are, for the most part, within direct fire range. Deception is difficult to achieve, since friendly forces may be under direct observation of the enemy. Obstacles are emplaced but are not as extensive as in the prepared defense.

## B. Support Elements

Differences in mission arise from the temporary nature of a hasty defense. Normally, the primary objective is to deny enemy access to a specific area. However, attrition of the enemy force is essential to any defense. In many cases, defensive positions are chosen to support resumption of offensive action rather than for a prolonged defense.

Combat support remains basically configured for continued offensive action. Artillery groupings may be organized to support the next offensive phase. Engineer mobile obstacle detachments lay minefields across critical avenues of approach. Maximum use is made of armored mine layers, armored engineer vehicles, and dozer blades attached to tanks to prepare obstacles and hasty positions. Engineer works are carried out in a sequence that insures readiness to repulse an enemy attack.

Combat service support also remains configured to support offensive action. Primary effort is devoted to preparing units for future offensive actions, with priority of support going to units selected to initiate offensive actions.

Chap 3

# (Defensive Operations) III. Withdrawal & Relief

*Ref: FM 100-2-1 The Soviet Army: Operations and Tactics (Jul '84), chap. 6.*

## I. Withdrawal

The Soviets view the withdrawal as a combat action designed to disengage troops from attack by superior enemy forces. The experiences of World War II taught the Soviets the complicated nature of retrograde operations under pressure. On the modern battlefield, a withdrawal will bring the full application of the enemy's combat power to destroy withdrawing units.

The Soviets can be expected to resort to deception, movement at night and during periods of reduced visibility, and covert preparations to avoid alerting the enemy.

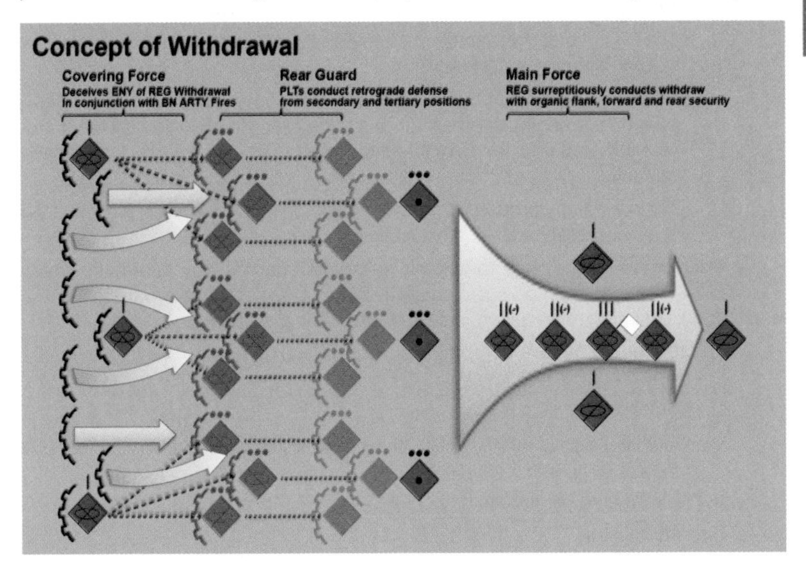


The Soviet commander's withdrawal order is detailed and includes the mission, routes, formation to be used, delay positions, control measures, and information on the new defensive position. Withdrawals are organized and executed under strict secrecy and security. The mission is to disengage the force. in a timely, organized manner without losing its combat capability. The force executing the withdrawal is divided into three groups.

### Covering Force

The covering force has the mission to deceive the enemy and to cover the initial withdrawal of the main body. This force normally comes from units along the forward edge of the defense. It normally consists of a reinforced platoon from each forward-deployed company.

## Rear Guard

The rear guard covers movement of the main body and fights a delaying action if the enemy attempts to maintain contact in the pursuit. It is organized to fight independently of the main body and covering force. Normally, it is organized as a combined arms force consisting of tank, motorized rifle, artillery, and engineer elements. Maximum use is made of artillery, mortar, and long-range ATGM fires through a series of delay positions to prevent enemy interference in the withdrawal of the main body.

## Main Body

The main body breaks contact and attempts to withdraw without disclosing its intentions to the enemy. Deception may be achieved by withdrawing under the cover of darkness or adverse weather conditions, by using supporting fires to cover noise, or by employing a ruse. A route reconnaissance and a reconnaissance of the new positions to be occupied are conducted and guides posted to expedite movement. Air strikes and artillery support are closely coordinated and planned to cover the withdrawal.



A regiment conducts a withdrawal in the following sequence:

- First echelon battalions designate platoons to act covering forces which attempt to portray a normal defensive posture to the enemy.
- The regimental commander designates a rear guard, normally a reinforced second echelon battalion.
- On order, the main body (first echelon battalions, minus covering forces, plus support elements) withdraws through the rear guard, in the following order: rear services first, then combat support elements, and finally the maneuver subunits.
- The main body proceeds, without pause, on multiple routes, all the way back to a new defensive position or assembly area.

Once the main body has completely passed through the rear guard, the covering force breaks contact on order and withdraws through the rear guard to join the main body. Minimum radio communications or listening silence is observed.

The rear guard fights a delaying action, leapfrogging to successive positions, using to the maximum:

- Smoke
- Mobile obstacle detachments to layminefields and to create obstacles across enemy avenues of approach
- Artillery fire concentrations
- Ambushes
- Attack helicopters
- Fixed-wing air strikes

If the enemy does not pursue, the rear guard assumes march formation and joins the main body as quickly as possible.

# II. Relief

The Soviet term "relief of troops" involves an organized transfer of positions, areas, and zones in a combat situation from one unit to another. The units being relieved have usually sustained considerable losses and are on the defense. A relief also may be conducted to enable a fresh unit to occupy the defense positions of the relieved unit in preparation for a renewed offensive. Because units being relieved are normally in direct contact with the enemy, they are subject to enemy fire and ground attacks. The relief is carefully organized and is executed quickly and secretly. It attempts to preserve as much of the unit's combat capability as possible. As a rule, a relief is conducted at night or during periods of reduced visibility.

# III. The Retrograde (U.S. Military Doctrine Perspective)

*Ref: The Small Unit Tactics SMARTbook (2nd Rev. Ed.), The Lightning Press, pp. 3-19 to 3-22.*

The retrograde is a type of defensive operation that involves organized movement away from the enemy. The enemy may force these operations or a commander may execute them voluntarily.

## I. Delay

This operation allows the unit to trade space for time, avoiding decisive engagement and safeguarding its elements. A delay is a series of defensive and offensive actions over subsequent positions in depth. It is an economy of force operation that trades space for time. While the enemy gains access to the vacated area (space), friendly elements have time to conduct necessary operations, while retaining freedom of action and maneuver. This allows friendly forces to influence the action; they can prevent decisive engagement or postpone action to occur at a more critical time or place on the battlefield. For either type of delay mission, the flow of the operation can be summarized as "hit hard, then move."

## II. Withdrawal

A withdrawal is a planned operation in which a force in contact disengages from an The commander uses this operation to break enemy contact, especially when he needs to free the unit for a new mission. Withdrawal is a planned operation in which a force in contact disengages from an enemy force. Withdrawals may or may not be conducted under enemy pressure. The two types of withdrawals are assisted and unassisted.

## III. Retirement

A retirement is conducted to move a force that is not in contact away from the enemy. Typically, the company conducts a retirement as part of a larger force while another unit's security force protects their movement. A retiring unit organizes for combat but does not anticipate interference by enemy ground forces. Triggers for a retirement may include the requirement to reposition forces for future operations or to accommodate other changes to the current CONOP. The retiring unit should move sustainment elements and supplies first, and then should move toward an assembly area that supports preparations for the next mission. Where speed and security are the most important considerations, units conduct retirements as tactical road marches.

The retiring unit generally moves toward an assembly area, which should support the preparations for the unit's next mission. When determining the routes the retiring force takes to the assembly area, the commander considers the unit's capability to support defensive actions if combat occurs during the retirement.

*Refer to The Small Unit Tactics SMARTbook (Leader's Reference Guide to Conducting Tactical Operations) for complete discussion of offensive and defensive operations. Related topics include tactical mission fundamentals, stability & counterinsurgency operations, tactical enabling operations, special purpose attacks, urban operations & fortifications, and patrols & patrolling.*

Defensive Operations

Soviet doctrine stresses the temporary nature of the defense and emphasizes the need for counterattacks as soon as it is feasible to initiate a renewed offensive. The relief operation is a means to achieve this end.

A battalion relief usually is conducted with the regimental commander establishing the relief sequence. The two battalion commanders (the one relieving and the one being relieved) conduct a joint reconnaissance of the defensive position. During this reconnaissance, they coordinate routes to and from the relief areas, traffic regulation posts, locations for guides to meet the relieving units, and the sequence of relief. In addition, the battalion commanders review the present system of fire and observation as well as obstacles and minefields that have been prepared for the position.

The commander of the battalion which is being relieved specifies to his subordinates the following:

- The sequence of turnover of the defense area
- Assembly area(s) after the relief
- Camouflage and security measures
- Instructions for guides to meet and accompany the arriving relief units
- The location of traffic regulation posts
- The times for commencing and completing the relief
- Actions in the event of an enemy attack during the relief

The commander of the battalion which is being relieved exercises overall control until the relief is completed. Should the enemy attack during the relief, the relieving battalion, under the command of the outgoing battalion commander, attempts to repel the attack.

At the appointed time, the relieving battalion moves to the relief area by concealed routes. The relief is carried out successively by platoons. The first to be relieved are motorized rifle and antitank subunits. They are followed by mortar, artillery, and tank subunits. Tanks may be reassigned and left in place if the relief is carried out by battalions of the same motorized rifle regiment. Once in position, the relieving subunits establish observation posts and their system of fire.

Relieved commanders transfer their positions, provide information on enemy activities and routines, and acquaint relieving commanders with the location of obstacles, minefields, and primary directions of fire. Established communications are maintained, and wire lines are left in place and passed on to relieving units.

All engineer installations, to include minefields and obstacles, are thoroughly checked and verified with respect to boundaries, passages, and degree of readiness.

If the enemy attacks, all available subunits-under the command of the commander being relieved - are used to repulse the attack. The reserve of the subunit being relieved may be used to counterattack. It is the last element to be withdrawn from the defensive area.

The relieving battalion commander checks the locations and weapon positions of his subunits to insure they are prepared for combat. The relieving battalion attempts to maintain the same routine and level of activities that existed before the relief. When the relieving commander reports to his superior that the relief is completed, the relief is officially terminated. The relieved battalion withdraws to assigned assembly areas and carries out its subsequent assigned mission.

Chap 3

# (Defensive Operations) IV. Small Unit Tactics

*Ref: FM 100-2-1 The Soviet Army: Operations and Tactics (Jul '84), chap 6, and FM 100-2-2 The Soviet Army: Special Warfare and Rear Area Support (Jul '84), chap 2 and 10.*

Defensive Operations

## I. Small-Unit Defensive Tactics

*Ref: Blank, Afghanistan and Beyond: Reflections on the Future of Warfare.*

The preeminence of RTA training has focused on the offense. Historically, the defense is viewed as a temporary position from which the force may build enough combat power to once again seek the offense. Defense is not an end state. Elaborate defensive networks are not the preferred RTA mode of operandi, and rarely have materiel resources been allocated to such a defense – instead preferring aggressive, hostile offensive actions as a form of defense.

However, recent Soviet experiences in Afghanistan (1979-1989) and Russian experiences in the Chechen Wars (1994-96 and again 2000-09) have significantly altered RTA perspectives of defense.

Notions of strategy, operations and tactics are compressed in low intensity conflicts and/or during operations in restrictive terrain such as mountains or jungles. Offensive actions at the strategic level may very well include a robust defense at the operational level to deny enemy maneuver along infiltration and supply routes. Likewise, a defense at an operational level often requires attacks in the forms of raids, sweeps and ambushes at the tactical level to disrupt enemy actions and diminish their capabilities. In this way, the distinctions between offense and defense operations have become blurred in RTA doctrine.

RTA commanders recognize that there are times when elaborate defenses are necessary for security. And when the conditions are correct, RTA build robust defenses.

# II. Strongpoint Defense

*Ref: FM 100-2-2 The Soviet Army, chap 2 and 3.*

Security measures often necessitate an area defense, which has the stated goal of denying enemy access to a given geographic point, route or area. The RTA defense has at its foundation the concept of strongpoints.

## A. Array the Combat Power of the Strongpoint Defense

The concept of the strongpoint is that the primary unit headquarters assumes the most defensible terrain, and from that terrain assigns subunit defenses in a cascading effect.

In this manner an RTA regiment may defend along a 2000-meter front. A battalion defends along a 700-meter front; and an RTA rifle company defends along a 300-meter front, although to interlock fires with adjacent units the each subunit actually plans a fire radius wider than their physical front.

*When engineer resources are available for strongpoint defense lumber and even steel plates may be available for construction of fighting positions. In the end, each fighting position is carefully concealed so that it cannot be detected from the immediate front or flank. (Courtesy of Hae-jung Larsen and OP EASTWIND.)*

The primary unit assigns subunits defensive positions to the left and right of the primary unit's frontal engagement. Additionally, alternate defensive positions are assigned to subunits, though rarely is a regiment or battalion assigned an alternate defensive position.

The strongpoint is then both the literal and figurative center of the defensive line. No alternative position is planned, and often the strongpoint becomes a "last stand" initiative. Commanders of strongpoint positions are forbidden to retreat or withdraw unless ordered to do so by higher command.

This is true of each subsequent subunit strongpoint, too, and the subtlety must not be overlooked. For example, the regiment will form a strong hold and cascade the subunit battalions to primary and alternative defensive positions. The battalion will

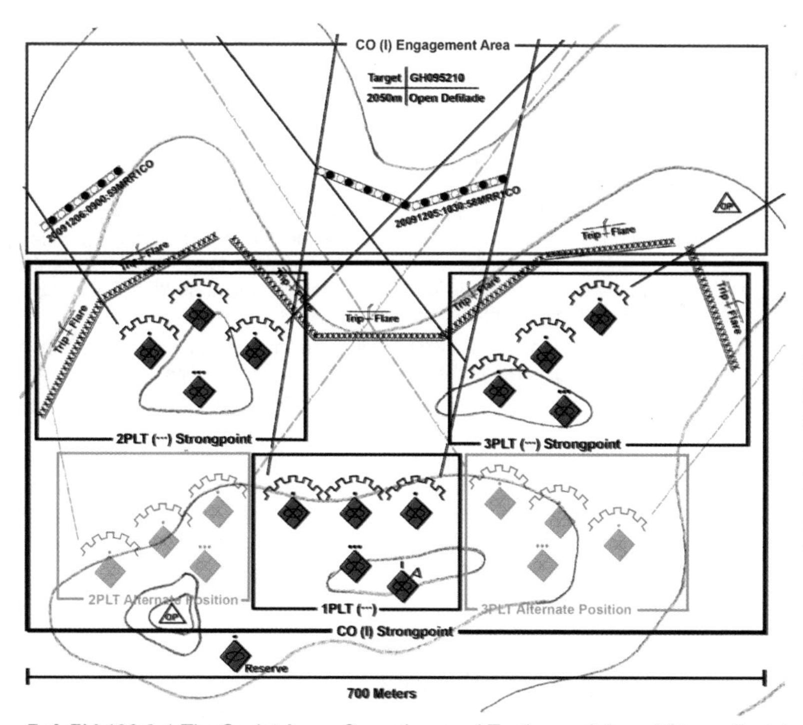


*Ref: FM 100-2-1 The Soviet Army: Operations and Tactics, p. 6-6, and Sharp, Soviet Infantry Tactics in World War II, pp. 74-78.*

then assume the strongpoint for the most defensible terrain in its sector, and then cascade subunit rifle companies to primary and alternative positions. Finally, the company will assume the strongpoint of the most defensible terrain in its assigned sector, and then cascade subunit platoons to primary and alternative positions.

Yet in order for any subunit to fall back to alternative defensive positions, that platoon, company or battalion must first obtain permission to do so from its higher command. This creates a stubborn defense in depth!

## B. Special Considerations for Strongpoint Defense

Special considerations of the strongpoint defense include the umbrella of support, interlocking sectors of fire, and cover of defilades.

1. Umbrella of support has implications for both logistics and fire support. The most immediate need for any commander is fire support into the assigned engagement area to bolster the defense. Fire support serves as the critical depth and strength of the defense.

Close Air Support (CAS), artillery, mortars indirect fires plus armored vehicle direct fire systems may be brought to bear against an attacking enemy within the engagement area. Supporting fires from higher echelons entail greater ranges and produce mass casualties against the enemy forces as they mass into their attack lanes. These weapon systems serve to augment the integral weapons of the RTA primary unit.

Logistical concerns for the umbrella of support include resupply of all materiel classes – ammunition, batteries, water, food rations, and medical supplies. But logistics also include services such as MEDEVAC that are critical to morale.

2. Interlocking sectors of fire are absolutely essential in eliminating gaps in the defensive line. This is particularly true when two sister units butt against each other's flank. Of the greatest concern are crew-served weapon systems. Each sector of fire must be assigned so that the arches overlap each other, preferably at the point of the forward wire obstacle to the front of the fighting positions.

3. Engineering obstacles serve to cover defilades as well as high-speed avenues of approach to the front of the defensive line. Engineering obstacles include liberal use of tangle foot wire approximately 50 meters forward of the fighting positions. Tangle foot does not present a visually formidable barrier compared to double-apron or triple-strand concertina; yet when emplaced properly tangle foot has a profound effect on slowing enemy forces in attack and/or infiltration. Indeed, RTA troops are expert at tangle foot wire obstacles.

Out just beyond the tangle foot wire are tripwire flares. These may include a mix of ground flares, aerial flares and screaming whistle pyrotechnics.

Farthest out are anti-personnel and anti-armor minefields. These may be command detonated, static, or scatter-type mines, or any combination thereof.

Regardless of the type or combination of engineering obstacle, all obstacles are covered by either direct fires in primary or alternative sectors of fire, or indirect fires from company and battalion mortars and regimental artillery. All obstacles are observed.

*RTA doctrine regarding the defense has appreciated significant gains since the 1980s. A blending of offensive and defensive perspectives allows for a strategic offense to include operational defense. Likewise, operational defense may very well mean tactical offensive actions. (Courtesy of Hae-jung Larsen and OP EASTWIND.)*

# C. Establish the Strongpoint Defense

1. The rifle company commander is tasked to a specific sector of the battalion defense. Immediately, the commander seeks the most defensible position within the company sector, locating one platoon plus a small reserve force with the company headquarters section at the company strongpoint.

2. The commander assigns the other two platoons a sector each within the company defense, typically cascading to the left, right and forward of the company strongpoint. Platoon commanders quickly assess the terrain and locate their platoon strongpoints on the most defensible position. They too cascade their squads in the most suitable manner to defend the platoon strongpoint.

3. Alternate defensive positions are identified for both of the forward platoons, though none is necessary for the platoon located with the company headquarters because they will not retreat from the company strongpoint without permission from the battalion commander.

4. Sectors of fire are next assigned to each platoon, each squad, and each fighting position. Subunit commanders create sector sketches to ensure the company commander's intent has been satisfied. In doing so, defilades and natural obstacles forward of each platoon are identified. From this information the commander will create a plan to employ engineer resources.

5. Fighting positions are dug. The time allotted for construction of fighting positions and vehicle redoubts are carefully calculated through algorithm worksheets. Engineer entrenching assets make this work much quicker.

6. As the fighting positions are being completed, wire obstacles and flares are emplaced without delay. Wire obstacles serve as the perimeter protective barricade, and flares serve as an early warning system for enemy attack. Aside from the fighting positions that protect the troops from fires, the wire obstacles and flares form the mainstay of the defense.

7. Indirect fires are coordinated and registered for all defilades and high-speed avenues of approach forward of the defensive position. The company must coordinate with battalion and regiment for these assets.

8. Because communication security is easily compromised with radio transmissions, telephone wire is laid between platoons to the company headquarters, and back to battalion and regiment.

9. Minefields are coordinated with regiment or division engineers. Mines serve to further protect high-speed avenues of approach and defilades forward of the defense.

10. Observation Posts (OP) are established to monitor enemy movement forward or the strongpoint defense and provide an early warning for the rifle company and platoon.

# III. Tactical Outpost

*Ref: Grau, The Bear Went Over the Mountain, chap. 4, and Sharp, Soviet Infantry Tactics, p.57.*

While all the principle elements of the tactical outpost mirror those of the strong-point defense, tactical outposts are typically held by regimental subunits at the rifle company or even platoon level. They are formed into 360° security perimeters; yet remain within the umbrella of support of the battalion and regimental indirect fires and logistical resupply.

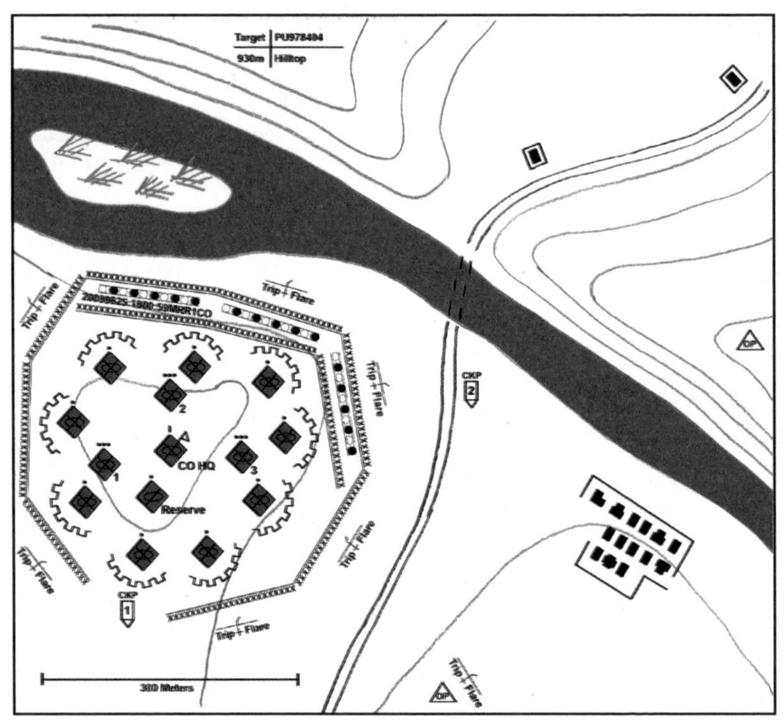


*Ref: Grau, The Bear Went Over the Mountain, p. 114, and Sharp, Soviet Infantry Tactics, p.57.*

## A. Array the Combat Power of the Tactical Outpost

For the platoon within the rifle company outpost, tactical considerations of the out-post look remarkably similar to the strongpoint defense. The company headquarters section and reserve force assume the most defensible terrain. The platoons are then cascaded in a 360° pattern, forming a perimeter with the company headquarters in the center.

Depending on the circumstances of the terrain and the nature of the threat, the rifle company typically establishes a tactical outpost measuring some 300 meters in diameter from wire barrier to wire barrier. Each rifle platoon forms a front of 100 to 200 meters.

Rarely are alternate positions assigned or used in the tactical outpost since the circular nature of the perimeter means there are dismally few options for retreat!

## B. Special Considerations for the Tactical Outpost

Critical considerations for the tactical outpost include the umbrella of support from higher command, and local security.

Tactical outposts remain within the umbrella of indirect fire support from battalion, regiment, and possibly even division mortars, artillery and CAS.  This is critical for the immediate defense of the outpost should it come under attack by a large enemy force.

*RTA forces may be assigned to an outpost for extended periods of time.  Outpost living is arduous, but often has better accommodations than temporary defensive fighting positions. (Courtesy of Hae-jung Larsen and OP EASTWIND.)*

Logistical resupply is certainly as important for sustained operations of the outpost. It is not uncommon for outposts to establish a helicopter landing pad for resupply when operating in the restricted terrain of mountains or jungles.  More typically vehicle convoy resupply such outposts.

Perhaps the single most immediate and on-going consideration is local security of the tactical outpost.  Commonly, outposts are located on the most dominant terrain, however this is not always feasible – perhaps because the most dominate terrain cannot be accessed by the subunit ground vehicles; or because the primary objective of the outpost cannot be achieved from the dominate terrain.  Whatever the case, if the tactical outpost is not located on the most dominate terrain, those high points must be mitigated by employing Observation Posts (OP) or they are covered by established target reference points for indirect fires.

Local security also dictates the need for robust fortifications and engineer obstacles such as wire barriers and minefields along the perimeter.  When possible, checkpoint operations are situated within effective firing ranges of the outpost so as to offer further security measures.

*Tactical outposts may appear defensive in nature at the operational level, but are actually a means of projecting offensive force into hostile territories. Here a squad leader conducts a Pre-Combat Inspection of his troops and equipment prior to departing the outpost on a presence patrol in a nearby village. (Courtesy of Hae-jung Larsen and OP EASTWIND.)*

Note that when an outpost is located nearby civilian traffic and villages, minefields are placed inside the perimeter wire obstacles. Alternatively, harmless trip flares are placed as early warning devices outside the wire. This adaptation has the humane rationale of reducing unintentional death and injury to civilian non-combatants; but also serves to deny enemy sappers access to thieve RTA landmine munitions. Added wire obstacles may be placed within the perimeter as well – both to create a more formidable defense against enemies, and to keep disoriented troops from mistakenly wandering into the minefields in periods of low visibility.

# C. Establish the Tactical Outpost

The tactical outpost is established in nearly identical manner as the strongpoint defense, though admittedly there exist a few unique considerations for a tactical outpost.

*RTA doctrine does not view tactical outposts and strongpoint defense as synonymous. Tactical outposts are thought of in terms of operationally offensive action, further blurring the line of defense and offense. Tactical outposts are used to control key terrain, supply routes, and even to influence civilian population traffic. (Courtesy of Hae-jung Larsen and OP EASTWIND.)*

1. The company commander is tasked to an outpost within the higher command's Area of Responsibility (AOR). Once on location, the commander seeks the most defensible position within the immediate surroundings, locating the headquarters section plus a reserve force in the center of the outpost.

2. The commander assigns all three platoons a sector within the company outpost, typically shaping either a triangular or circular perimeter around the company strongpoint. Platoon commanders quickly assess the terrain and locate their platoon strongpoints on the most defensible position. They too cascade their squads in the most suitable manner to defend the platoon's sector of the outpost.

3. Sectors of fire are next assigned to each platoon, each squad, and each fighting position. Subunit commanders create sector sketches to ensure the company commander's intent has been satisfied. In doing so, defilades and natural obstacles forward of each platoon are identified. From this information the commander will create a plan to employ engineer resources.

4. Fighting positions and trench works are dug. The time allotted for construction of fighting positions and vehicle redoubts are carefully calculated through algorithm worksheets. Engineer entrenching assets make this work much quicker.

5. As the fighting positions are being completed, wire obstacles and flares are emplaced without delay. Wire obstacles serve as the perimeter protective barricade, and flares serve as an early warning system for enemy attack. Aside from the fighting positions that protect the troops from direct and indirect enemy fires, the wire obstacles and flares form the mainstay of the outpost's perimeter defense.

6. Indirect fires are coordinated and registered for nearby dominant terrain, defilades and high-speed avenues of approach to the tactical outpost. The company commander must coordinate with battalion and regiment for these assets.

7. Minefields are coordinated with regiment or division engineers. Mines serve to further protect avenues of approach and defilades along the outpost's defenses.

8. External positions such as OP and checkpoints (CKP) are established to monitor and control all traffic into and out of the tactical outpost's AOR.

# IV. Rearguard Retrograde

*Ref: FM 100-2-2 The Soviet Army: Special Warfare and Rear Area Support, chap. 12, and Frasche, The Soviet Motorized Rifle Battalion, chap. 7.*

The third form of RTA defensive tactic is the rearguard. RTA doctrine prescribes a rearguard as an ongoing task – regardless of whether the regiment is conducting offensive or defensive actions.

As the word indicates, a rearguard protects the regimental rear area from spoiling attacks and envelopments by enemy forces. More often the case is that the rear guard protects interior Lines of Communication (LOC).

During offensive operations, the rear guard may also be brought forward to assist with final assaults against pinned and isolated enemy pockets of resistance, thereby defeating the enemy in detail. Lastly during defensive operations, the rearguard is responsible for buying time and space for the regiment to regroup in the event of a tactical withdraw. In western military terms this is known as a retrograde.

Retrograde actions may be thrust upon the rearguard due to enemy activities, or the RTA commander may voluntarily execute a retrograde in order to entice a massed enemy to remain in contact long enough that the regiment or battalion may bring greater resources to bear and defeat the massed enemy. This lesson was forged on the battlefields of the Second World War, but proved to be just as relevant to clandestine warfare in Afghanistan and Chechnya.

Furthermore, the bronegruppa was born during the Soviet War in Afghanistan. This was partly due to RTA commanders' stubborn refusal to surrender armored vehicles – a rare commodity during the Second World War, and one that had served RTA commanders so well in the years since. The compromise was to dismount ground troops from the vehicles in action against the enemy in restrictive terrain, but then to bring the bronegruppa to bear with its inherent heavy firepower at an appropriate time.

The bronegruppa proved to be a brilliant compromise not only for the hammer and anvil attack, but it was equally proficient for the role of rearguard. The bronegruppa lends maneuver as well as firepower to small unit tactics in delaying retrograde actions.

## A. Array the Combat Power of the Rearguard

The regimental commander assigns the front line battalions in defense. Depending on the situation, he may designate a rifle company or even an entire rifle battalion to rearguard. In doing so, the regimental commander determines the left, right, forward and rear limits of the regimental rear area.

In turn, the battalion commander tasked to rear guard designates and assigns each rifle company a defensive sector and lines of resistance within the regimental rear area. Each company commander reconnoiters their assigned sector and in most cases will further assign platoons a defensive sector and lines of resistance within the company defensive sector. Indeed, in extreme circumstances the platoon commander will also assign individual squads a defensive sector and lines of resistance.

The cascading effect as well as the decentralized nature of the rearguard creates a fluid defensive posture. This is atypical for the top-down heavy command structure of RTA forces, but the rearguard provides a noteworthy exception to the norm.

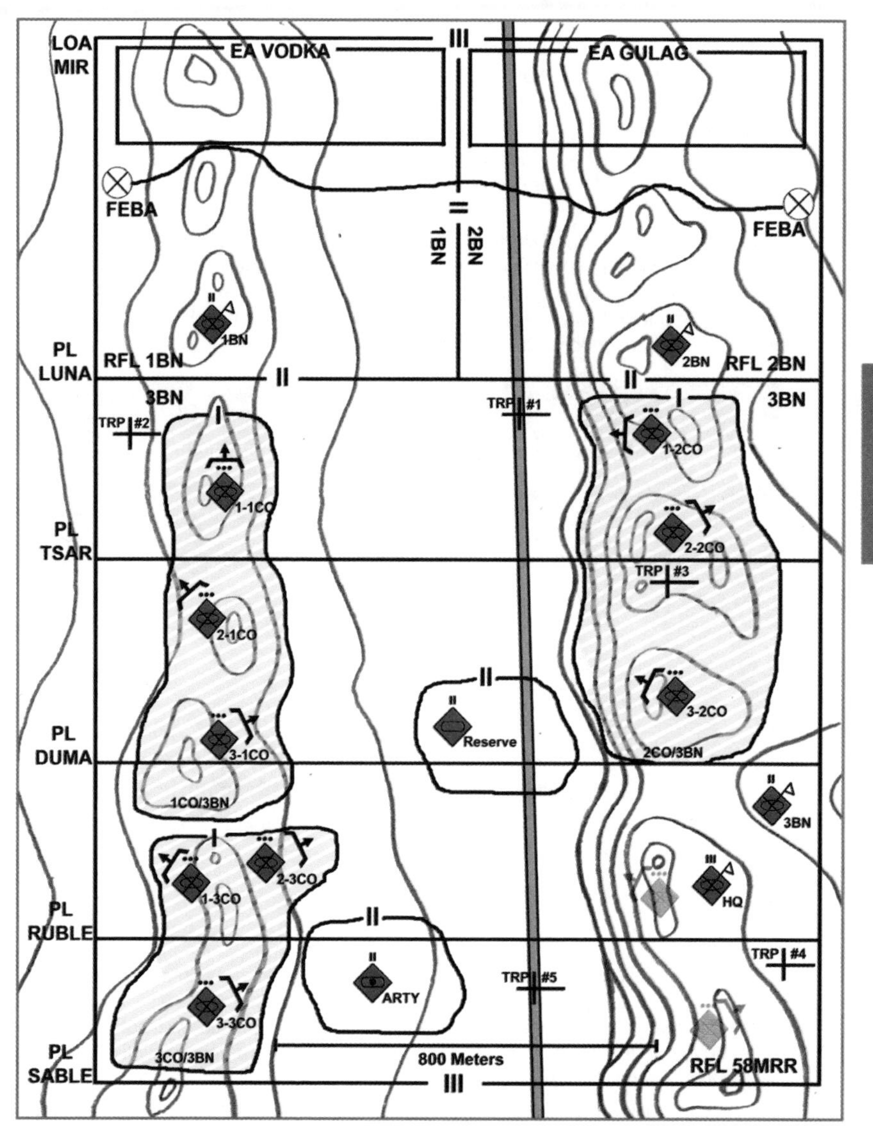


Ref: Frasche, The Soviet Motorized Rifle Battalion, chap. 7, fig. 66, and Grau, The Bear Went Over the Mountain, pp. 130-133, and Sharp, Soviet Infantry Tactics, pp. 78-79.

Defensive Operations

## B. Special Considerations for Rearguard

The rearguard is anything but static. Instead it is a fluid situation when implementing retrograde actions. That said, fire and maneuver coordination become paramount in the planning phase of the rearguard.

Lines of resistance, phase lines, primary and alternate defensive positions, primary directions of fire, and artillery target reference points must all be coordinated carefully.

Lines of resistance include multiple anticipated routes of enemy attack. Attack by fire positions are established along these routes by company, platoon and/or squad. The distance between each attack by fire positions does not exceed the effective range of the integral machineguns! This is necessary so that each attack by fire position obtains supportive fires from adjacent subunits.

*The rearguard functions as a mobile defense when in retrograde. Carefully planned and coordinated fires coupled with maneuver are the critical characteristics of the rearguard. Short patrolling operations allow the subunits to become very familiar with the surrounding terrain and help them identify attack angles and avenues. (Courtesy of Hae-jung Larsen and OP EASTWIND.)*

For a squad medium machinegun that distance will not exceed 800 meters, though for the heavy machineguns of the bronegruppa the distance could easily be doubled. However, ideally the distance between each attack by fire position will not be further than 300 to 400 meters from the next, so that small arms fire from individual troops can support each subsequent position.

The critical consideration for the rearguard is that it maintains fluidity in its fires and maneuver. The rearguard does not die for land! Superior terrain has little intrinsic value to the rearguard, and subunits will fade from their attack by fire positions when threatened.

Attacks are pulsed and a very high rate of tempo and from multiple vantage points to wear down an attacking enemy force. Attack by fire; dislocate when threatened; deliver direct or indirect avenging fires on the enemy as they regroup on each position; and then seek the enemy's flank or rear to conduct a counterattack. This is an extremely fluid action.

The rearguard in retrograde action is almost impossible for any single commander to control. Each commander – from the regiment down to the platoon – offers specific guidance and control measures in the planning and preparation phase. But during execution of the retrograde, each subunit commander is expected to show preparedness, flexibility, and initiative.

# C. Establish the Rearguard Retrograde

1. Upon receipt of the rearguard mission by battalion higher command, the company commander conducts reconnaissance within the company sector to determine the best attack by fire positions along the anticipated enemy routes of attack.

2. The commander creates a fire and maneuver plan with phase lines, primary directions of fire, and alternate positions for each platoon. The company commander assigns platoon sectors to each platoon commander, and identifies the primary and alternate location of the company headquarters and mortars section. The company commander will also designate within the company sector target reference points along the lines of resistance for regiment artillery.

3. Platoon commanders consult to ensure each platoon is able to support adjacent and subsequent platoon positions with direct fires, identify and de-conflict multiple routes of egress, plus designate multiple target reference points along the lines of resistance for company and battalion mortars.

4. With those considerations confirmed, the platoon commanders assigned each squad an attack by fire position within the platoon sector, ensuring each position can provide supporting fires for the next adjacent position. The squads are assigned a primary direction of fire and an anticipated route of egress to an alternate platoon position as a contingency plan. Signals for withdraw are established by the platoon commander for each squad.

5. For the platoon's alternate position the platoon commander assigns guides to remain at the position in order to direct retreating squads into new attack by fire positions. Guides are typically a two-man team composed of a junior sergeant and an experienced soldier.

6. If the bronegruppa is to be used independently, multiple routes of egress and attack by fire positions must be identified for the platoon bronegruppa. Guides are not usually employed for the bronegruppa, unless the retrograde occurs during nighttime conditions.

7. Covered and defilade routes of counterattack are as important for the platoon commander to identify as routes of egress to alternate attack by fire positions. These are calculated guesses, of course, because the exact position of the enemy force will be unknown. Yet commanders of the company, platoon and even squad leaders must walk their sector to identify potential counterattack lanes as part of their contingency plan should their subunit have to withdraw from their assigned attack by fire position.

8. Obstacles are incorporated into company and platoon defensive sectors. However because the rearguard occupies the regimental rear area, lethal obstacles such as anti-personnel and anti-tank land mines are used only at the discretion of the regimental commander. In the rare instance that minefields are approved for use, they are visibly marked so that friendly troops can avoid them. More commonly natural obstacles are sought and may be further bolstered by non-lethal engineer capabilities such as tangle foot wire and tank pits. Tripwire flares are put out each night, and retrieved each morning.

9. Local reconnaissance patrols and even ambushes can be planned into day-to-day security measures for the rearguard. This prevents the rearguard from becoming static while it protects the regiments LOC, and ultimately anticipates a retrograde action. Of course all such patrols are coordinated at company level within the company sector so as to avert fratricide.

# V. Small Unit Retrograde (U.S. Military Doctrine Perspective)

*Ref: The Small Unit Tactics SMARTbook (2nd Rev. Ed.), The Lightning Press, p. 3-22.*

Retrogrades conducted under pressure of enemy contact are extremely dangerous combat operations. This is partly due to the fact that the enemy is almost always much larger than friendly forces, and almost always is on the offensive. But retrogrades are also dangerous because they often require friendly forces to break up into multiple elements, synchronize the fight, and then coordinate a link-up under austere conditions.



Retrograde operations are conducted to improve a tactical situation or to prevent a worse situation from developing. Companies normally conduct retrogrades as part of a larger force but may conduct independent retrogrades (withdrawal) as required such as on a raid. Retrograde operations accomplish the following:

- Resist, exhaust, and defeat enemy forces
- Draw the enemy into an unfavorable situation
- Avoid contact in undesirable conditions
- Gain time
- Disengage a force from battle for use elsewhere in other missions
- Reposition forces, shorten lines of communication, or conform to movements of other friendly units
- Secure more favorable terrain

The delay and withdraw retrograde operations require an enormous amount of coordinated fires. In turn this means that communication between maneuvering and displacing friendly elements becomes paramount. Without it, fratricide becomes certain.

## Reconstitution

Combat leaders must recognize that troops do not like to retrograde. Retrogrades can negatively affect the participating soldiers' attitude more than any other type of operation because they may view the retrograde as a defeat. A commander must not allow retrograde operations to reduce or destroy unit morale. Leaders must maintain unit aggressiveness. By planning and efficiently executing the retrograde and ensuring that soldiers understand the purpose and duration of the operation, the commander can counter any negative effects of the operation on unit morale. After completing a retrograde operation, the commander may reconstitute the force.

*Note: FM 4-100.9 establishes the basic principles of reconstitution.*

*Refer to The Small Unit Tactics SMARTbook (Leader's Reference Guide to Conducting Tactical Operations) for complete discussion of offensive and defensive operations. Related topics include tactical mission fundamentals, stability & counterinsurgency operations, tactical enabling operations, special purpose attacks, urban operations & fortifications, and patrols & patrolling.*

# Specialized Warfare

*Ref: FM 100-2-2 The Soviet Army: Special Warfare and Rear Area Support (Jul '84), introduction and chaps 2 to 4.*

The term "specialized warfare," used in the title of this FM, is intended to be an abbreviated, collective description of combat actions which, in US terminology, may be described as "special operations" or "operations in special conditions." These are arbitrary categorizations used only to describe combatactions other than those general forms of Soviet ground forces operations and tactics discussed in FM 100-2-1. Use of the term "special" does not imply that the combat actions discussed in this FM represent abnormal forms of operations or tactics. They are all an integral part of Soviet military doctrine. Special operations include airborne, heliborne,and amphibious operations, and unconventional warfare in the enemy rear.

## Specialized Warfare





## I. Airborne Operations

During World War II, the Soviets gained some experience with airborne operations in combat. Because they lacked the transport aircraft required for large-scale operations. they employed the airborne troops mainly as infantry. Since the war, the Soviets have completely reequipped their large airborne force and built a large fleet of transport aircraft to support it. Airborne units played key roles in Soviet intervention in Czechoslovakia (1968) and Afghanistan (1979). The airborne force currently consists of seven divisions.

Heliborne operations are relatively new to the Soviets. They have built an impressive fleet of transport and gunship helicopters and have trained assault troops. However, until the Afghanistan intervention, they lacked actual combat experience with this type of operation. Motorized rifle or airborne troops or an air assault brigade assigned to a front, could conduct heliborne operations.

*See pp. 4-3 to 4-6 for further discussion.*

# II. Heliborne Operations

RTA heliborne units offer lightning strikes and tactical flexibility to their parent organization. RTA reconnaissance battalions are often assigned helicopter capabilities. Such units achieve peer status with the best militaries across the globe.

Typical missions for RTA heliborne units include attacks against enemy command and control nodes; destruction of enemy air defense or artillery assets; seizure of bridgeheads; securing mountain passes; or a vertical envelopment in pursuit of retreating enemy.

*See pp. 4-7 to 4-10 for further discussion.*

# III. Amphibious Operations

Amphibious operations are primarily the responsibility of the Soviet naval infantry (marines), a small but growing force. During World War II, the Soviet Army and Navy conducted many amphibious operations, mainly on river and inland seas within the Soviet Union. They have never conducted massive amphibious assault operations like those conducted by the US in the Pacific and the Allies in North Africa and Europe during World War II. In recent years, the Soviet naval infantry has been revitalized and reequipped. It currently has three independent regiments and one understrength division and is supported by a growing fleet of amphibious ships and small aircraft carriers. This elite force trains in joint exercises with airborne units, and it undoubtedly has an intervention or power projection mission.

The Soviets have a variety of special purpose units that are trained and equipped for unconventional warfare (UW) missions. Because of their politcal sensitivity, UW activities are managed at the highest level of government authority. They are directed by the Committee for State Security (KGB) and the General Staff's Main Intelligence Directorate (GRU).

*See pp. 4-11 to 4-14 for further discussion.*

# III. Unconventional Warfare (Special Ops)

Special operations certainly will be conducted in wartime, and some of these will play important roles in peacetime intervention and power projection beyond Soviet borders.

Operations in special conditions include river crossings, mountain and desert warfare, and combat in extreme cold, in cities, and at night. Soviet ground forces are well equipped and trained for river crossings. The Soviets consider the capability to cross water barriers from the march on a broad front with minimal delays an essential element in maintaining a rapid rate of advance in an offensive. River crossings are a consistent feature of Soviet field exercises.

While no particular Soviet divisions are identified as being tailored or trained specifically for mountain or desert warfare,some divisions are suited for combat in these environments as a result of their base locations. The Soviets undoubtedly are gaining more experience in mountain warfare from their increased use of military force in power projection, such as in Afghanistan.

Soviet ground forces also are well prepared for combat in extreme cold. The majority of Soviet divisions are located in areas with harsh winters.

Based on their World War II experience and recognition of the urbanization of Europe the Soviets realized that combat in cities would be common to most military operations. Their training reflects this realization.

One of the principles of Soviet operational art and tactics is the prosecution of combat relentlessly, under all conditions of visiblity. With this principle, the Soviets strive to be capable of continuous combat, during daylight, or at night.The Soviets conduct much of their training during hours of darkness.

*See pp. 4-15 to 4-18 for further discussion.*

# (Specialized Warfare)
# I. Airborne Operations

*Ref: FM 100-2-2 The Soviet Army: Special Warfare and Rear Area Support (Jul '84), chap 2.*

Red Team Armies (RTA) regularly employ airborne units as vertical envelopment to shape the success of major offensive action along the front line or area of operations. Airborne operations focus on the seizing of key facility such as bridgeheads, seaports or airfields; to establish blocking positions along key terrain; and/or to disrupt enemy logistical supply along lines of communication.

Surprise is the principle advantage of RTA airborne forces. Seldom do airborne forces conduct the frontal attacks that have become the hallmark of RTA doctrine.

Instead, landing zones are designated in undefended or suppressed areas of the battlespace. Airborne drops appreciate high priority of air assets, suppression of enemy counter fires, and ample artillery support.

RTA airborne regiments seek a single drop zone, however when multiple drop zones are required battalion integrity is maintained. The heavy drop of vehicles and heavy weapons immediately precedes the dropping of parachutists.

RTA commanders will rarely if ever risk reinforcements into the same drop zone, but in extreme circumstances may allow for air-delivered resupply. Upon securing the drop zone RTA artillery can begin immediately targeting the objective with fires.

*[Note: The type of artillery (engagement range) determines the maximum possible distance of the drop zone from the objective.]*

# I. Preparation of Airborne Forces

RTA airborne forces are mechanized or motorized. Each airborne battalion maintains integral artillery, engineer, and air defense assets to create their own umbrella of combat support.

Airborne regiments are prized units of the RTA. Morale is high because they almost invariably receive the best equipment and training. Troops undergo a selective screening process. Most unconventional warfare and reconnaissance units undergo parachutist training.

# II. Airborne Forces in the Offense

Surprise, speed, and violence of action are critical to the success of RTA airborne operations. Airdrops have expressed objectives to seize in support of follow-on conventional land forces.

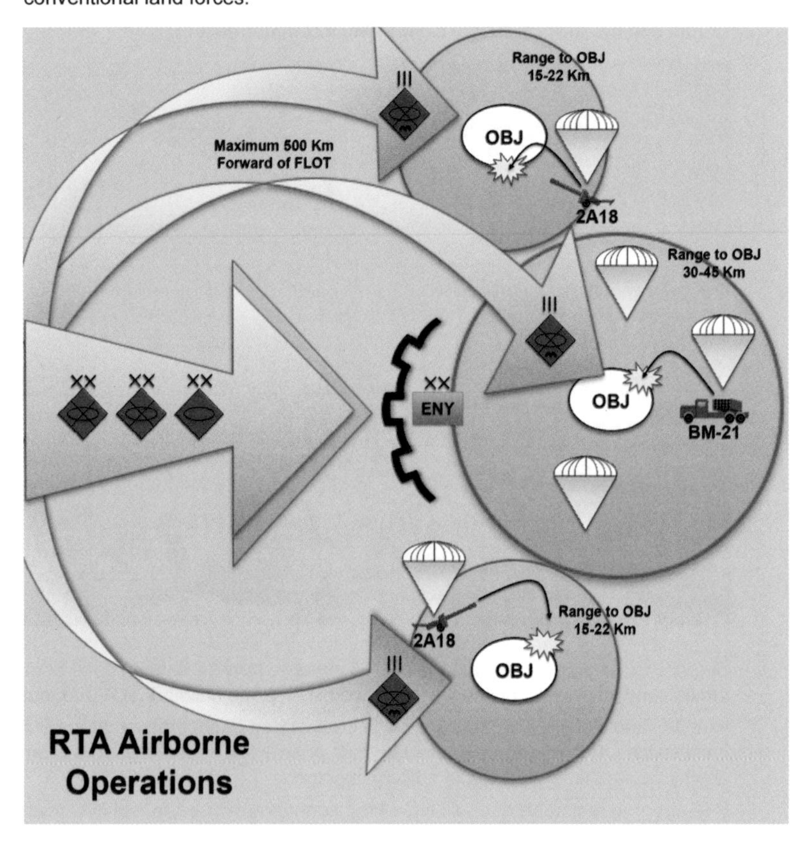


*RTA conduct airborne vertical insertions no farther than 500 kilometers (300 miles) beyond their forward line of troops. Airborne operations shape land-borne attacks with the explicit objective to seize key terrain and to establish blocking positions. Once blocking positions are established, airborne regiments may dispatch rifle companies to conduct special purpose attacks to disrupt the enemy's combat service support and rear area supply lines.*

# Airborne and Air Assault Operations (U.S. Military Doctrine Perspective)

*Ref: JP 3-18 Joint Forcible Entry Operations (Nov '12), App. B.*

Joint airborne and air assault operations involve the air movement and delivery of specially trained combat forces and logistic support into an objective area to execute a mission. Airborne and air assault forces provide the commander with the unique ability to quickly respond on short notice and mass rapidly on critical targets. Airborne operations are executed by specially trained forces and can be launched at a considerable distance from the target area with such speed as to cause tactical or operational surprise and prevent effective action by the enemy. Airborne forces can secure and/or destroy critical installations, facilities or terrain; reinforce US and multinational forces; and conduct a show of force or attack an adversary in isolated areas. Air assault operations increase mobility and freedom of action by providing operational and tactical mobility for both the offense and defense.

Air operations enable forces to reduce time and space limitations normally encountered in movement of assault forces by land, cross terrain obstacles, bypass hostile areas, and attack, destroy, and/or seize objectives deep in enemy territory. Each component can significantly contribute to the successful execution of airborne and air assault operations.

## Concept

Airborne and air assault forces are capable of conducting operations in support of strategic, operational, and tactical objectives. They land intact with weapons, ammunition, and other combat equipment and are prepared for combat immediately. Airborne forces aggressively seize and hold objectives until linkup is accomplished. An airborne operation usually terminates upon seizure of the objective, linkup with other ground forces, or extraction. Air assault operations are deliberate, precisely planned, and vigorously executed to strike over extended distances.

## Characteristics

Airborne and air assault forces share many of the same capabilities. They can extend the battlefield, move, and rapidly concentrate combat power quicker than land forces. Airborne and air assault forces also share the same limitations. They are dependent on the availability of airlift assets, fire support, and combat service support resources; they are highly vulnerable to enemy attack by ground and air forces while en route to the LZ and/or DZ; and are equally assailable when operating in open terrain against an armored threat or WMD. Environmental conditions and adverse weather can also impact performance. There are four phases of airborne operations: marshalling, air movement, landing, and ground tactical phases. Air assault operations have five phases: staging, loading, air movement, landing, and ground tactical phases.

*Army Field Manual (FM) 90-26, Airborne Operations, provides more specifics on airborne and air assault operations.*

*Refer to The Joint Forces Operations & Doctrine SMARTbook (Guide to Joint, Multinational & Interagency Operations) for complete discussion of joint operations and unified action, the range of military operations and operation plan phases. Additional topics include joint doctrine fundamentals, joint operation planning, joint logistics, joint task forces, information operations, multinational operations, and IGOs/NGOs.*

Time spent in battalion assembly areas is kept to a minimum. Commanders confirm their unit strength and receive situation reports from deployed reconnaissance units. Yet because airborne operations are conducted almost invariably deep within enemy territory and require speed and surprise, commanders may conduct offensive action without complete reconnaissance.

Objectives of RTA airborne forces are most commonly bridgeheads, airfields, seaports or mountain passes. In attacking these objectives airborne forces often seek an enveloping or flanking maneuver, while deploying supporting fires. Artillery plays a critical role in both suppressing and disrupting enemy defenses.

The assaulting force maneuvers as closely to the objective as possible before forming into the attack formation. Due to the noise of armored vehicles, the attack position is nominally established at 1,000 meters, but closer when possible.

RTA airborne forces may attack in either a single echelon or double, depending on the relative strength of the enemy position. A rifle company typically attacks along a front of 200 meters to a maximum of 500 meters wide.

Once the objective is successfully captured, RTA airborne units immediately assume a defensive position to wait for follow-on forces.

# III. Airborne Forces in the Defense



Once the RTA airborne regiment has seized the objective, its mission is to defend it until the arrival of ground forces advancing from the front line or along a line of attack through the area of operations.

The unit establishes a series of strongpoint defenses that form into a 360-degree front. Critical assets such as artillery and air defense systems are protected within the nucleus of the perimeter to offer better application of fires against enemy attack.

RTA airborne units continue to develop their defense position with engineer assets. Priority is given to hull-down vehicle positions to fire in direct support of infantry positions and minefields. Units make maximum use of natural obstacles, as there is seldom the opportunity to drop additional supplies such as barbed wire and construction materials.

From the defended objective, RTA airborne regiments may dispatch a number of rifle companies or platoons to conduct special purpose attacks against enemy supply lines and critical resources. Raids and ambushes further disrupt the enemy's ability to coordinate counterattacks against the RTA airborne force or resist the impending RTA attack along the front lines.

In rare cases RTA airborne units are required to fight their way back to front lines instead of continue a defense. In such an event the regiment or battalion conducts a movement to contact using the approach march method, maximizing the use of reconnaissance units as forward vanguards. Link up with the RTA front lines is a critical enabling task for such a mission.

# (Specialized Warfare)
# II. Heliborne Operations

*Ref: FM 100-2-2 The Soviet Army: Special Warfare and Rear Area Support (Jul '84), chap 3.*

Heliborne regiments are essentially the only "light" infantry regiments of the RTA. They have no integral armored vehicles because too few helicopters have such lift capability. And while heliborne regiments can lift their artillery assets, they rarely do. Instead, heliborne units remain within the umbrella of fires from a larger unit to benefit from artillery, armor, and air defense support.

RTA heliborne units offer lightning strikes and tactical flexibility to their parent organization. RTA reconnaissance battalions are often assigned helicopter capabilities. Such units achieve peer status with the best militaries across the globe.

RTA heliborne formations are limited in numbers. Relatively slow speeds and altitude limitations leave them incredibly vulnerable to enemy air defense fires, minimizing the size, scope and frequency of heliborne operations.

Given the multi-mission flexibility of rotary wing aircraft – fast attack, observation, air lift supply, medical evacuation – RTA commanders are reluctant to allocate helicopters to high risk missions outside the umbrella of RTA artillery and air defense support.

*[Note: The type of artillery (engagement range) determines the maximum possible distance of the heliborne objective.]*

## I. Preparation of Heliborne Forces

While in the past the short requirement of training in heliborne operations meant that virtually any RTA unit might be temporarily divorced from its armored vehicles to conduct heliborne operations; modern RTA forces select heliborne units on a competitive basis. The various capabilities and considerable expense of helicopter assets means only elite forces are assigned to RTA heliborne operations.

Heliborne units are virtually the only light infantry assets known to RTA forces, with the rare exception of alpine units. In special circumstances vehicles are assigned to heliborne units. Yet they are light skinned trucks and motorcycles that serve as logistic carriers and reconnaissance platforms, not as attack vehicles.

This means that while training unique to the helicopter is achieved in literally just a half day, the emphasis on dismounted patrolling operations requires specialized equipment and ongoing tactical training that can take months to complete.

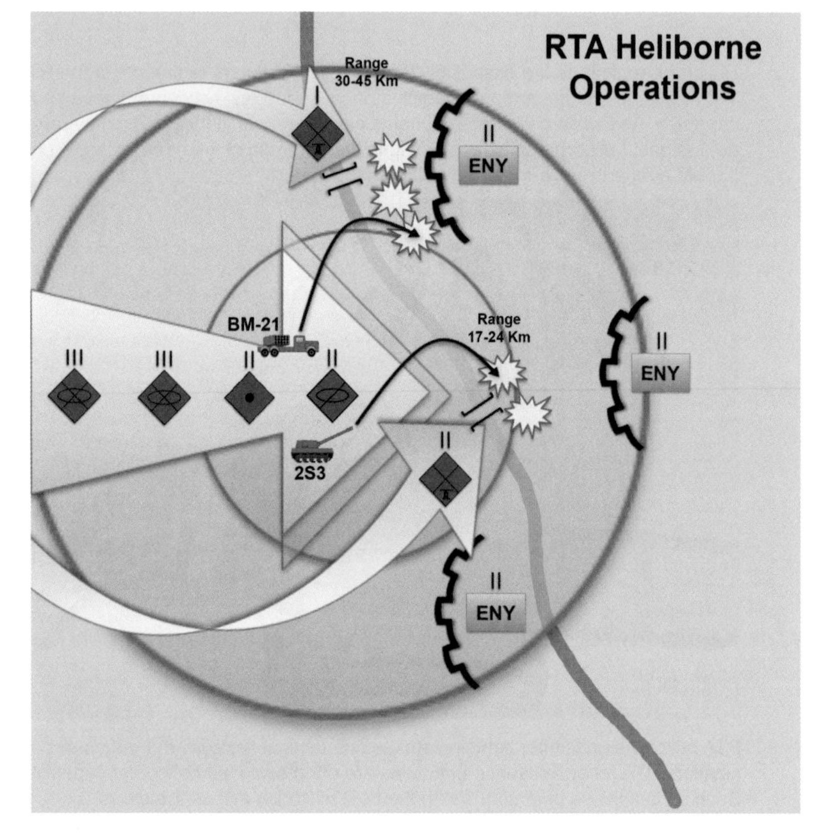


*RTA heliborne operations shape ground-based attacks by seizing key terrain or facilities within the umbrella of support of the decisive action. In this illustration a heliborne battalion is dispatched to the primary objective – to secure a bridgehead. Another heliborne rifle company is tasked to secure a secondary bridgehead.*

# II. Heliborne Forces in the Offense

RTA heliborne attack doctrine in practice suggests that operations are almost invariably conducted within artillery range of the principle regiment or division. In some cases heliborne units have airlifted their artillery, engineer, and air defense assets deep into enemy territory to create their own integral umbrella of support, very similar to airborne units. However, this is indeed rare.

Furthermore, RTA heliborne units are typically company or battalion-size missions in part due to the limited number of available helicopters. These units would not have the offensive power or force protection of a full regiment or division. Operations outside the umbrella of support of the principle unit leave heliborne forces extremely vulnerable to enemy fires and counterattack.

# Air Assault Operations (U.S. Military Doctrine Perspective)

*Ref: FM 3-90 Tactics (Jul '101; superseded), App.C.*

Joint force commanders conduct entry operations at the operational level of war. Commanders operating at the tactical level conduct airborne or air assault operations to gain a positional advantage or to envelop or turn the enemy. Airborne and air assault operations are types of entry operations that use a vertical envelopment to insert a force into an area of operations (AO).

Air assault operations are those in which assault forces (combat, combat support, and combat service support) using the firepower, mobility, and total integration of helicopter assets, maneuver on the battlefield under the control of the ground or air maneuver commander to engage and destroy enmy forces or to seize and hold key terrain. They are often highrisk, high-payoff operations.

An air assault task force (AATF) can dramatically extend the commander's ability to influence operations within his AO and to execute operations in locations beyond the capability of more conventional forces. The air assault force retains the flexibility to rapidly redeploy to conduct subsequent offensive or defensive operations. Air assault operations closely resemble airborne operations. Air assault forces are most vulnerable during the takeoff from PZs and the landing at LZs in unsecured areas.

The assault force uses the firepower, mobility, and total integration of helicopter assets to maneuver throughout the AO. Its purpose is to engage and destroy enemy forces or to seize and hold key terrain. Joint doctrine regards air assault operations as a subset of airborne operations. Air assault operations are not administrative movements of soldiers, weapons, and materiel by Army aviation units. An air assault is a deliberate, precisely planned, and vigorously executed combat operation designed to allow friendly forces to strike over extended distances and terrain barriers to attack the enemy when and where he is most vulnerable. The commander plans these operations using the previously described reverse planning process.

The substantial mobility of an air assault force enables its commander to achieve surprise and deception and to conduct operations throughout his AO. However, air assault operations conducted in locations geographically remote from supporting forces may place the air assault force at increased risk if its ISR systems do not accurately detect enemy forces positioned to disrupt the air assault. Air assault units are well suited for use as reaction forces and in search and attack operations when information about the enemy's location, strength, and disposition is vague.

The large-scale use of helicopters in air assault operations greatly multiplies the mobility of ground units and contributes directly to an increase in combat effectiveness. Their use allows the ground commander to take advantage of the speed and flexibility of Army aircraft to accomplish a variety of tasks. For example, during a river-crossing operation, an air assault can help secure the crossing site or bridgehead line.

*Army Field Manual (FM) 90-26, Airborne Operations, provides more specifics on airborne and air assault operations.*

*Refer to The Joint Forces Operations & Doctrine SMARTbook (Guide to Joint, Multinational & Interagency Operations) for complete discussion of joint operations and unified action, the range of military operations and operation plan phases. Additional topics include joint doctrine fundamentals, joint operation planning, joint logistics, joint task forces, information operations, multinational operations, and IGOs/NGOs.*

Instead, RTA heliborne units are leveraged most commonly as a raiding force. The helicopter can deliver small tactical teams to virtually any objective regardless of terrain. Heliborne units insert remarkably close to their objective and arrive with unit integrity in tact, immediately ready to fight. Often, heliborne units land beside their objective while coordinated artillery fire suppresses the enemy objective.

Typical missions for RTA heliborne units include attacks against enemy command and control nodes; destruction of enemy air defense or artillery assets; seizure of bridgeheads; securing mountain passes; or a vertical envelopment in pursuit of retreating enemy.

Heliborne units are also well suited for guerilla warfare including highly mobile patrolling operations in reconnaissance, ambush and raids. Such capabilities lend well to specific operating environments such as mountainous or tropical regions.

# III. Heliborne Forces in the Defense

RTA heliborne units have a limited role in defensive operations due to a lack of armored vehicle assets. In unrestricted terrain such as farmlands, grasslands, deserts or even relatively flat forests, heliborne units grounded in a defensive position are quickly outflanked, out-maneuvered, and out-gunned. Even with their attack helicopters, heliborne units are extremely vulnerable to armored attack.

In the defense, heliborne units tend to be rotated to rear areas. They may serve as mobile reserves or forward reconnaissance. In the most desperate conditions, heliborne forces may be divided to augment mechanized regiments on the front line.

Yet heliborne units often play a vital role as outposts or in retrograde defenses, particularly in mountainous and tropical regions. In such operating environments the agility of helicopter airlift and resupply are critical in establishing key defensive outposts along internal lines of communication.

In such environments, the terrain provides reliable protection from the enemy's armored formations and airlift capabilities ensure a continuous resupply and reinforcement. It is in these restrictive environments that RTA heliborne operations first proved their resilience in the defense.

# (Specialized Warfare) III. Amphibious Operations

*Ref: FM 100-2-2 The Soviet Army: Special Warfare and Rear Area Support (Jul '84), chap 4.*

Amphibious units are extremely rare within Red Team Armies (RTA). In part this is because so few RTA maintain a "blue water" navy capable of projecting their forces globally. Yet a small number of RTA maintains naval infantry regiments with the ability to conduct amphibious operations.

Amphibious operations are conducted to gain entry of ground forces along costal regions, or to surround and destroy enemy forces or facilities in such areas.

## I. Preparation of Amphibious Forces

RTA naval infantry regiments are proficiently trained on amphibious operations. These units are incredibly few in number, and enjoy a high esprit de corps. By contrast, RTA army regiments likely have no training in amphibious operations – unless there is the time, space, and opportunity to prepare RTA army units for a specified mission.

RTA naval infantry regiments are equipped with amphibious vehicles such as the venerable PT-76 light tank, K-61 tracked personnel carrier, and BTR-60P wheeled personnel carrier – all of which have swimming capabilities. These vehicles are issued to the first assault wave to secure the initial beachhead.

Follow on amphibious forces use larger Dyugon-class or Zubr-class landing vessels to off load main battle tanks plus heavy armored infantry, artillery and engineer vehicles.

Amphibious operations require extensive inter-service training and coordination between RTA naval, air, and ground forces.

# II. Amphibious Forces in the Offense

Offensive missions unique to naval infantry forces include the seizure of a beachhead to gain entry, or to secure islands, seaports, and even coastal airfields.

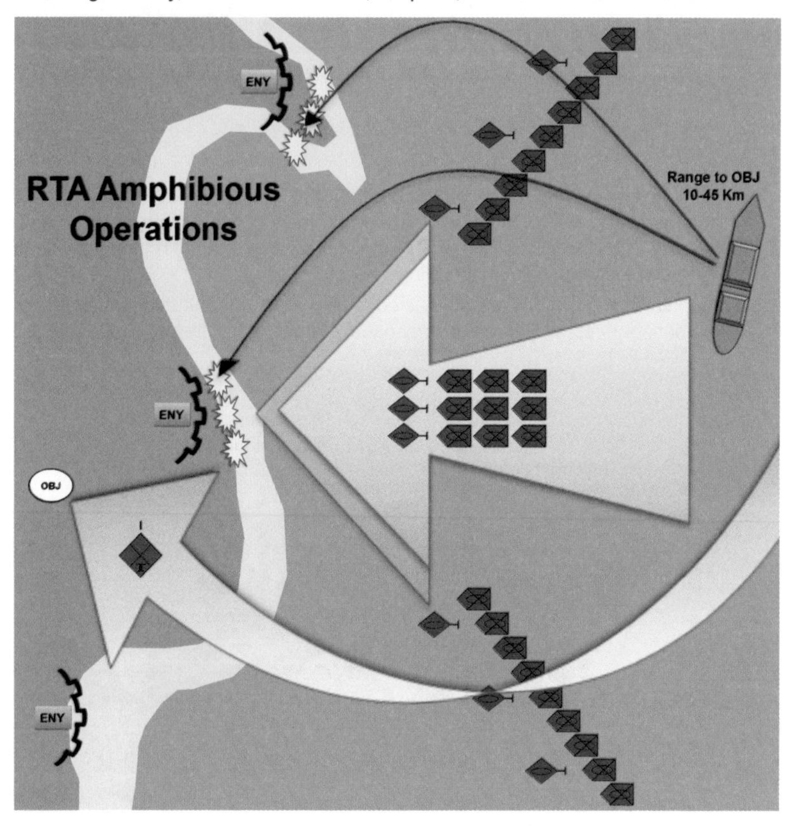


*RTA army or naval infantry units may conduct amphibious operations using amphibious ferries, swimmable tanks, or armored fighting vehicles. Shaping operations may take the form of vertical insertion of airborne or heliborne units, and naval artillery fires. Air superiority must be achieved over the beachhead.*

Air cover must achieve superiority over the beachhead landing area. The naval fleet and amphibious operations are vulnerable to enemy attack by air. Additionally, anti-submarine capabilities must augment the taskforce.

RTA amphibious operations against fortified enemy positions or facilities are often detected well in advance of the amphibious force due to the sheer size and importance of the naval fleet. When this is the case, the naval infantry will employ the smaller swimmable vehicles to present smaller targets to enemy weapon systems, and to negotiate enemy defensive obstacles. Larger vessels ferry follow-on ground forces to the beachhead once it is secured.

Alternatively, when the beachhead is not well defended or when complete surprise is achieved, only the larger landing vessels are employed to maximize speed and minimize risk due to poor sea conditions.

In either case, airborne and/or heliborne units conduct simultaneous vertical envelopment to seize key terrain and infrastructure; to destroy critical enemy weapons

# Amphibious Operations (U.S. Military Doctrine Perspective)

*Ref: JP 3-02 Amphibious Operations (Jul '14).*

An amphibious operation is a military operation launched from the sea by an amphibious force (AF) to conduct landing force (LF) operations within the littorals. The littorals include those land areas (and their adjacent sea and associated air space) that are predominantly susceptible to engagement and influence from the sea.

Amphibious operations use maneuver principles to transition ready-to-fight combat forces from the sea to the shore in order to achieve a position of advantage over the enemy. During combat operations, maneuver, in conjunction with fires (organic and supporting), is essential to gaining access where the enemy least expects it.

## Amphibious Raid

An amphibious raid is an operation involving a swift incursion into or the temporary occupation of an objective to accomplish an assigned mission followed by a planned withdrawal. An amphibious raid may be conducted to temporarily seize an area in order to secure information, confuse an adversary, capture personnel or equipment, or to destroy a capability. An amphibious demonstration is a show of force intended to influence or deter an enemy's decision. An amphibious demonstration's intent is to deceive the enemy, causing the enemy to select an unfavorable course of action.

## Amphibious Assault

An amphibious assault involves the establishment of an LF on a hostile or potentially hostile shore. An amphibious assault requires the swift buildup of combat power ashore, from an initial zero capability to full coordinated striking power as the attack progresses toward AF objectives. The assault begins on order after sufficient elements of the assault echelon arrive in the operational area and specified operational criteria for landing are met. For an assault, the action phase ends when conditions specified in the initiating directive are met, as recommended by the CATF and CLF and approved by the JFC or designated commander.

## Amphibious Withdrawals

Amphibious withdrawals are operations conducted to extract forces in ships or craft from a hostile or potentially hostile shore. They may be conducted under enemy pressure or under operational urgency in permissive, uncertain, or hostile environments to obtain forces needed elsewhere or to remove forces whose mission is completed. AFs support to crisis response and other operations focuses on providing a rapid response to crises, deterring war, resolving conflict, promoting peace, and supporting civil authorities in response to domestic crises.

## Other Operations

AFs routinely conduct support to other operations such as security cooperation, foreign humanitarian assistance, noncombatant evacuation operations, peace support operations, recovery operations, or protecting US facilities and personnel abroad.

*Refer to The Marine Expeditionary Unit (MEU) SMARTbook, a reference for MEU and PHIBRON Commanders, MEU and PHIBRON staffs and the commanders and staffs of the ARG-MEU team. Topics include: MEU mission, organization, and capabilities; MEU staff functions; mission planning; mission essential tasks; standing mission briefs; MEU liaison and survey elements; appendices and reference guides; and glossary.*

Specialized Warfare

and command centers; and to establish blocking positions to prevent enemy reinforcements from reaching the beachhead.

Naval artillery fire against coastal targets supports the landing. Fires are concentrated on enemy artillery, obstacles and fortified positions. Fires may also be tasked to smoke screening missions for select sections of the beachhead.

Minesweeping ships may precede the amphibious force to clear obstacles and establish marked approach lanes. Minesweepers may also be tasked to provide smoke screens for the assault wave.

Assault formations for the first wave may form into a line, wedge, echelon or even multiple columns. All variations of the formation include swimmable tanks forward with personnel carriers and tracked ferries behind. RTA vehicle crews train to fire their weapons at targets of opportunity while afloat.

RTA amphibious forces do not dismount on shore unless they are tasked to specific functions such as removing enemy obstacles, destroying enemy fighting positions, or securing key terrain. Instead, each rifle company or battalion is tasked to a specified objective inland, and the assault continues to press toward objectives that establish the initial limit of advance. At that time units rendezvous on or just past the objective and reconsolidate.

With the beachhead secured and an initial front established, the naval infantry units provide protective cover for follow-on ground forces in the larger landing vessels. Follow-on ground forces with heavier armored vehicles will capitalize on entry through the beachhead to attack critical enemy infrastructure and cut off or block enemy forces along the coastal area.



# III. Amphibious Forces in the Defense

Other than a protective perimeter established around the beachhead landing, RTA naval infantry forces do not engage in conventional defensive operations. That is, naval infantry are not conceived in RTA doctrine for continued inland ground operations because they are supported directly by the fleet taskforce. Extended inland operations would leave the fleet vulnerable to enemy counterattack.

However, after the amphibious assault, naval infantry forces do provide a protective defense perimeter of the beachhead to allow the immediate landing of follow-on ground forces. Depending on the size of the invasion, naval infantry regiments may be required to continue defending the beachhead for an extended period of time.

Naval infantry forces are trained in establishing classic RTA strongpoint defenses around the beachhead area, seizing key terrain and critical infrastructure such as seaports, airports, bridges, railheads, crossroads junctions, and even coastal towns.

Engineer and construction battalion assets are provided by the naval fleet taskforce to augment the establishment of defenses. The fleet continues to provide an umbrella of support for artillery and air defense, plus logistical resupply.

Once the beachhead has served its purpose of gaining entry and all ground forces have been dispatched to the coast, naval infantry forces withdraw. The fleet taskforce then departs the area.

# (Specialized Warfare)
# IV. Unconventional Warfare

*Ref: FM 100-2-2 The Soviet Army: Special Warfare and Rear Area Support (Jul '84), chap 5.*

Red Team Armies (RTA) leverage conventional tactics in unconventional operating environments. The overarching objective for unconventional warfare (UW) is to weaken the targeted opponent or antagonist to shape the victory for follow-on conventional forces.

UW involves partisan warfare, subversion, and sabotage conducted in periods of armed conflict and peace. Almost invariably, UW is conducted covertly as clandestine operations.

## I. Preparation of UW Force

RTA establishes select organizations for UW inside the military and paramilitary forces. Additionally, military reconnaissance battalions and companies are often employed in UW because they are often the more capable military units.

UW forces receive specialized training in camouflage and infiltration, surveillance, explosives and improvised weapons, hand-to-hand combatives, and communication technologies. Specialized medical and language training are also common.

UW forces also stand in contrast to RTA conventional forces in that they rarely deploy with mechanized vehicles. Instead they are more commonly infiltrated by either aerial insertion or waterborne insertion techniques. They may dress in special camouflage uniforms, foreign military uniforms, or in civilian attire.

UW forces employ a wide array of tactical equipment that may be issued or acquired from indigenous resources. This holds true for weapons, communication systems, and even vehicles.

# II. UW in the Offense

RTA conducts UW in the form of advisory training teams, espionage, surveillance, and special purpose attacks – most notably raid and ambush – to destroy or capture enemy resources. UW operations entail a full spectrum of participation from low intensity to high intensity open warfare.

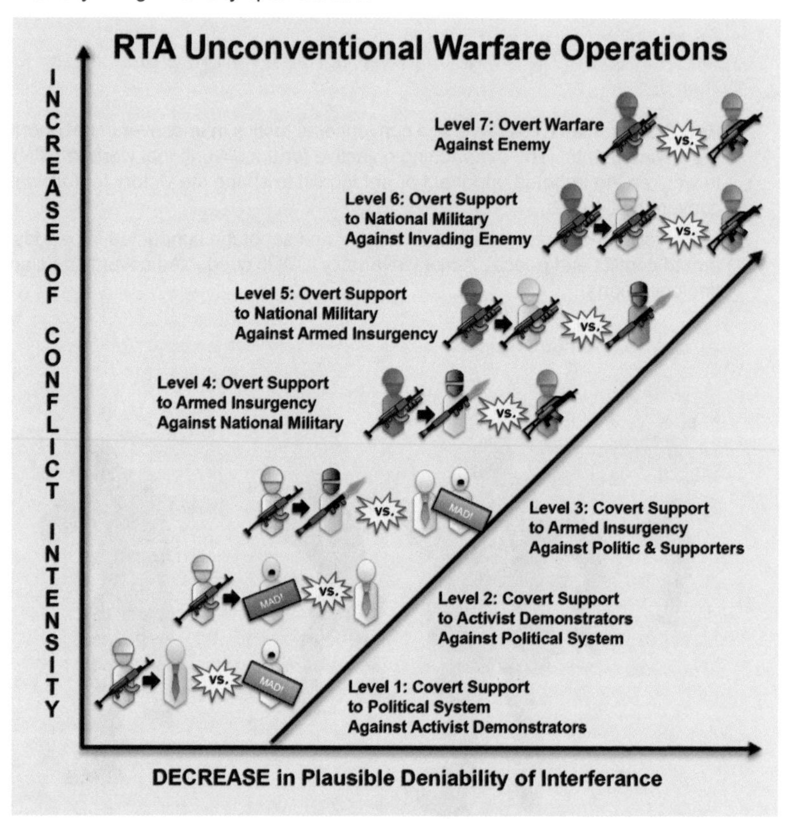


## 1. Covert Support to Political System

RTA UW forces play a role in political support and protection of foreign politicians who are partial to their political beliefs. Often this support is openly known. However sometimes it is more politically expedient that such support remain surreptitious. Such was the case of Soviet Union support to Cuban military capabilities during the height of the Cold War.

## 2. Covert Support to Anti-Government Activist

RTA UW forces may assume a supportive role against foreign political systems when anti-government forces are ideological aligned with RTA causes. In Vietnam during the 1950s and 60s RTA from WARPAC nations and China sent weapons, equipment, and advisors to both North Vietnam while encouraging anti-government movements in South Vietnam.

## 3. Covert Support to Armed Insurgency

RTA UW forces may discreetly support armed insurgencies of foreign nations when ideologically aligned or when the outcome suits the purposes of the RTA nation. Such was the case of Chinese and Soviet support to guerillas in Rhodesia in the 1970s.

# Special Operations (U.S. Military Doctrine Perspective)

*Ref: JP 3-05 Special Operations (Jul '14).*

Special operations require unique modes of employment, tactics, techniques, procedures, and equipment. They are often conducted in hostile, denied, or politically and/or diplomatically sensitive environments, and are characterized by one or more of the following: time-sensitivity, clandestine or covert nature, low visibility, work with or through indigenous forces, greater requirements for regional orientation and cultural expertise, and a higher degree of risk. Special operations provide JFCs and chiefs of mission (COMs) with discrete, precise, and scalable options that can be synchronized with activities of other interagency partners to achieve United States Government (USG) objectives. These operations are designed in a culturally attuned manner to create both immediate and enduring effects to help prevent and deter conflict or prevail in war. They assess and shape foreign political and military environments unilaterally, or with host nations (HNs), multinational partners, and indigenous populations. Although special operations can be conducted independently, most are coordinated with conventional forces (CF), interagency partners, and multinational partners, and may include work with indigenous, insurgent, or irregular forces. Special operations may differ from conventional operations in degree of strategic, physical, and political and/or diplomatic risk; operational techniques; modes of employment; and dependence on intelligence and indigenous assets.

SOF often conduct distributed operations with small operational and logistics footprints far from major bases. SOF employ sophisticated communications systems and a road array of infiltration, support, and exfiltration techniques to penetrate and return from hostile, denied, or politically and/or diplomatically sensitive areas.

While special operations can be conducted unilaterally in support of specific theater or national objectives, the majority are planned and conducted in support of theater campaigns. Special operations typically complement—not compete with nor substitute for—conventional operations.

Special operations can be a single engagement, such as direct action (DA) against a critical target; as a protracted operation or series of activities such as support to insurgent forces through unconventional warfare (UW); or support to a HN force through foreign internal defense (FID) or security force assistance (SFA). Military information support operations (MISO) can be used during special operations to influence selected target audiences' behavior and actions. Civil affairs operations (CAO) also provide essential support to a JFC or country team. Special operations, synchronized with MISO and CAO, can create effects disproportionate to the size of the units involved.

Special operations are inherently joint because of the integration and interdependency that is established among ARSOF, NAVSOF, AFSOF, and MARSOF to accomplish their missions. SOF conduct joint and combined training both within the SOF community, with CF, and with interagency and multinational partners.

*Refer to The Joint Forces Operations & Doctrine SMARTbook (Guide to Joint, Multinational & Interagency Operations) for complete discussion of joint operations and unified action, the range of military operations and operation plan phases. Additional topics include joint doctrine fundamentals, joint operation planning, joint logistics, joint task forces, information operations, multinational operations, and IGOs/NGOs.*

### 4. Overt Support to Armed Insurgency

RTA UW forces may openly support armed insurgents and guerillas of foreign nations when ideologically aligned or when the outcome suits the needs of the RTA nation. Cuban intervention in Angola from the mid-1970s through the 1980s began with UW forces, although at its peak included 25,000 conventional Cuban military forces.

### 5. Overt Support to Foreign Military against Internal Unrest

RTA UW forces may be leveraged in the early states of open military support to foreign states under the auspice of aid to foreign nation internal stability. This was the rationale provided by Russia in early 2014 as its neighboring nation Ukraine split into pro-Western and pro-Russian factions. Russian UW forces moved quickly into Crimea, initially in unmarked uniforms and vehicles, to shape the success of follow-on conventional Russian forces that seized the Crimean peninsula.

### 6. Overt Support to Foreign Military against Invasion

RTA UW forces conduct advanced shaping operations against enemy invasion of allied foreign states. This was the case when in 2008 when Georgian military forces moved into the disputed region of South Ossetia, which was allied with Russia, to put down rebellious factions who opposed Georgian rule. The initial Georgian advance was halted by the contributions of South Ossetia militia backed by Russian UW forces. Russian conventional forces then attacked southward, well into the nation of Georgia with devastating effect.

### 7. Overt Warfare against Opposing Enemy

RTA UW forces may function as a disruptive force to shape a military advance in open warfare. In the summer of 1950, North Korea invaded South Korea with UW forces from the North Korean Army conducting espionage against the South Korean military. Their actions caught the South Korean Army off guard and greatly reduced the South's ability to affect a military response. North Korean UW forces also rallied sympathetic civilians from the South Korean populous to aid in material support to the invading army.



## III. UW in the Defense

UW forces do not conceptually espouse a defensive doctrine. UW forces must be managed through operations for rest and retraining rotations. However they do not function in defensive positions or tactics, per se.

Yet because UW forces commonly operate in deep in enemy territory, when the enemy is conducting major offenses against RTA, UW forces conduct espionage missions that target the enemy's vulnerable lines of communication and logistics.

The intent is to disrupt the enemy's coordinating communications and resupply. When possible UW forces team with local partisans to force the enemy to redirect combat units to regions the enemy believed already pacified. Such was the case in many of the Eastern European nations, plus Ukraine and Belarus regions in the Soviet Union that fell victim to the German invaders during the Second World War.

UW forces may also be tasked to special missions internally that are often referred to as the "scorched earth" defense. The intent is to deny all usable indigenous resources to an advancing enemy. In the weeks after the German invasion of 1941, Joseph Stalin ordered that food sources, agriculture and infrastructure be destroyed as the Soviet Army withdrew to deny these resources to the invading enemy. Moreover, Stalin ordered paramilitary UW forces (NKVD) to round up political prisoners of the state for summary execution and/or deportation eastward.

RTA UW forces in defense may, or may not, resort to violent acts of desperation. Still, clearly there is not a doctrine of UW forces in defense, and such forces may conduct themselves professionally with dignity or pose a more serious threat.

# Chap 5 Tactical Enabling Tasks

*Ref: ADP 3-90, Offense and Defense (Aug '12), ADRP 3-90, Offense & Defense (Aug '12) and FM 3-90-2 Reconnaissance, Security and Tactical Enabling Tasks (Mar '13).*

The tactical level of war is the level of war at which battles and engagements are planned and executed to achieve military objectives assigned to tactical units or task forces (JP 3-0). Activities at this level focus on the ordered arrangement and maneuver of combat elements in relation to each other and to the enemy to achieve combat objectives. It is important to understand tactics within the context of the levels of war. The strategic and operational levels provide the context for tactical operations. Without this context, tactical operations are reduced to a series of disconnected and unfocused actions.

## Tactical Enabling Tasks





## Tactical Enabling Tasks

Commanders direct tactical enabling tasks to support the conduct of decisive action. Tactical enabling tasks are usually shaping or sustaining. They may be decisive in the conduct of stability tasks. Tactical enabling tasks include tasks such as reconnaissance, security, troop movement, relief in place, passage of lines, encirclement operations, and urban operations.

*Refer to The Small Unit Tactics SMARTbook (Leader's Reference Guide to Conducting Tactical Operations) for complete discussion from U.S. military doctrine of offensive and defensive operations, tactical mission fundamentals, stability & counterinsurgency operations, tactical enabling operations, special purpose attacks, urban operations & fortifications, and patrols & patrolling.*

# Tactical Mission Tasks (U.S. Doctrine)

*Ref: FM 3-90, Tactics (Jul '01), app. C.*

There is no direct reference that discusses/defines Red Team Army tactical mission tasks, but the following chart from U.S. doctrine provides context and an overview of the types of tasks conducted in the course of tactical operations. Tactical mission tasks describe the results or effects the commander wants to achieve - the *what* and *why* of a mission statement. There is no definitive list of words or terms and is not limited to the tactical mission tasks listed below. The *what* is an effect that is normally measurable. The *why* of a mission statement provides the mission's purpose or reason.

## Effects on Enemy Force

Block
Canalize
Contain
Defeat

Destroy
Disrupt
Fix
Interdict

Isolate
Neutralize
Penetrate
Turn

## Actions by Friendly Forces

Assault
Attack-by-Fire
Breach
Bypass
Clear
Combat Search and Rescue
Consolidation & Reorganization

Control
Counterreconnaissance
Disengagement
Exfiltrate
Follow and Assume
Follow and Support
Linkup

Occupy
Reconstitution
Reduce
Retain
Secure
Seize
Support-by-Fire
Suppress

## Types and Forms of Operations

### Movement to Contact
Search and Attack

### Attack
Ambush
Demonstration
Feint
Raid
Spoiling Attack

### Exploitation
### Pursuit
### Offensive Maneuver
Envelopment
Frontal Attack
Infiltration
Penetration
Turning Movement

### Area Defense
### Mobile Defense
### Retrograde Operations
Delay, Withdrawal, Retirement

### Reconnaissance Operations
Zone
Area (including point)
Route
Recon in force
Forms of security
- Screen
- Guard
- Cover
- Area

### Security Operations
### Information Operations
### Combined Arms Breach Ops
### Passage of Lines
### Relief in Place
### River Crossing Operations
### Troop Movement
Administrative Movement
Approach March
Road March

## Purpose (in order to)

Divert
Enable
Deceive
Deny
Prevent

Open
Envelop
Surprise
Cause
Protect

Allow
Create
Influence
Support

# (Tactical Enabling Tasks) I. Reconnaissance

*Ref: FM 100-2-1 The Soviet Army: Operations and Tactics (Jul '84), chap 7.*

The tactical concepts of Soviet ground forces require timely, accurate, and continuous information on the enemy, terrain, and weather. Reconnaissance, as defined by the Soviets, is the collection of information about the location, activity, disposition, composition, size, armament, combat readiness, and intentions of the enemy. The Soviets recognize that reconnaissance will be met by enemy countermeasures and deception. They employ multiple, overlapping collection means to insure success of their reconnaissance efforts.

*Map reconnaissance is still the absolute minimum requirement. Yet even when tasking reconnaissance assets to named areas of interest (NAI), map recon is used in the planning of those missions. (Courtesy of Hae-jung Larsen and OP EASTWIND.)*

## I. Reconnaissance Elements

The effective ranges of the reconnaissance means at front level vary at each level of command. These ranges are also dependent on weather and terrain.

Aerial reconnaissance by high performance aircraft normally is conducted by aviation units at front and army level. Aviation units conduct visual, photo, and electronic intercept and direction-finding reconnaissance missions. Ranges of reconnaissance aircraft vary. Missions of 350 to 400 km usually are flown by pairs of aircraft to support armies or divisions. Long-range missions in excess of 400 km also are flown in support of front operations. Visual reconnaissance is a secondary mission of all aircraft in the divisional tactical area. In-flight observations are transmitted to the maneuver elements on the tactical air net.

Helicopters flying in the vicinity of the FEBA depend on local air superiority. When air superiority is denied, helicopters are used to emplace observation posts or reconnaissance patrols rather than perform as air reconnaissance platforms. All helicopters performing any missions may be expected to pass tactical information to those headquarters and units with whom they have radio communications.

From front to regiment, there are chemical defense units which monitor nuclear and chemical contamination. Chemical defense troops from these units provide direct combat support to the maneuver units down to company level. Equipped with radiological-chemical reconnaissance vehicles, these troops monitor radiation and chemical agents and mark contaminated areas. Helicopters or fixed-wing aircraft also may conduct NBC reconnaissance.

Soviet artillery from front to division has organic target acquisition units which obtain and transmit meteorological and topographic information. The division artillery regiment has a target acquisition battery which gathers information from a topographic survey platoon, sound/flash ranging platoon, a reconnaissance platoon, a surveillance radar section, and a meteorological section.

Engineer units from front to regimental level may be used in reconnaissance detachments. Engineer specialists normally accompany maneuver unit reconnaissance patrols. The Soviets are particularly aware of the need for engineer intelligence to assist in maintaining a rapid rate of advance. The reconnaissance resources of the division's combat engineer battalion also include mine detection equipment and the means or detailed bank and bed survey of water obstacles.

Airborne or airmobile forces may be employed behind enemy lines to locate enemy headquarters, communications systems, and nuclear weapons. They also may be given the mission to attack these targets.

# II. Reconnaissance Organizations



To obtain timely intelligence Soviet commanders sometimes organize and dispatch reconnaissance groups. These groups may be formed by the commander from army through regiment. A reconnaissance group is a temporary tactical subunit formed for the execution of a specified reconnaissance mission. The composition of such groups, usually reinforced platoons or companies, depends on the situation and the assigned mission. In an attack, a division could form a reconnaissance group consisting of a motorized rifle company, reinforced with a platoon of tanks and engineer and NBC reconnaissance squads.

## Reconnaissance Detachment

A reconnaissance detachment is a temporary tactical subunit of reinforced company or battalion strength. The basic subunit (motorized rifle or tank) is almost always reinforced With elements of the other arm to make it a balanced combat force. Depending on the mission, specialized reconnaissance elements such as artillery, engineers, or NBC may be assigned or attached. A reconnaissance detachment of battalion strength is assigned a zone approximately 7 kilometers wide and 35 kilometers in depth, or it may be assigned an axis of advance. A reconnaissance detachment fulfills its mission by observation, by ambush, and by direct attack if necessary.

## Separate Reconnaissance Patrol

A separate reconnaissance patrol is a temporary tactical subunit composed of a reinforced squad or a platoon. It normally is assigned a specific objective and or route instead of a zone. A squad-sized patrol may operate away from its parent unit at a distance of 8 kilometers during the day and 3 kilometers at night, while a platoon-sized patrol may operate at a distance of up to 15 kilometers during the day and up to 5 kilometers at night. A separate reconnaissance patrol accomplishes its mission by observation, but may engage in limited combat if necessary. Limited combat in this case means that the patrol may use reconnaissance by fire to determine enemy positions when no other means are available.

## III. Principles of Soviet Reconnaissance

*Ref: FM 100-2-1 The Soviet Army: Operations and Tactics (Jul '84), p. 7-1.*

### Aggressiveness

The decisive actions and initiative used by commanders and headquarters to obtain necessary information by all means available.

### Continuity

The conduct of reconnaissance at all times regardless of the intensity of combat, time of day, or weather conditions. Established contact with the enemy must not be broken and observation must be continuously maintained.

### Timeliness

The gathering and reporting of reconnaissance information in sufficient time to counter enemy actions.

### Reliability

The degree to which the intelligence information accurately portrays the enemy situation. This involves verifying the intelligence with data from other sources and assigning additional reconnaissance missions to confirm or deny the information.

### Accuracy

The accurate determination of coordinates of important enemy targets such as missile installations, nuclear capable artillery, nuclear storage sites, etc.

## B. Typical Reconnaissance Patrol Tasks

- Identify, locate, and report on enemy headquarters, nuclear weapon systems, troop locations, communication centers, and movement of enemy units
- Determine the disposition of enemy defenses, locate enemy boundaries and artillery positions, and provide topographical information on approaches to enemy defensive positions
- Report enemy emplacement of demolitions and the location of minefields
- Determine obstacle-crossing sites and provide hydrographic information on water obstacles
- Monitor areas of suspected NBC contamination
- Identify routes for advance, withdrawal, and lateral communications
- Identify key terrain
- Identify possible sites for friendly communication installations

## Combat Reconnaissance Patrols

Combat reconnaissance patrols in reinforced small subunit strength are employed to attack known or suspected enemy positions to gain information. Their mission is to cause the enemy to react and thereby reveal his dispositions, strength, and fire plan. The patrol conducts its reconnaissance by feints or demonstrations employing fire and maneuver against actual or suspected enemy positions. These positions generally are assigned to the patrol as reconaissance objectives by the controlling headquarters.

*Mounted reconnaissance moves quickly. It can develop the situation for the commander in short order. Yet mounted reconnaissance is exposed and often vulnerable to enemy countermeasures. Furthermore, the information gain by mounted reconnaissance typically has a very short shelf life. (Courtesy of Hae-jung Larsen and OP EASTWIND.)*



## Reconnaissance in Force

A reconnaissance in force is employed when ordinary air and ground reconnaissance activities fail to provide sufficient intelligence on which to base a plan of attack. Like the combat reconnaissance patrol, the reconnaissance in force is intended to force the enemy to expose his defensive system. Its specific objectives are to fix the true trace of enemy defense and to locate troop concentrations and weapons; to determine the enemy defensive fire system and the types and locations of fortifications and obstacles; to locate tactical reserves, boundaries between units, and secondary troop dispositions; to capture prisoners and documents; and to seize and hold important objectives which permit surveillance of the defensive position until the main force attack takes place. The subunit which conducts a reconnaissance in force for a division is normally a reinforced battalion and for regiment, a reinforced company. Reconnaissance in force is conducted to convince the enemy that an all-out attack is under way. The attack is made on a comparatively wide frontage and is accompanied by feints and demonstrations by subunits in contact in other sectors.

# IV. Counducting Reconnaissance Operations

*Ref. FM 100-2-1 The Soviet Army: Operations and Tactics, chap 11.*

Reconnaissance within RTA forces does not vary significantly in concept or doctrine from that of western militaries. Reconnaissance teams have the expressed goal of providing situational awareness for the commanders they serve. They achieve this goal using a variety of vehicle platforms and unit TTP.

# A. Reconnaissance Principles (U.S. Military Doctrine Perspective)

Reconnaissance teams are well trained in the "how to" of reconnaissance tactics. Less understood are management requirements for ISR assets. Seven principles guide effective reconnaissance:

## 1. Conduct Continuous Reconnaissance

Effective reconnaissance is an on-going responsibility before, during, and after the conduct of operations. Commanders must know what the enemy is doing in each phase of the operation, to include afterwards. It's important for the commander to understand how the enemy responds.

## 2. Do Not Hold Reconnaissance in Reserve

Reconnaissance assets must be rested and maintained. This requirement of course means that ISR assets are not dispatched 100 percent of the time, around the clock. However, commanders must not hold a refreshed and serviced ISR asset in reserve. This practice gains nothing for the commander in terms of situational awareness.

## 3. Orient Reconnaissance on an Objective

The objective must be feasible for the type of ISR assigned. Yet most critically ISR assets must be assigned a specific objective. Do not make the mistake of "casting a wide net" hoping to discover something of importance. Focus the reconnaissance effort on specific objectives with appropriate ISR assets assigned according to their capabilities.

## 4. Report Information in a Timely Manner

All information has an expiration date and time. If the enemy is aware that our ISR asset has compromised them, they will work to change or mitigate that information. Do not hold or husband information. Pass it up to higher command quickly while it still has meaningful relevance to ongoing operations.

## 5. Retain Maneuver

ISR assets that become decisively engaged in combat lose maneuver. Maneuver is critical to reconnaissance in order that the ISR asset may develop the commander's situational awareness quickly.

## 6. Gain and Maintain Contact

Find the enemy and observe them! Do not make the mistake of assuming that all "contact" equates to armed engagement. Observing the enemy force is a form or contact, too. If the enemy moves, maneuver to regain contact immediately.

## 7. Develop the Situation

At the very minimum report the enemy unit size, activity, and location or direction of movement. The more information reported on the enemy disposition the better. Enemy obstacles are also a legitimate objective for reconnaissance. At a minimum report the location, type and extent of the obstacle, and whether or not it is covered by enemy fire. Finally, if there is nothing to report, report that, too. This is particularly true if the enemy or civilian populations are not where they are anticipated. An absence of enemy or civilian populations can be just as critical to the commander's situational awareness and decision-making as their presence.

# B. Special Considerations for Reconnaissance Operations

Every military commander must determine how quickly he needs to gain situational awareness, and measure that desire against the potential for opportunity loss. This is certainly true of RTA commanders as well.

At the heart of the question is the ability of the reconnaissance team to gain and maintain elusiveness, either through speed or stealth.

RTA reconnaissance forces are almost invariably mounted. Or at least they have that option. Reconnaissance vehicles move quickly toward a Named Area of Interest (NAI) – a suspected enemy force, obstacle, or natural chokepoint. Because the vehicle moves quickly, so too does information regarding that NAI. The commander gains situational awareness quickly.

Furthermore, while some tacticians are quick to overstate the vulnerability of an armored reconnaissance vehicle, it should be pointed out that such reconnaissance vehicles bring two assets to bear that no foot patrol could ever dream of. First, vehicles bring heavy firepower in the form of machinegun, automatic grenade launchers, and/or cannon. Second, they bring highly mobile protective armor that presents a form of elusiveness.

It is incredibly difficult to disable a vehicle that moves quickly! This is true regardless of whether or not the enemy is aware of such vehicle. Think in terms of jet aircraft. Yes, the ground troops are aware of the noisy aircraft flying above, but there is little a rifleman or even tank can do about the jet. Shooting at this aircraft is all but hopeless without the most sophisticated weapons and troops properly trained in the use of said weapon.

Albeit to a lesser extent, the same is true for ground troops facing fast moving armored vehicles conducting reconnaissance. The vehicle can find adequate cover quickly, or simply move out of range of the enemy guns with relative ease and speed.

It is all the more difficult to disable an enemy vehicle that can also suppress the opponent with well-placed heavy firepower. This makes getting an accurate kill shot all the more difficult, again adding to the element of elusiveness.

That is the strength of mounted reconnaissance. However, the trade-off is that the enemy is very much aware that they've just been compromised by an opponent's reconnaissance. They'll quickly change or alter their position to mitigate the danger.

In this way, mounted reconnaissance is quick to develop the situational awareness for their commander, but the information has a very short expiration time. The commander must act immediately, or lose the opportunity to gain the upper hand.

The spectrum opposite of that is reconnaissance by stealth. Stealthy reconnaissance might employ small thin-skinned vehicles, but rarely. More commonly stealthy reconnaissance involves slow moving foot patrols to achieve elusiveness.

Dismounted foot patrol reconnaissance does not move fast. It does not have firepower to suppress an enemy force. Indeed, if a foot patrol is detected and caught by a large enemy force, it is almost certainly doomed to catastrophic failure.

The other side of that coin is that slow moving foot patrols often observe the enemy without the enemy being aware of their presence. Stealthy reconnaissance can stay on objective longer, giving greater detail of the enemy disposition. And more commonly than not, stealthy reconnaissance often escapes undetected, so their information has a longer expiration date – the enemy unaware that they've been compromised makes no radical changes to their routine or position.

Stealthy reconnaissance often requires days to achieve its objectives, whereas the speed of mounted reconnaissance may require just hours or minutes to achieve its objectives. Careful deliberation must be given to time allotments of on-going operations, as well as to the likely success of each type of reconnaissance. There is no single best solution.

*Dismounted reconnaissance is stealthy but slow. It is elusiveness and often the enemy is completely unaware of its presence. Yet time considerations and risk must be balanced when selecting the method of reconnaissance. (Courtesy of Hae-jung Larsen and OP EASTWIND.)*

Reconnaissance units are elite amongst RTA forces. Such units have rich histories and their troops tend to have high morale because of the unit's past performance and strict training regimen. In terms of discipline and proficiency, reconnaissance troops are a higher quality than the typical conscript troop within RTA forces.

To be certain, most reconnaissance units have remarkable success in one military campaign or another. In general, RTA reconnaissance units have been instrumental in battlefield success when used within the boundaries of their own national borders during conflicts involving civil war or when repelling an invading foreign military.

RTA reconnaissance forces have been less successful when employed as part of an RTA force projected beyond their own national boundaries. True, RTA reconnaissance forces have enjoyed some success in foreign wars. They played key roles in Soviet invasions of Hungary in 1956 and again in Czechoslovakia in 1968 to quell uprisings. Both of these invasions represent successful Soviet projections of military power.

Such success noted, RTA reconnaissance units have a spotty history when projected outside their own national borders. Yet failures of reconnaissance forces often have less to do with their training and doctrine – and far more to do with circumstances beyond the control of reconnaissance subunit commanders.

Perhaps the most significant obstacle to success for reconnaissance units has been a failure of senior RTA commanders to understand the role and function of assigned reconnaissance subunits. Instead of collecting intelligence for the regiment, battalion or company commander, RTA forces tend to place an over-reliance upon air reconnaissance assets instead. Reconnaissance subunits are frequently tasked to frontline offensive actions or held in reserve for counterattack.

Holding reconnaissance assets in reserve breaks a cardinal rule for reconnaissance. Furthermore, sending specialized forces into direct action also serves to rapidly dwindle through battlefield attrition the number of reconnaissance troops available – troops who cannot be replaced quickly enough due to the specialized nature of their training.

Therein lies the second most significant obstacle for reconnaissance troops. RTA forces commonly (though not always) operate at less than full compliment of forces. It is one thing to discuss the table of organizational allowances for a regiment; it is quite another matter entirely to look at the historic data regarding the number of troops that go to war with an RTA regiment. In Afghanistan and Chechnya for example, Soviet/Russian regiments were commonly undermanned at 70 percent. In extreme cases regiments were fielded with just 50 percent of their allotted personnel.

Spread so thin within the battlespace, all reconnaissance assets become invaluable – critical even. Yet RTA history shows that just when commanders most desperately need to field their reconnaissance subunits, they often instead hold them in reserve, or task them to direct action against enemy forces; favoring the highly trained reconnaissance subunits over the conscript frontline troops for direct action.

Once engaged in combat, reconnaissance units lose the principle of maneuver that is so fundamental to their work as intelligence gatherers. Additionally, casualties inflicted upon their undersized units cannot be immediately replaced with qualified (e.g. trained) troops. Instead they are replaced with unqualified conscript troops, and the spiral down to inefficiency begins.

Yet RTA reconnaissance forces have enjoyed almost unparalleled battlefield success when capable regiment, battalion, or company commanders grasp the role and function of ISR assets and competently manage their assigned reconnaissance subunits.

# (Tactical Enabling Tasks)
# II. River Crossings

*Ref: FM 100-2-2 The Soviet Army: Special Warfare and Rear Area Support (Jul '84), chap 6.*

Soviet military theorists place great emphasis on high advance rates by armor-heavy columns in the offense. The Soviets stress that this high advance rate would be important in the European theater with its "relatively small" operational depth. Such an offensive would be impossible without overcoming Europe's many north-south water obstacles. A 1965 Soviet study revealed that in the European theater, forces would encounter water obstacles up to 100 meters wide every 35 to 60 kilometers, between 100 and 300 meters wide every 100 to 150 kilometers, and greater than 300 meters wide, every 250 to 300 kilometers.

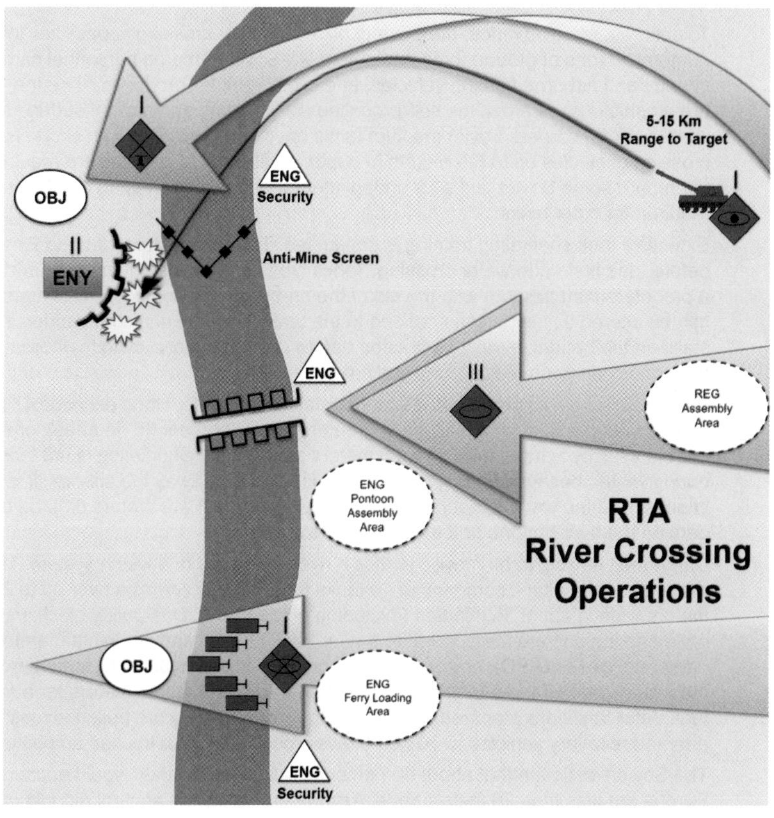


*RTA engineer support plays a critical role in river crossing operations that are necessary to maintain the momentum of surprise, speed and violence of action. Heliborne units attack enemy strong points, and amphibious vehicles ferry vehicles across the river. Engineer units establish pontoon bridges, and in specific cases may create cut-away sections of the riverbank to allow submersion tank crossings. Air superiority must be achieved at the local point of river crossing.*

In response to these challenges, Soviet planners have devoted tremendous resources to improving the river crossing capabilities of their combat equipment. They have provided their ground forces with large stocks of specialized bridging and assault crossing equipment. River crossing figures prominently in most Soviet exercises.

### Keys to Successful River Crossings

- Early planning and thorough organization
- Destruction of the enemy in the area of the water obstacles
- Speed and surprise
- Broad front crossings
- Swift development of the attack on the far bank
- Continuation of the attack throughout the crossing
- Skillful and rapid engineer employment
- Air defense

# I. Equipment and Organization

To ensure a rapid advance, the Soviets have built river crossing capabilities into numerous types of ground force equipment. All Soviet armored personnel carriers, infantry and airborne fighting vehicles, and scout vehicles produced since the 1960s are amphibious, as are some self-propelled (SP) artillery and tactical surface-to-air missile (SAM) carriers.Soviet medium tanks have been provided with snorkels for crossing obstacles up to 5.5 meters in depth. As little as 15 minutes are required to prepare some Soviet tanks for underwater fording, although up to a half hour is required for older tanks.

Extensive tank snorkeling training is conducted. Tank crews train for up to 2 months before their first underwater crossing. Tanks cross underwater in first gear and follow a predetermined azimuth with the aid of the on-board gyrocompass. This direction can be altered by instructions radioed to the tanks from the unit commander. If a tank stalls on the bottom, it must be flooded before crew members using their breathing apparatus can open the hatches and escape.

A snorkeling tank cannot cross a water obstacle if the entry slope exceeds 47 percent (25 degrees), if the exit slope is greater than 27 percent (I5 degrees), or if the current velocity is more than about 3 meters per second. Snorkeling is not feasible during winter, because drifting or unbroken ice could rip away the snorkel. It is also impossible if the water is deeper than 5.5 meters, if there are craters or large boulders on the river bottom, or if the bottom is too soft.

Unmanned tanks can be moved across a river by means of a winch system. This system permits a tank company of 10 tanks to be moved across a river up to 200 meters wide in about 35 minutes (excluding preparation). One pulley block and an anchoring unit are transported to the far bank in a tracked amphibian, armored personnel carrier (APC), or power boat. It must be installed 30 to 45 meters from the water's edge if three tanks cross simultaneously or 10 to 15 meters for a single tank. After tanks are prepared for underwater crossing, they are pulled across by two armored recovery vehicles whiletheir crews cross in APCs or tracked amphibians.

The Soviets estimate that about 60 percent of all obstacles they would encounter in Europe are less than 20 meters wide. Accordingly, there are several models of both tank- and truck-launched gap bridges for rapidly crossing ravines, partially blown bridges, antitank ditches, road craters, and similar obstacles. Gap bridging is used frequently in combination with ponton bridges to provide shore-connecting spans or to extend the bridge to sufficient length.

Each Soviet motorized rifle and tank regiment has one tank-launched bridge (MTU) per tank battalion; i.e., one MTU per motorized rifle regiment and three per tank regiment. Mounted on a T-54/55 tank chassis, the MTU assault bridge is 12.3 meters long. The folded ramp sections of the new MTU-20 (which has become the Soviet standard) extend the bridges length 20 meters. Both spans have a 50-ton carrying capacity and can be launched in 3 to 5 minutes without crew exposure.

Some Soviet regiments may have received a Czech-designed scissors bridge (MT-55) with an electro-hydraulic control system that permits bridge emplace-ment in 1.5 minutes. The MT-55 span is 17 meters long and can support loads up to 50 tons. The launcher has a gap-measuring device and infrared equipment for bridge laying at night.

Each motorized rifle and tank regiment also has a set of four truck-launched scissors spans (TMM). The TMM set, with its four 10.5-meter spans, can erect 42 meters of class 60 (capable of supporting 60 tons) bridging in 20 to 40 mintues.

The engineer battalion organic to each Soviet tank and motorized rifle division provides the division commander with flexible river-crossing support. Equipment organic to the battalion includes PMP ponton bridging (frequently used to make ferries), power boats, GSP self-propelled ferries, tracked amphibious transporters, tank-and truck-launched gap bridging, and limited stocks of fixed wooden bridges.

The assault crossing company of a Soviet division's engineer battalion has GSP tracked ferries and K-61 or PTS tracked amphibians. PKP amphibious trailers may be assigned to units equipped with PTS. Tracked amphibians are used primarily to transport artillery, air defense, or logistical elements across water barriers. (The Soviet 122-mm SP howitzer is amphibious.)

The Soviet PMP ribbon bridge is revolutionary both in its simplicity and rapid emplacement time. Its accordion-like pontons are launched when the trucks on which they are transported are braked at the water's edge. They are opened automatically by a torsion bar mechanism, rotated manually 90 degrees, and quickly joined to form a continuous strip of floating roadway. Soviet motorized rifle and tank divisions have a half set of 16 PMP and two end (ramp) sections in their engineer battalion.

Army and front have river crossing capabilities in their organic engineer regiments or brigade. Ponton brigade regiments and assault crossing battalions also provide river crossing support.

Assault crossing battalions that provide amphibious transport and ferry support to army or front elements can be allocated to divisions to speed up crossing operations. There is one battalion in each army, with up to three in a front If equipped with the PTS and PKP trailer, the battalion's two tracked amphibious companies are able to transport two towed artillery battalions simultaneously. Each GSP ferry can transport one Soviet medium tank.

To provide the logistic support necessary for planned rapid offensives, the Soviets have expended considerable resources to field a variety of line of communications (LOC) bridging. LOC bridges are essential for the orderly introduction of divisions and combat forces of successive echelons, as well as uninterrupted resupply of combat units. They are emplaced by troops of the Military Transportation Service. In anticipation of wartime interdiction of existing bridges, the Soviets and their allies have stock-piled obsolescent bridging and prefabricated bridge sections near strategic crossings.

# II. Tactical River Crossings

There are two basic types of Soviet tactical river crossings, the assault crossing from the march and the prepared river crossing. The Soviets prefer the crossing from the march, which is often the expected method. Normally, the Soviets only conduct the prepared crossing out of necessity within direct enemy contact.

# A. Assault Crossing from the March

*Ref: FM 100-2-2 The Soviet Army: Special Warfare and Rear Area Support (Jul '84), pp. 6-3 to 6-7.*

An assault crossing from the march is conducted with forces moving toward the river in dispersed, normally march, formation, across a wide frontage, at top speed. Forward detachments or airborne or heliborne forces may seize favorable crossing sites in advance. All measures are taken to insure that crossing is conducted as swiftly as possible and that the offen-sive is continued on the opposite shore.

A decision to conduct a crossing from the march is made as early as possible to allow maximum time for appropriate organization of forces and crossing equipment, and for reconnaissance of crossing sites.

The Soviets prefer crossing sites with gently sloping banks, fords, and a bend towards the attackers. Soviet commanders use maps, aerial photographs, engineer and combat patrols, radar, signal, and human intelligence to determine the following:

- River width, depth, and current
- Entry and exit gradients
- Composition of river bottom
- Bank composition and height
- Obstacles on banks
- Approach and exit routes
- Critical terrain features overlooking both banks
- Possible fording, ferrying, bridging, and snorkeling sites
- Information on enemy defenses

The number of reconnaissance patrols depends on the width of the river and the number of required crossing sites; patrols can vary from squad to platoon size. Reconnaissance patrols operate up to 50 kilometers forward of a division's main body.

Engineer reconnaissance units are equipped with tracked amphibians, scout cars, or APCs. They often mount a profilograph (a device used to determine width and depth of rivers) or the newer echo depth finder. Although such equipment significantly reduces exposure and reconnaissance time, it appears that most Soviet engineers use less sophisticated gear-a variety of bottom probes, range finders, and hydro-metric propellers or simply floats of some type and a stopwatch for measuring velocity. A sapper platoon assigned a reconnaissance mission would also typically have six mine detectors, grapnels with cables, radiation detectors, and light diving equipment.

Armored personnel carriers, preferably BMPs, make a rapid amphibious crossing to seize a bridgehead on the far shore. Their crossing normally is covered by smoke and supported from the rear shore by all available fires. Heliborne or, less probably, airborne forces, may be used to seize and hold a bridgehead on the far shore. Once the bridgehead is established, tanks cross by ferry, by fording, or by snorkeling. Artillery and other combat support equipment crosses on tracked amphihians. Later, tactical bridging is emplaced for follow-on forces.

The Soviets consider units engaged in a river crossing to be especially vulnerable to enemy aviation. They emphasize the need for tactical air defense at river crossing sites before a crossing is attempted. In some tactical situations they may choose to move part of their air defense assets across first to maximize the range of these weapons in protecting subsequent units making the crossing. Placement and movement sequence of air defense assets will vary as the Soviet commander assesses each new tactical situation.

Subunits acting as forward detachments advance as quickly as possible to the river, by-passing enemy forces whenever possible, to seize near-shore crossing sites or to swim the river to seize a far-shore bridgehead. A forward detachment differs from an advance guard, which has the responsibility of clearing a route for advancement of its main force. Forward detachments attempt to slip through enemy lines to force and hold crossing sites. Advance guards follow and fight through any enemy encountered to make way for the main forces.

Based on reconnaissance, the Soviet commander organizes his unit to insure the most expedient crossing and continuation of the offense. The Soviets stress that tactical air support is more critical during river crossing operations than during other types of ground operations.

A motorized rifle battalion acting as a forward detachment usually is reinforced with a tank company, an artillery battalion, ferry and tracked amphibians, and air defense, anti-tank, and chemical defense subunits ranging from squad to company size. When acting as a forward detachment a motorized rifle battalion would be 2 or 3 hours in front of the main body.

Advance guards destroy enemy forces to insure unhindered advance by the main force. As they approach the water barrier, advance guards exploit the success of forward detachments or air landed elements, forcing the obstacle from the march and developing the attack into the depth of enemy defenses when possible.

Depending on the tactical situation, a division crosses a major waterbarrier with one, two, or three regiments in the first echelon in a zone 20 to 30 kilometers wide. A division's combat elements can cross a 200-meter-aide river in approximately 5 or 6 hours, using equipment organic to the division. If reconnaissance and site preparation time is included, a division's total crossing time may approximate 9 hours. A division might receive reinforcement from army or front engineer units.

The Soviets believe river crossings can be managed successfully with equipment presently organic to their maneuver units. However, some Soviet theorists express concern that present levels may prove inadequate to conduct successive crossings of two or more major water obstacles. One way to solve this problem is to leapfrog divisions. Army-and front-level engineer units have augmentation potential sufficient to establish a significant number of ponton bridges.

Combat bridging is further supplemented by LOC sectional bridging. According to Soviet estimates, LOC bridging can be erected by road construction troops in as little as 8 hours after the initial assault crossing. It is left in place for subsequent use by front-level units.

# B. Prepared River Crossings

*Ref: FM 100-2-2 The Soviet Army: Special Warfare and Rear Area Support (Jul '84), p. 6-8.*

Apparently because they expect to cross most rivers from the march at lightly defended or unoccupied sites, the Soviets devote considerably less attention to the enemy-opposed prepared crossing. Such a crossing requires detailed planning and preparation, centralized control, and massive suppression of enemy fires. They conduct a prepared crossing from a position in contact. The prepared crossing is used as a last resort, when an assault crossing from the march fails or is not possible.

A prepared crossing requires intensive reconnaissance. By day, troops observe enemy defensive positions and activity. Under cover of darkness engineer and reconnaissance patrols measure the river, inspect obstacles, and pinpoint crossing areas.

During preparation, troops make maximum use of existing fortification as well as cover and concealment of personnel and equipment. They prepare roads and cross-country routes for movement to crossing sites, as are assembly areas and artillery positions. Such work is performed at night under the guise of improving the defense.

Twice as many troops as had occupied defensive positions normally launched the initial assault in a prepared river crossing. It generally takes place either at night or under a smoke screen. An artillery preparation is fired against enemy strongpoints. Airborne or heliborne forces may be used to block enemy reinforcements. Some artillery is employed in the direct fire role to neutralize enemy weapons remaining in the enemy defensive sector.

The prepared crossing is conducted similarly to the assault crossing. Numerous APC's swim across on a broad frontage supported by all available direct and indirect fires. Tanks and other heavy weapons and equipment follow. Bridging is emplaced only when bridge sites are secure from enemy observation and direct fire.

Chap 5

# (Tactical Enabling Tasks) III. Troop Movement

*Ref: FM 100-2-2 The Soviet Army: Special Warfare and Rear Area Support (Jul '84), pp. 13-13 to 13-14.*

## I. Troop Movement

Troop movement is the movement of troops from one place to another by any available means. The ability of a commander to posture friendly forces for a decisive or shaping operation depends on the commander's ability to move that force. The essence of battlefield agility is the capability to conduct rapid and orderly movement to concentrate combat power at decisive points and times. Successful movement places troops and equipment at their destination at the proper time, ready for combat. The three types of troop movement (as defined in U.S. military doctrine) are administrative movement, tactical road march, and approach march.

## II. Convoy Operations

RTA doctrine does not radically or even significantly differ in tactical concept from western militaries regarding the tasks inherent to convoy operations. And to be certain, RTA forces routinely conduct such operations.

### A. Coordination of Convoy Operations

Upon receipt of the convoy security mission, the RTA commander must develop a plan. This will include identification of a suitable route and careful coordination with the supporting units – especially when air assets are assigned in support of the convoy.

Coordination for the passage/reentry of lines is made with the host unit and the receiving unit. Special equipment and weapons of the gun trucks are obtained, and a plan for the exact order of march appropriate to the ratio of gun trucks to cargo trucks is created.

Upon issuing the convoy order, back-brief and rehearsals are conducted. At a minimum, actions on enemy contact are rehearsed – react to ambush, react to IED/mines, vehicle recovery, vehicle cross load, plus medical aid and litter drills. All of these tasks must be capably conducted while under fire and in direct contact with enemy forces.

Finally a plan is established and coordinated for Intelligence, Surveillance and Reconnaissance (ISR) assets. Reconnaissance is an ongoing task for convoy operations on a basis of before, during, and after the mission.

*Convoy security requires a specific number of "gun trucks" with capable armament and armor to fight off enemy ambushes. The order of march becomes a critical consideration, with a specific emphasis on forward and rear security vehicles. (Courtesy of Hae-jung Larsen and OP EASTWIND.)*

## B. Special Considerations for Convoy Operations

The leaders location within the convoy is critical. The RTA commander must position himself to best control the convoy and communicate with the security gun trucks. RTA commanders tend to default to the front of the column, though this is ill advised even within their own doctrine. Rather than the lead or trail vehicle, the commander is better placed toward the center of the convoy column in an ambiguous vehicle (e.g. avoid the vehicle with the most antennas).

Medical teams/trucks and vehicle maintenance/recovery trucks must also be located carefully within the order of march. Typically these vehicles are located toward the rear of the convoy column and brought forward as needed.

Forward reconnaissance vehicles must clear and/or secure all chokepoints along the convoy route. For sake of security and maneuver, forward reconnaissance teams maintain an appropriate distance interval between themselves and the main convoy column. Lastly but most critically, the convoy security commander and subunit teams must gain and maintain situational awareness at all times.

Chap 5

# (Tactical Enabling Tasks)
# IV. Relief in Place

*Ref: FM 100-2-1 The Soviet Army: Operations and Tactics, p. 6-11, and Frasche, The Soviet Motorized Rifle Battalion, chap. 7, fig. 67.*

As defined by U.S. military doctrine, a relief in place is an operation in which, by the direction of higher authority, all or part of a unit is replaced in an area by the incoming unit. A commander conducts a relief in place as part of a larger operation, primarily to maintain the combat effectiveness of committed units. A relief in place may also be conducted--

- To reorganize, reconstitute, or re-equip a unit that has sustained heavy losses
- To rest units that have conducted sustained operations
- To establish the security force or the detachment left in contact (DLIC) during a withdrawal operation
- To allow the relieved unit to conduct another operation

RTA forces have employed Relief in Place/Transfer of Authority (RIP/TOA) in every major conflict. Yet, as noted earlier, for smaller conflicts of short duration there has been little attention paid to RIP/TOA and the nuanced demands of such coordination is often lost or overlooked.

*From regiment commander to platoon leader, each must thoroughly brief their subunit leaders. Here a platoon commander briefs his squad leaders on how the unit will conduct the RIP/TOA of a sister platoon. (Courtesy of Hae-jung Larsen and OP EASTWIND.)*

That said, RIP/TOA is very much a part of RTA doctrine. The primary focus of this tactic is to relieve the frontline unit without inflicting fratricide casualties, and without tipping off the enemy as to such actions. If the enemy is aware that a RIP/TOA is underway, they very well may attack during this vulnerable transition. Operational security is critical.

## A. Coordination of the Relief in Place

Relief in place is a somewhat similar situation to the passage of lines. Yet in a relief in place, one stationary unit will retire and fall back from a defensive position after another unit has replaced the forward unit on the line.

Again, coordination emphasizes mitigation of the danger of fratricide. This is especially due to the tendency for relief in place to be conducted in secrecy under conditions of darkness or limited visibility. Coordination considerations include Restricted Firing Lines (RFL), Assembly Areas (AA), recognition signals, relief and egress routes, plus maneuver phase lines as well as the Forward Line of Troops (FLOT). Often battlefield deception in terms of noise and light discipline or artillery barrage are incorporated into the plan for the relief in place.

Command personnel from both the forward unit and the relief unit must meet and coordinate the relief in place of subunits. This is true regardless of whether or not an order has been issued for the relief in place from higher command. Ultimately the feasibility of that order/plan and final coordination falls on the shoulders of the forward unit commander and the relieving unit commander.

## B. Special Considerations for the Relief in Place

The forward unit commander has command authority until the relief in place is complete. This is because the forward unit commander knows the lay of the land and is/has been in contact with the enemy. If the enemy attacks during a relief in place, the forward unit commander has authority and the relieving unit falls subordinate to the forward unit commander until such time as the enemy is repulsed and the relief in place is complete.

Sharing intelligence on friendly positions, friendly and enemy obstacles, lay of the terrain, and the enemy situation is absolutely critical to success. The relieving unit must quickly gain situational awareness, and the forward unit possesses such situational awareness already.

### Hasty or Deliberate

A relief is either deliberate or hasty, depending on the amount of planning and preparations. The major differences are the depth and detail of planning and, potentially, the execution time. Detailed planning generally facilitates shorter execution time by determining exactly what the commander believes he needs to do and the resources needed to accomplish the mission. Deliberate planning allows the commander and his staff to identify, develop, and coordinate solutions to most potential problems before they occur and to ensure the availability of resources when and where they are needed.

In a deliberate relief, units exchange plans and liaison personnel, conduct briefings, perform detailed reconnaissance, and publish orders with detailed instructions. In a hasty relief, the commander abbreviates the planning process and controls the execution using oral and fragmentary orders.

# (Tactical Enabling Tasks)
# V. Passage of Lines

*Ref: FM 100-2-1 The Soviet Army: Operations and Tactics, chap 5.*

As defined in U.S. military doctrine, passage of lines is an operation in which a force moves forward or rearward through another force's combat positions with the intention of moving into or out of contact with the enemy. A passage may be designated as a forward or rearward passage of lines (JP 1-02). A commander conducts a passage of lines to continue an attack or conduct a counterattack, retrograde security or main battle forces, and anytime one unit cannot bypass another unit's position. It involves transferring the responsibility for an area of operations between two commanders. That transfer of authority usually occurs when roughly two-thirds of the passing force has moved through the passage point. If not directed by higher authority, the unit commanders determine—by mutual agreement—the time to pass command.

RTA doctrine does not significantly differ from western military doctrine in regards to passage of lines or relief in place. Such lessons were born from the battlefields of the First and Second World Wars and heavily mechanized forces around the world have since implemented effective Tactics, Techniques and Procedures (TTP).

*Refer to The Small Unit Tactics SMARTbook (Leader's Reference Guide to Conducting Tactical Operations) for complete discussion of passage of lines from U.S. military doctrine. Related topics include offensive and defensive operations, tactical mission fundamentals, stability & counterinsurgency operations, tactical enabling operations, special purpose attacks, urban operations & fortifications, and patrols & patrolling.*

A passage of lines occurs under two basic conditions. A forward passage of lines occurs when a unit passes through another unit's positions while moving toward the enemy. A rearward passage of lines occurs when a unit passes through another unit's positions while moving away from the enemy. Reasons for conducting a passage of line include—

- Sustain the tempo of an offensive operation
- Maintain the viability of the defense by transferring responsibility from one unit to another
- Transition from a delay or security operation by one force to a defense
- Free a unit for another mission or task

Passage of lines consists of essentially two tasks, (1) coordinating the time and place of the *departure*, and (2) coordinating the time, place and signals of the *reentry* through the Forward Line of Troops (FLOT).

Where there is notable difference between western forces and RTA on this topic is that RTA forces from many nations simply don't train in such tactics. Their tactical warfighting – though capable – is limited to operations of very short duration and distance. Instead of conducting a passage of lines or relief in place to continue the fight, less developed nations with RTA forces simply push their troops to mission completion or culmination, rather than handing off the fight to an adjacent friendly unit.

## A. Coordination of the Passage of Lines

Passage of lines is a situation in which one friendly unit will pass through another forward unit in order to continue the momentum of operations. The forward unit may be permanently halted in a defensive position, or it may be temporarily halted as ordered, or due to some culminating variable. In either case, the unit to the rear passes through the forward unit.

Coordination emphasizes mitigation of the danger of fratricide. This coordination includes Restricted Firing Lines (RFL), Assembly Areas (AA), recognition signals, passage points and passage lanes, plus maneuver phase lines as well as the Battle Handover Line (BHL).

Most critical is that the command personnel from both the forward unit and the passing unit must meet and coordinate the passage of various subunits. This is true regardless of whether or not an order has been issued for the passage of lines from higher command. Ultimately the feasibility of that order/plan and final coordination falls on the shoulders of the forward unit commander and the passing unit commander.

## B. Special Considerations for the Passage of Lines

The forward unit commander has command authority until the passage is complete. This is because the forward unit commander knows the lay of the land and is/has been in contact with the enemy. If the enemy attacks during a passage of lines, the forward unit commander has authority and the passing unit falls subordinate to the forward unit commander until such time as the enemy is repulsed and the passage of lines is complete.

Sharing intelligence on friendly positions, friendly and enemy obstacles, lay of the terrain, and the enemy situation is absolutely critical to success. The passing unit must quickly gain situational awareness, and the forward unit possesses such situational awareness already.

Chap 5

# (Tactical Enabling Tasks) VI. Checkpoints

*Ref: FM 100-2-1 The Soviet Army: Operations and Tactics, chap 5.*

## I. Checkpoints/Roadblocks

Roadblocks and checkpoints (CPs) are a means of controlling movement on roads, tracks, and footpaths. A roadblock is used to block or close a route to vehicle or pedestrian traffic. Checkpoints may have a more limited and specific purpose, usually apparent from their title, as vehicle CP, personnel CP etc. For simplicity, they are all referred to as roadblocks. Roadblocks are set up for one or more of the following reasons:

- Maintain a broad check on road movement to increase security and the assurance of the local population
- Frustrate the movement of arms or explosives
- Assist in the enforcement of movement control of people and material
- Gather information and related data on suspected persons, vehicles, and movement

*Even with mitigating factors in force, troops expose themselves to considerable risk when conducting checkpoint operations. Ultimately, troops must close with vehicle and foot traffic to interview personnel and enforce laws and regulations. Troops become alert to the specifics of body language and contextual awareness. (Courtesy of Hae-jung Larsen and OP EASTWIND.)*

Checkpoint layout, construction, and operating should reflect METT-TC factors, including the amount of time available for emplacing it.

# A. Coordination of Checkpoint Operations

Checkpoint operations are a form of security achieved through civilian traffic control plus law, order, and regulation enforcement. There are essentially two types of checkpoints – vehicle and pedestrian checkpoints.

Critical coordination of checkpoints includes local security via sentry positions and Quick Reaction Force (QRF) that are equipped with both lethal and non-lethal weapon in overwatch. Additionally the checkpoint requires a communication network; protective barriers; entry point and initial search zone prior to the entry; approach lanes; search and holding areas; and posted signs.

*The guard tower offers situational awareness not just of the approach and search areas of the checkpoint, but also serves to coordinate the various search teams and Quick Reaction Force (QRF). The guard post is the communication center. (Courtesy of OP EASTWIND.)*

*Checkpoints must be resourced with enough combat power to fend off attack. For vehicle checkpoints that means anti-armor weapons, but non-lethal weapons must also be considered. This is especially true for pedestrian traffic checkpoints. (Courtesy of OP EASTWIND.)*

Special equipment necessary for checkpoints includes communication systems, wire barriers and blast barriers, adequate weaponry to stop vehicle and pedestrian assault, appropriate lighting systems, and signs for both warnings and specific instructions.

Signs should be in both the native language and RTA force language. Signs should denote the speed limit of approach, initial vehicle search area, vehicle inspection and dismount point, plus male and female search areas. All specific instructions should also be covered via signs.

*Because checkpoints involve a temporary position and relatively small numbers of troops, they are often preferred targets for guerilla and insurgent forces. Each checkpoint position must be robust – protective walls, reliable communication, and adequate weaponry. (Courtesy of OP EASTWIND.)*

*A protective barrier is essential for troops in security overwatch of the checkpoint. This force protection consideration shields troops from suicide bombers in vehicle or foot traffic. It also serves to protect from small arms fire. (Courtesy of OP EASTWIND.)*



## B. Special Considerations for Checkpoint Operations

Checkpoints are vulnerable to enemy attack. Checkpoints require enough troops as a function of force protection. The QRF is positioned and concealed away from the checkpoint to prevent escapes and respond to enemy attacks, and various overwatch positions are properly armed with weapons appropriate to either pedestrian or vehicle traffic – or both.

Checkpoint personnel search pedestrians, vehicles, drivers, and cargo. Interpreters and local law enforcement are present if at all feasible. When available, female RTA troops are included at checkpoints to search and question women and children. A checkpoint offers a unique opportunity for RTA forces to interface with the local populace and get a sense of their health and economic situation, socio-political grievances, and immediate concerns regarding ongoing RTA operations.

A checkpoint rest plan must designate and position resting troops to safely rest and quickly respond to any attack. The rest position obviously doubles as a reserve force, but should not be tasked to QRF. The QRF must be alert and able to deploy at a moments notice. Furthermore, whereas the rest position must be carefully guarded internally, the QRF may be positioned just outside of the checkpoint, secure and carefully hidden from sight.

The site selection of a checkpoint should prevent bypass or avoidance; an area where the terrain restricts the traffic is desirable. However, the area should not be so restrictive as to present a safety hazard for civilian traffic, or prevent the QRF from maneuver.

# B. Types of Checkpoints/Roadblocks

All RTA forces conduct checkpoint operations to enforce laws and regulations, and to control foot and vehicle traffic where necessary. RTA doctrine does not significantly depart from Western doctrine in checkpoint operations. Where there are notable differences such issues stem from cultural norms and discipline, or lack thereof, amongst various RTA forces. This is particularly true for checkpoint operations in such cases when command discipline breaks down. Graft becomes rampant and checkpoints may degenerate into venues for petty criminal extortion of the civilian traffic.

Checkpoint operations become critical in low intensity conflicts. Checkpoints are a viable means to separate insurgent antagonists from the populations they endeavor to control. When employed correctly, checkpoints also go a long way in preventing insurgents and terrorists groups from moving among the population disguised as non-combatants. Finally, for cordon and search operations within population centers, checkpoints may function as the cordon.

## Deliberate

Permanent or semi-permanent checkpoints/roadblocks placed on a main road, perhaps near a border, on the outskirts of a city, or on the edge of a controlled area. View deliberate roadblocks as a deterrent to movement. They are unlikely to be productive sources of information/contraband material once their positions and activities are observed.

## Hasty

Make checkpoints/roadblocks easy to set up and dismantle. Ground troops, already on patrol, or a rapid reaction force deployed by helicopter can deploy the roadblock. Two vehicles placed diagonally across and road with a search area in between is a simple roadblock. In a rural area, helicopters can place hasty roadblocks, in which case, forces can improve obstacles, such as narrow bridges or level crossing gates, with a single coil of barbed wire.

## Triggered

This is a variation of the hasty checkpoints/roadblocks, usually used under circumstances where it is often easy for anyone to take avoiding action on sighting a block in operation. This roadblock is particularly effective in defeating the use of convoys and 'scout cars' by hostile groups. Allowing a suspected 'scout car' to pass through the roadblock triggers the roadblock to catch the target vehicle. Units operating the roadblock must occupy covered and concealed positions and wait for selected targets. Additionally, they can stop and search personnel out of sight of anyone approaching on the road. As with hasty roadblocks, a covert protection force and a helicopter borne reaction force are required. Foot and vehicle insertion, from a carefully sited patrol base, are most common.

## Reactionary

This is a version of the hasty checkpoints/roadblock, but is used in reaction to an incident or attack in another area. Ground or helicopter based, this roadblock is useful in interdicting hostile activity following the occurrence.

*Refer to The Stability, Peace and Counterinsurgency SMARTbook (Nontraditional approaches in a Dynamic Security Environment) for further discussion of checkpoints and roadblocks in chap 5 (small unit "competencies, skills & tasks"). Related topics include peace and counterinsurgency operations; civil-military operations; engagement, security cooperation, and security force assistance, multinational operations and IGO/NGO coordination.*

Chap 6

# Small Unit Drills

*Ref: The Small Unit Tactics SMARTbook, 2nd Rev. Ed., The Lightning Press, pp. 1-1 to 1-6.*

## I. The Tactical Level of War (U.S. Doctrine)

Through tactics, commanders use combat power to accomplish missions. The tactical-level commander employs combat power to accomplish assigned missions.

The tactical level of war is the level of war at which battles and engagements are planned and executed to achieve military objectives assigned to tactical units or task forces (JP 3-0). Activities at this level focus on the ordered arrangement and maneuver of combat elements in relation to each other and to the enemy to achieve combat objectives. It is important to understand tactics within the context of the levels of war. The strategic and operational levels provide the context for tactical operations. Without this context, tactical operations are reduced to a series of disconnected and unfocused actions.

Tactical operations always require judgment and adaptation to the unique circumstances of a specific situation. Techniques and procedures are established patterns that can be applied repeatedly with little or no judgment in a variety of circumstances. Tactics, techniques, and procedures (TTP) provide commanders and staffs with a set of tools to use in developing the solution to a tactical problem.

### Individuals, Crews, and Small Units

Individuals, crews, and small units act at the tactical level. At times, their actions may produce strategic or operational effects. However, this does not mean these elements are acting at the strategic or operational level. Actions are not strategic unless they

*Refer to The Small Unit Tactics SMARTbook (Leader's Reference Guide to Conducting Tactical Operations) for complete discussion from U.S. military doctrine of offensive and defensive operations, tactical mission fundamentals, stability & counterinsurgency operations, tactical enabling operations, special purpose attacks, urban operations & fortifications, and patrols & patrolling.*

contribute directly to achieving the strategic end state. Similarly, actions are considered operational only if they are directly related to operational movement or the sequencing of battles and engagements. The level at which an action occurs is determined by the perspective of the echelon in terms of planning, preparation, and execution.

### Battles, Engagements, and Small-Unit Actions

Tactics is the employment and ordered arrangement of forces in relation to each other. Through tactics, commanders use combat power to accomplish missions. The tactical-level commander uses combat power in battles, engagements, and small-unit actions. A battle consists of a set of related engagements that lasts longer and involves larger forces than an engagement. Battles can affect the course of a campaign or major operation. An engagement is a tactical conflict, usually between opposing, lower echelons maneuver forces (JP 1-02). Engagements are typically conducted at brigade level and below. They are usually short, executed in terms of minutes, hours, or days.

# II. The Science and Art of Tactics

The tactician must understand and master the science and the art of tactics, two distinctly different yet inseparable concepts.

## A. The Science

The science of tactics encompasses the understanding of those military aspects of tactics—capabilities, techniques, and procedures—that can be measured and codified. The science of tactics includes the physical capabilities of friendly and enemy organizations and systems, such as determining how long it takes a division to move a certain distance. It also includes techniques and procedures used to accomplish specific tasks, such as the tactical terms and control graphics that comprise the language of tactics. While not easy, the science of tactics is fairly straightforward. Much of what is contained in this manual is the science of tactics—techniques and procedures for employing the various elements of the combined arms team to achieve greater effects.

Mastery of the science of tactics is necessary for the tactician to understand the physical and procedural constraints under which he must work. These constraints include the effects of terrain, time, space, and weather on friendly and enemy forces. However—because combat is an intensely human activity—the solution to tactical problems cannot be reduced to a formula. This realization necessitates the study of the art of tactics.



## B. The Art

The art of tactics consists of three interrelated aspects: the creative and flexible array of means to accomplish assigned missions, decision making under conditions of uncertainty when faced with an intelligent enemy, and understanding the human dimension—the effects of combat on soldiers. An art, as opposed to a science, requires exercising intuitive faculties that cannot be learned solely by study. The tactician must temper his study and evolve his skill through a variety of relevant, practical experiences. The more experience the tactician gains from practice under a variety of circumstances, the greater his mastery of the art of tactics.

Military professionals invoke the art of tactics to solve tactical problems within his commander's intent by choosing from interrelated options, including—

- Types and forms of operations, forms of maneuver, and tactical mission tasks
- Task organization of available forces, to include allocating scarce resources
- Arrangement and choice of control measures
- Tempo of the operation
- Risks the commander is willing to take

# (Small Unit Drills) I. Movement & Formations

*Ref: FM 100-2-2 The Soviet Army, chap. 2.*

*RTA forces employ elements of speed and guard as redundant forms of security on the march. Here a reconnaissance team uses the diamond formation while moving through wooded terrain. (Courtesy of Hae-jung Larsen and OP EASTWIND.)*

## I. Small Unit Battle Drills

*Ref: Grau, The Bear Went Over the Mountain, pp. 200-201.*

Battle drills can be described as micro tactics, or the building block formations that lend to the larger tactical plan of fire and maneuver. Yet within the battle drill there is no plan to develop or issue. Each battle drill is so thoroughly rehearsed that every troop knows immediately what to do. They have an objective, a focus, without question. The only decision required of the commander is the order of which battle drill to execute.

Red Team Armies (RTA) profoundly relies on battle drill. Such reliance may be rationalized due to the vast language diversity that creates communication barriers within a large number of RTA nations; or it may be due to the relatively low education ratio of a few of the RTA nations.

Whatever the rationale, it is important to understand that decision-making authority is rarely ever delegated down below the RTA commander. Because of this tendency, simple, redundant, and exhaustively rehearsed battle drills serve the commander well under the pressure of battle. They offer uncomplicated and easily understood orders.

Yet the point must also be made that no two RTA units will conceive the same battle drill precisely as the other. Variations, and often significant variations are common in battle drill given different types of terrain, enemy capabilities, and internal limitations.

# II. Movement Techniques & Battle Formations

*Ref: FM 100-2-2 The Soviet Army, chap. 2.*

Unlike their Western counterparts, RTA commanders do not merely choose between the speed of a dense formation or the guard of dispersed formation as means of security while on the march. Instead they employ both formation types redundantly.

On the march RTA forces post a point guard well ahead of their formation, and a rear guard well behind their formation. They do this regardless of unit size.

## A. The Motorized Rifle Company

The general rule of thumb is that the unit on the march, in this case a company, employs subunits two levels down as teams for point and rear guard. That means a company will usually post a squad on point guard and a squad on rear guard.

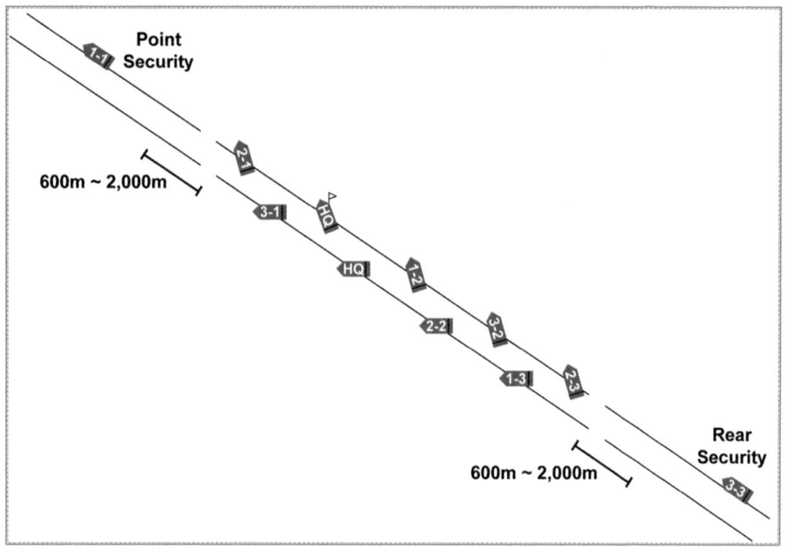


*Ref: FM 100-2-2 The Soviet Army, pp. 2-7 and 2-8.*

### 1. Array the Company

The point and rear guard of an RTA rifle company are deployed as far as two kilometers forward and behind the main body in open terrain and during daylight hours. In urban, mountainous or forested terrain the distance of the point and rear guard may be decreased to 600 meters. And during nighttime operations or periods of low visibility such as snow or sand storms the distance can be as little as just 100 meters forward and to the rear of the main body.

The commander and remainder of the rifle company are centered between the point and rear guards in a fairly dense, close-order march. A dense formation allows the company commander greater control over the main body as compared to a dispersed formation. It allows for greater speed if necessary. And it is more comfortable for the troops, allowing them to arrive at the objective less exhausted than the disciplined demands of a slow, deliberate open-order march.

### 2. Actions on Contact

Mounted - When halted for any reason, vehicles assume a herringbone formation by alternating the primary direction of the vehicle slightly left or right and pulling to the shoulder of the road.

Upon order of the commander, platoons may be directed to assume overwatch positions to the immediate left and right of the column to fend off an enemy attack, to avoid enemy indirect fires, or to pull security for details such as engineer road repair and vehicle maintenance and recovery.

The point and rear guards maintain their positions. They await further order of the commander and may be recalled immediately to counterattack an enemy force.

Dismounted – When halted for any reason, troops move immediately to the side of the road alternating left and right between individual troops. Troops take a knee to lower their profile and await further order.

Upon order of the company commander, platoons may be directed to assume overwatch positions to the most immediately defendable terrain to fend off an enemy attack or to avoid enemy indirect fires.

The point and rear guards maintain their positions. They await further order of the commander and may be recalled immediately to counterattack an enemy force.

## B. The Motorized Rifle Platoon

The RTA rifle platoon employs subunits two levels down as teams for point and rear guard. That means a platoon will usually post a weapon crew or reconnaissance team of three troops on point guard and another on rear guard.

### 1. Array the Platoon

The point and rear guard of the platoon are deployed no farther than the platoon can support with its integral firepower. For dismounted platoons that would be no more than 600 meters, but for mounted platoons it could be as far as two kilometers away from the platoon main body in open terrain and during daylight hours. In urban, mountainous or forested terrain the distance of the platoon guards may be decreased to 100 meters. And during nighttime operations or periods of low visibility such as snow or sand storms the distance can be as little as just 50 meters forward and to the rear of the main body.

The commander and remainder of the rifle platoon are centered between the point and rear guards in a fairly dense, close-order march. A dense formation allows the platoon commander greater control over the main body as compared to a dispersed formation. It allows for greater speed if necessary. And it is more comfortable for the troops, allowing them to arrive at the objective less exhausted than the disciplined demands of a slow, deliberate open-order march.

## 2. Actions on Contact

**Mounted** - When halted for any reason, vehicles assume a herringbone formation by alternating the primary direction of the vehicle slightly left or right and pulling to the shoulder of the road.

Upon order of the platoon commander, squads vehicles may be directed to assume an echelon front, left or right of the column and dismount to fend off an enemy attack, to avoid enemy indirect fires, or to pull security for details such as engineer road repair and vehicle maintenance and recovery. In the case of indirect fires, the troops may remain buttoned up within the armored vehicles, depending on the situation.

ECHELON RIGHT

ECHELON LEFT

*Ref: The herringbone is the default formation for armored column halts. However, echelon right and echelon left drills are employed to react to enemy contact or when used in overwatch. Grau, The Bear Went Over the Mountain, vignette 38 pp. 145-147.*

The point and rear guards maintain their positions. They await further order of the platoon commander and may be recalled immediately to counterattack an enemy force.

**Dismounted** – When halted for any reason, troops move immediately to the side of the road alternating left and right between individual troops. Troops take a knee to lower their profile and await further order.

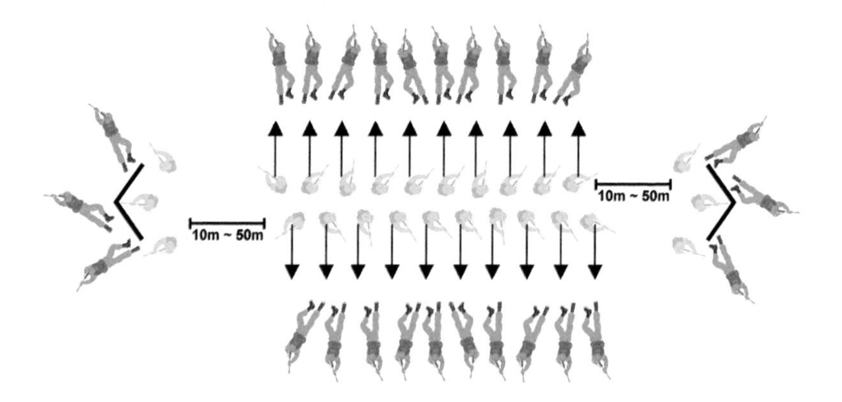


Upon order of the platoon commander, squads may be directed to assume overwatch positions to the most immediately defendable terrain to fend off an enemy attack or to avoid enemy indirect fires.

The point and rear guards maintain their positions. They await further order of the platoon commander and may be recalled immediately to counterattack an enemy force.

## C. The Rifle Squad

A mounted squad does not dismount a front or rear guard, and instead remains as single unit for maneuver. Squads mounted in armored vehicles never operate independently from their platoon. As such, this section discusses dismounted squad drill only.

With only 8 to 10 troops, the dismounted rifle squad cannot deploy both a weapon crew forward and behind its formation. The squad leader is left with two options, either he requests more troops from the platoon for the sake of force protection, or he foregoes the rear guard. In the latter case only a point guard is deployed.

*The point security team assumes a wedge formation, while the rest of the squad walks in column or double column. Rear security also forms a reverse wedge when employed. (Courtesy of Hae-jung Larsen and OP EASTWIND.)*

## 1. Array the Squad

The point guard and rear guard, when used, are deployed no farther than the squad's integral firepower can support. In open terrain and during daylight hours a dismounted squad generally sends the guard a distance no greater than 400 meters. More commonly in urban, mountainous or forested terrain the squad point and rear guards maintain a distance of 30 to 50 meters from the squad main body. And in periods of darkness or limited visibility, the point and rear guards may be as little as 10 meters away.

## 2. Actions on Contact

Squad Halt – When the dismounted squad is halted for any reason, all troops stop and lower their profile by going to knee and facing left or right into their prescribed sectors of fire. When halted longer than three minutes, or upon order, all troops move two paces out from their kneeling position and toward their prescribed sector of fire, and go prone.

Point and rear guard merely hold their current positions and go prone. This creates a cigar-shaped 360-degree security position for long term halts. The cigar-shaped security position is also suitable for assault positions and Objective Rally Points (ORP).

*When halted troops kneel. After three minutes or as ordered, they'll form a 360$^0$ security halt. (Courtesy of Hae-jung Larsen and OP EASTWIND.)*

# (Small Unit Drills)
# II. Dismounted Drills

*Ref: Sharp, Soviet Infantry Tactics of World War II, chap. 3, and Grau, The Bear Went Over the Mountain.*

*While the MRR places enormous emphasis on armored formations, commanders regularly dismount the troops to act in concert with or separate of the bronegruppa. Here, too, RTA forces rely thoroughly on prescriptive battle drill. (Courtesy of Hae-jung Larsen and OP EASTWIND.)*

## I. Immediate Action Drills – Dismounted Squad



Dismounted squads may engage the enemy to the squad's immediate front or either flank. As such there are three battle drills, one for each contingency. Additionally the fourth and fifth battle drills allow the squad to extract itself from contact with the enemy.

RTA unit standard operating procedure (SOP) usually dictates that if the enemy has not engaged the squad and there is no immediate danger of being fired upon, the pointman gives the hand signal to halt the squad upon visual contact of an enemy force. All troops stop and lower their profile by going to knee or going prone, whichever is more suitable. The squad leader is then called forward to assess.

There is no benefit in yelling or conducting immediate fires if the enemy is unaware of the squad's presence. In fact, there can be great benefit if the squad is able to achieve stealth and surprise in their maneuver.

However, the following five battle drills assume the enemy has already fired or is about to fire upon the rifle squad. There is an immediate danger. The urgency of this situation merits loud yelling and even individual initiative such as giving the command to initiate any of the first three battle drills below. The last two battle drills, Break Contact and React to Indirect Fire, are issue only by the most senior leader present.

# A. Contact Front

This battle drill may be ordered by any troop within the squad who sees the enemy preparing to fire on his comrades, though usually the pointman gives the order.

1. The drill is ordered by yelling "Contact Front!"
2. Squad members repeat the command "Contact Front!" and rush forward.
3. Squad members form a frontal arched line and conduct an attack by fire.
4. If a rear guard is present, it goes prone instantly to secure the rear or flank.

*Ref: Sharp, Soviet Infantry Tactics in World War II, p.19. The point guard or squad leader orders "Contact Front!" Every member of the squad repeats the order as they sprint forward to assume an arched line and gain tenacious fire superiority. (Courtesy Courtesy of Hae-jung Larsen and OP EASTWIND)*

Small Unit Drills

# B. Contact Right

This battle drill may be ordered by any troop within the squad who sees the enemy preparing to fire on his comrades, such as if the squad enters the kill zone of an enemy ambush. More commonly the squad leader gives the order.

1. The drill is ordered by yelling "Contact Right!" or "Contact Left!"
2. Squad members repeat the command "Contact Right/Left!" and rush the flank.
3. Squad members form an arched line to the flank and conduct an attack by fire.
4. Point and rear guards go prone instantly to secure the flanks and attack by fire.

*The squad leader, point guard or rear guard orders "Contact Right!" Every member of the squad repeats the order as they sprint to the right flank and assume an arched line to gain tenacious fire superiority. (Courtesy of Hae-jung Larsen and OP EASTWIND)*

Small Unit Drills

# C. Contact Left

This battle drill may be ordered by any troop within the squad who sees the enemy preparing to fire on his comrades, such as if the squad enters the kill zone of an enemy ambush. More commonly the squad leader gives the order.

1. The drill is ordered by yelling "Contact Right!" or "Contact Left!"
2. Squad members repeat the command "Contact Right/Left!" and rush the flank.
3. Squad members form an arched line to the flank and conduct an attack by fire.
4. Point and rear guards go prone instantly to secure the flanks and attack by fire.

Small Unit Drills

# D. Break Contact

A rifle squad on the march cannot retreat from the battlefield without permission from higher command. However, the squad leader may wish to disengage from a superior or better-positioned enemy force to preserve his squad and to maneuver to a new angle of attack. Only the squad leader issues this battle drill.

1. The squad leader yells "Break Contact!"
2. Squad members repeat the command "Break Contact!" and prepare to move.
3. The leader orders the guard to support by fire "Front Guard-Hold!"
4. Squad members repeat the command "Front Guard-Hold!"
5. The leader orders the squad to a direction/distance "3 O'clock, 30 Meters!"
6. Squad members repeat the command "3 O'clock, 30 Meters!" and fall back.
7. The leader forms the squad online to suppress the enemy and orders "Front Guard-Fall back!"
8. Squad members repeat the command "Front Guard-Fall Back!" and cover the guard's withdraw with suppressive fires against the enemy.

*Sequence (c) through (h) may be repeated until the squad can safely withdraw and seek a new angle of attack against the enemy force.*

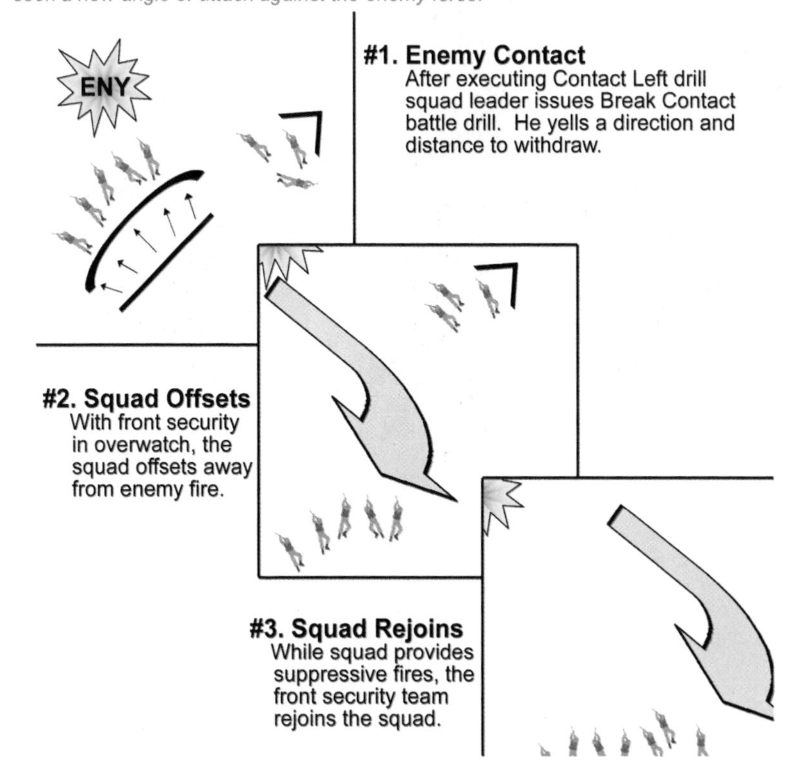


*Ref: Grau, The Bear Went Over the Mountain, p.75 and 200. Bound and overwatch, or in this case its reverse application in the Break Contact drill was not part of RTA doctrine prior to the Soviet-Afghan War of the 1980s. The point security team (or rear security team when used) functions as the second team in bound and overwatch.*

Small Unit Drills

# E. React to Indirect Fire

Again, a rifle squad cannot retreat from the battlefield without permission from higher command. Yet in the instance of enemy artillery fire or air bombardment, the squad leader will displace his squad immediately to preserve the force!

1. The squad leader yells "Incoming!"
2. Squad members repeat the command "Incoming!" and move immediately off the road or trail to go prone.
3. At the first available lull in fire the squad leader orders a direction and distance to safety "6 O'clock, 200 Meters!"
4. Squad members repeat the command "6 O'clock, 200 Meters!" and fall back.
5. At the designated rally point, the squad forms a 360-degree security position and conducts reconsolidation and head count.

*Sequence (a) through (e) may be repeated until the squad is no longer in the impact area of the enemy artillery or attack aircraft.*

*Upon indirect fire, all troops go prone to limit exposure to flak projectiles. If walking on a road during aerial attack, troops move immediately off the road and then go prone. At the first lull in the attack the squad leader yells a direction and distance. All troops repeat the direction and distance while running to the designated point. (Courtesy of Hae-jung Larsen and OP EASTWIND.)*

# (Small Unit Drills)
# III. Mounted Drills

*Ref: Frasche, The Soviet Motorized Rifle Battalion, chap. 6 and 8.*

*Mounted infantry squads can be engaged by numerous enemy weapons systems from any single or even multiple sides. The following three drills enable the squad to dismount from an armored vehicle in order to address such threats. Again, prescriptive drill builds an infantry motorized squad that is as responsive and deliberate in action as any artillery unit or aircrew. (Courtesy of Hae-jung Larsen and OP EASTWIND.)*



## I. Immediate Action Drills –Mounted Squad

Because there are numerous vehicles assigned to various Motorized Rifle Regiments, there are easily as many variations of seating/mounting arrangements. Of significant consideration is whether the squad dismounts to the rear, side or top of the vehicle.

Most armored vehicles mount and dismount the rifle squad from the rear of the vehicle – BMP, BMD, and most of the BTR-series vehicles. For sake of example, this section will discuss rear dismount options.

As a general rule of thumb the squad leader dismounts first. That desire must be balanced with the squad leader's ability to gain situational awareness, which means in fact the squad leader positions himself inside the vehicle where he feels he can best see any situation as it develops and control his troops.

The next troop out of the vehicle is either the deputy leader or a machinegunner. The trick here is to reverse load the vehicle. Those troops out first – the squad leader, deputy leader, and machinegunner should mount into the vehicle last.

Whatever the case, mount and dismount drills must be consistent and rehearsed exhaustively until it becomes second nature.

The effort of this drill is to dismount in an orderly manner to prevent injury to squad members. The vehicle provides some level of protection from enemy direct fire. The squad leader must balance the need to protect troops and the need to protect the vehicle when deciding which dismount drill is most appropriate.

*When discussing dismount options, the point of reference is always from aboard the vehicle and in reference to the direction the nose of the vehicle is pointing. The machinegunner or track commander determines the place to halt the vehicle, whereas it is the responsibility of the driver to safely negotiate the passage of the vehicle to that point.*

# A. Dismount Front

When the squad leader wants to place firepower forward, he issues the order to dismount front.

1. Upon vehicle halt, the leader yells, "All Clear!"
2. The squad visually confirms that the door is clear for opening and yells "All Clear!"
3. Either the driver or nearest troop disconnects the rear door latch.
4. The squad leader yells, "Dismount Front!"
5. The squad repeats, "Dismount Front!" and begins to move in two files out the rear door.
6. The squad leader exits the vehicle and positions to the immediate left or right of the door, depending on his preference. The next troop (deputy leader or machinegunner) positions to the opposite side of the door. Both assume a weapons-up overwatch position and may begin engaging enemy targets.
7. The next two troops follow out the rear door in a fluid motion and assume a prone position to the immediate flanks of the vehicle and orient their fires forward.
8. All subsequent troops exit the rear of the vehicle following in this fluid manner until they form online extending out both flanks of the vehicle.
9. With troops online, the squad leader can now move the dismounted squad to the front, firing and bounding in concert while the bronegruppa provides cover and suppressive fires against the enemy.

*Ref: Frasche, The Soviet Motorized Rifle Battalion, chap. 8, fig. 92. As a general rule of thumb, the mounted RTA force does not dismount until it is upon its objective. It then executes a dismount drill – in this illustration a Dismount Front. (Courtesy of Hae-jung Larsen and OP EASTWIND.)*

Small Unit Drills

# B. Dismount Right

When the squad leader wants to place firepower to the right of the vehicle, he issues the order to dismount right.

1. Upon vehicle halt, the leader yells, “All Clear!”
2. The squad visually confirms that the door is clear for opening and yells “All Clear!”
3. Either the driver or nearest troop disconnects the rear door latch.
4. The squad leader yells, “Dismount Right!”
5. The squad repeats, “Dismount Right!” and moves single file out the rear door.
6. The squad leader exits the vehicle and positions to the immediate right of the door. The squad leader immediately assumes a weapons-up overwatch position and may begin engaging enemy targets.
7. The next troop (deputy leader or machinegunner) follows out the rear door in a fluid motion and assumes a prone position to the immediate right flank of the vehicle. Each troop orients their fires forward.
8. All subsequent troops exit the rear of the vehicle following in this fluid manner until they form online extending out the right flank of the vehicle.
9. With troops online, the squad leader can now move the dismounted squad to the front or right, firing and bounding in concert while the bronegruppa provides cover and suppressive fires against the enemy.

*Ref: Frasche, The Soviet Motorized Rifle Battalion, p. 69 and 79. Tactical training for the rifle subunits is prescriptive and repetitive. Subunits must be able to execute each prescribed drill within demanding time parameters. In this case, the squad reacts to a “meeting engagement”.*

# C. Dismount Left

When the squad leader wants to place firepower to the left of the vehicle, he issues the order to dismount left.

1. Upon vehicle halt, the leader yells, "All Clear!"
2. The squad visually confirms that the door is clear for opening and yells "All Clear!"
3. Either the driver or nearest troop disconnects the rear door latch.
4. The squad leader yells, "Dismount Left!"
5. The squad repeats, "Dismount Left!" and moves single file out the rear door.
6. The squad leader exits the vehicle and positions to the immediate left of the door. The squad leader immediately assumes a weapons-up overwatch position and may begin engaging enemy targets.
7. The next troop (deputy leader or machinegunner) follows out the rear door in a fluid motion and assumes a prone position to the immediate left flank of the vehicle. Each troop orients their fires forward.
8. All subsequent troops exit the rear of the vehicle following in this fluid manner until they form online extending out the left flank of the vehicle.
9. With troops online, the squad leader can now move the dismounted squad to the front or right, firing and bounding in concert while the bronegruppa provides cover and suppressive fires against the enemy.

*While the mounted squad will typically press through an enemy engagement until it has reached its objective, specific circumstance such as being stuck in an enemy ambush kill zone dictate the use of the dismount drill to maximize firepower. (Courtesy of Hae-jung Larsen and OP EASTWIND.)*

# II. On Point: Evolution of RTA Platoon & Squad Tactics

Red Team Armies (RTA) spent virtually all of the Cold War decades preparing for a large-scale mechanized battle in the European theater. This manifested enormous formations in which a 2,300-man regiment was considered a "small tactical unit".

In these regiments the RTA rifle platoon was kept so close to company command that line-of-sight communication was all that was necessary. RTA rifle squads did not separate at all. It was the smallest unit of maneuver and would remain in formation with the platoon, huddled inside an armored infantry vehicle until the squad was literally on top of the objective. The squad would dismount at the last possible minute to conduct mopping up attacks along a broken enemy defense.

*Does the evolving nature of RTA small unit infantry tactics mean a larger role and shared decision-making authority for junior officers and sergeants? (Courtesy of Hae-jung Larsen and OP EASTWIND.)*

By the close of the 1980s as the Soviet Army withdrew from Afghanistan, platoon and squad tactics had gone through subtle but important changes under the baptism of fire. Most critically, the bronegruppa was born and tactics were developed around it that allowed the platoon to dismount independent of the bronegruppa. Also, platoons and squads had learned to coordinate bound and overwatch techniques with point and rear security teams functioning as the alternate bound or overwatch.

Just as American forces had learned in Vietnam, the Soviet experience in Afghanistan nudged RTA forces slowly away from linear tactics. Too, Mujahideen tactics did not lend well to RTA doctrine of attacking large, entrenched European forces. To counter such tactics meant that Soviet commanders had to dispatch smaller and smaller subunits, placing greater emphasis on junior officers.

The emphasis on decentralized operations played a critical role in platoon and squad tactics. This can be seen in dismounted operations independent of the bronegruppa. Note that the dismounted platoon formation in the Movement Techniques and Battle Formation section of this book mirrors an expectation and counter contingency of the parallel ambush – a small unit infantry tactic finely tuned in the latter half of the Soviet-Afghan War.

Chap 7

# Urban & Regional Environments

*Ref: FM 100-2-2 The Soviet Army: Special Warfare and Rear Area Support (Jul '84), chap 7 to 10.*

U.S. Army doctrine addresses five regional environments: desert, cold, temperate, mountain, and jungle. Another area of special consideration involves urban areas*.

## Relative Units of Control, Action & Maneuver

| | Unit of Control | Unit of Action | Unit of Maneuver | Relative Command & Control |
|---|---|---|---|---|
| Desert Region | JTF | BDE | BN/CO | Decreasing Unit Size |
| Cold Region | BDE | BN | CO/PLT | |
| Temperate Region | BDE | BN | CO/PLT | |
| Urban Area | BN | CO | PLT/SQD | |
| Mountain Region | BN | CO | PLT/SQD | |
| Jungle Region | CO | PLT | SQD/TM | Increasing Unit Autonomy |

## I. Urban Operations

The continued trend worldwide of urban growth and the shift of populations from rural to urban areas continues to affect Army operations. The urban environment, consisting of complex terrain, dense populations, and integrated infrastructures, is the predominant operational environment in which Army forces currently operate. ATTP 3-06.11, Combined Arms Operations in Urban Terrain (Jun '11), establishes doctrine for combined arms operations in urban terrain for the brigade combat team (BCT) and battalion/squadron commanders and staffs, company/troop commanders, small-unit leaders, and individual Soldiers.

*See pp. 7-3 to 7-6.*

## II. Mountain Operations

With approximately 38 percent of the world's landmass classified as mountains, the Army must be prepared to deter conflict, resist coercion, and defeat aggression in mountains as in other areas. Throughout the course of history, armies have been significantly affected by the requirement to fight in mountains. FM 3-97.6 (90-6), Mountain Operations (Nov '00), describes the tactics, techniques, and procedures that the U.S. Army uses to fight in mountainous regions. It provides key information and considerations for commanders and staffs regarding how mountains affect

personnel, equipment, and operations. It also assists them in planning, preparing, and executing operations, battles, and engagements in a mountainous environment. Army units do not routinely train for operations in a mountainous environment. The jungle environment includes densely forested areas, grasslands, cultivated areas, and swamps. Jungles are classified as primary or secondary jungles based on the terrain and vegetation.

*See pp. 7-7 to 7-10.*

## III. Desert Operations

Arid regions make up about one-third of the earth's land surface, a higher percentage than that of any other climate. Desert operations demand adaptation to the environment and to the limitations imposed by terrain and climate. Success depends on the appreciation of the effects of the arid conditions on Soldiers, on equipment and facilities, and on combat and support operations. FM 90-3/FMFM 7-27, Desert Operations (Aug '93), is the Army and Marine Corps' manual for desert operations. It is the key reference for commanders and staff regarding how desert affects personnel, equipment, and operations. It will assist them in planning and conducting combat operations in desert environments.

*See pp. 7-11 to 7-14.*

## IV. Cold Region Operations

When conducting military operations in cold regions, leaders, Soldiers, and Marines must plan to fight two enemies: the cold and the opposing force. Despite the difficulties that cold regions pose, there are armies that have prepared for and can conduct large-scale, sustained operations in cold environments. In contrast, few U.S. Army units or personnel have trained extensively in cold region operations. ATTP 3-97.11/ MCRP 3-35D, Cold Region Operations (Jan '11), is the Army's doctrinal publication for operations in the cold region environment. This manual will enable leaders, Soldiers, and Marines to accurately describe cold region environments, their effects on military equipment, impacts these environments have on personnel, and most importantly, how to employ the elements of combat power in cold region environments. It provides the conceptual framework for conventional forces to conduct cold region operations at operational and tactical levels.

*See pp. 7-15 to 7-18.*

## * Jungle Operations

Jungles, in their various forms, are common in tropical areas of the world—mainly Southeast Asia, Africa, and Latin America. The climate in jungles varies with location. Close to the equator, all seasons are nearly alike, with rains throughout the year; farther from the equator, especially in India and Southeast Asia, jungles have distinct wet (monsoon) and dry seasons. Both zones have high temperatures (averaging 78 to 95+ degrees Fahrenheit), heavy rainfall (as much as 1,000 centimeters [400+ inches] annually), and high humidity (90 percent) throughout the year. Severe weather also has an impact on tactical operations in the jungle. FM 90-5, Jungle Operations (Aug '93), is the Army's field manual on jungle operations.

# Mission Command Considerations

Commanders of tactical forces will recognize a general tendency of command and control to vary from centralized to decentralized operations that is specific to any given regional or area environment. Such trends represent an historic norm, however the trends are not etched in stone as formalized doctrine. Still, it may help to consider battle command as it fluctuates from unit reliance on highly centralized control of desert operations, to unit autonomy in highly decentralized control of jungle operations.

Chap 7

# (Urban & Regional Environments)
# I. Urban Operations

*Ref: FM 100-2-2 The Soviet Army: Special Warfare and Rear Area Support (Jul '84), chap 10.*

Red Team Army (RTA) doctrine readily anticipates urban warfare as the norm, and not the exception. In fact, armed conflict can be viewed through RTA doctrine as the conquest of one population center after another, in sequence.

Nowhere does RTA doctrine codify rules of engagement for urban operations. However historically speaking, the rules of engagement for RTA forces operating in urban areas suggest an inverse correlation with regard to civil consideration. The correla-

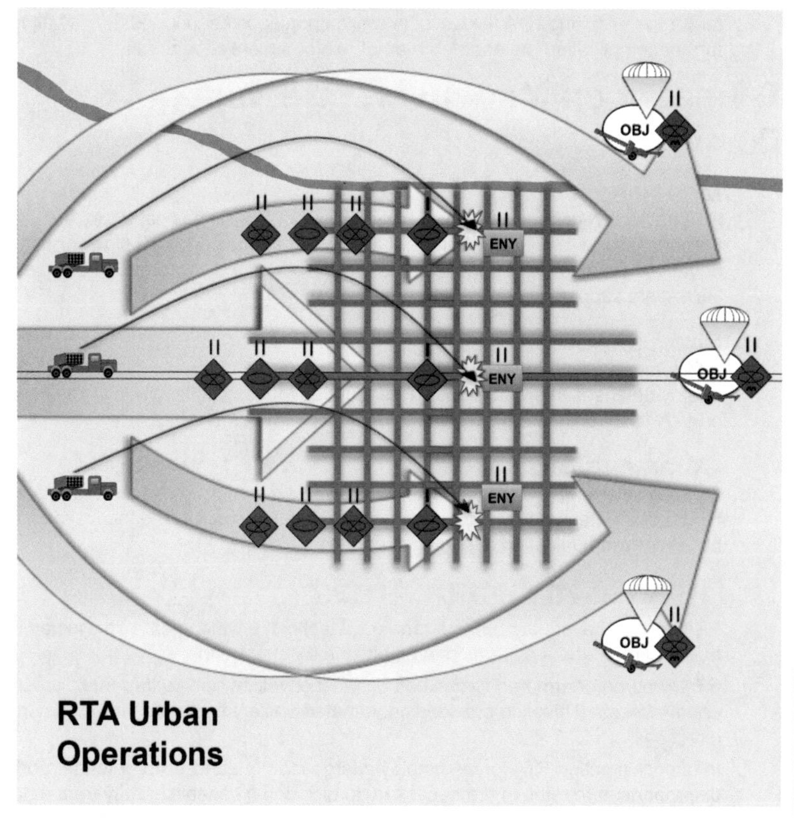


*RTA doctrine for urban operations is battle-proven. In defense strongpoint positions make excellent use of cover, concealment, and canalized approaches. The regiment places two battalions forward and holds one in reserve. In offense each regiment conducts a movement to contact with the reconnaissance company as a forward vanguard. RTA forces use a synchronous combination of tank, mechanized infantry and artillery for the main attack and shaping attacks. An airborne regiment is vertically inserted to form blocking positions in the enemy's rear area.*

Urban & Regional

tion appears predicated upon the nature of the larger mission – offensive capture, defensive security, or stability occupation.

When RTA forces are tasked with occupation and stability operations in an urban area, these missions are often conducted with deference to civil considerations. That is, the rules of engagement are significantly restricted so as to minimize collateral damage to the civilian populous and property. The overarching intent is to stabilize the socio-political or physical infrastructure. Death and destruction must be applied with judicious caution.

Yet when RTA forces are tasked with the defense of an urban area, military operations take precedence over civil considerations. The civilian populous is not necessarily evacuated from their homes and businesses, and indeed civilians may continue to be a valued resource for logistics and the construction of defensive structures. However spies and espionage by civilian collaborateurs become a very real threat. Martial law, blackout periods, and redirection of traffic are enforced. The rules of engagement are significantly more permissive.

Under the task of attacking and capturing an urban area, RTA forces allow for aggressive rules of engagement. Civil considerations are minimized. It may prove better for the attacking RTA forces if the civilian populous abandoned the city altogether, further complicating the enemy's plan of reinforcement or withdraw.

# I. Impact on Maneuver, Fire Support & Command

## Maneuver

RTA doctrine recognizes that movement through urban areas canalizes armored formations, and results in greater expenditure of ammunition with slower rates of advance. Dismounted troops lead the attack with supporting armored vehicles in immediate support.

## Fire Support

RTA forces depend greatly upon sustained high rates of fire to suppress and reduce enemy defenses in urban areas. This requires massed artillery and close air support. Artillery units are moved to the outskirts of the urban area.

## Command & Control

Building structures may significantly hamper radio communication in urban areas. However the dense nature of urban fighting negates much of the tactical considerations of communication over long distances.

# II. Offense in Urban Areas

RTA doctrine favors the hammer and anvil tactic of envelopment. This is particularly true for urban areas and has proven historically successful.

RTA Airborne or armored formations conduct envelopments to trap and disrupt enemy forces. This also provided coordinated artillery fires onto target from multiple directions.

In offensive action RTA forces employ a large ratio of attacker-to-defender and disproportionate rates of fire necessary to dislodge a capable enemy from a defense in urban areas. Again, RTA forces are historically very competent in these types of operations, although they tend to overwhelm their opponents with sheer numbers and frontal assaults. High casualty rates are anticipated.

When conducting offensive actions, RTA divisions operating in urban areas tend to attack in double columns along a 4 km front. Regiments attack along a 2 km front in two columns. Battalions attack along a 600-meter front, also in two columns.

# Urban Operations (U.S. Military Doctrine Perspective)

*Ref: The Small Unit Tactics SMARTbook (2nd Rev. Ed.), The Lightning Press, pp. 7-4 to 7-5.*

Commanders conducting major urban operations use their ability to visualize how doctrine and military capabilities are applied within the context of the urban environment. An operational framework is the basic foundation for this visualization. In turn, this visualization forms the basis of operational design and decisionmaking. To accurately visualize, describe, and direct the conduct of operations in an urban environment, commanders and their staffs must understand the basic fundamentals applicable to most urban operations.

## Fundamentals of Urban Operations

The impact of the urban operations environment often differs from one operation to the next. However, some fundamentals apply to urban operations regardless of the mission, geographical location, or level of command. Some of these fundamentals are not exclusive to urban environments. Yet, they are particularly relevant to an environment dominated by man-made structures and a dense noncombatant population. Vitally, these fundamentals help to ensure that every action taken by a commander operating in an urban environment contributes to the desired end-state of the major operation.

- Maintain close combat capability
- Avoid the attrition approach
- Control the essential
- Minimize collateral damage
- Preserve critical infrastructure
- Separate noncombatants from combatants
- Restore essential services
- Understand the human dimension
- Create a collaborative information environment
- Transition control

## Key Tactical Considerations

Commanders and planners of major operations must thoroughly understand the tactical urban battle as well as the effects of that environment on men, equipment, and systems. The complexity of urban environment changes and often compresses many tactical factors typically considered in the planning process. These compressed tactical factors include—

- Time
- Distances
- Density
- Combat power
- Levels of war
- Decision making

*Refer to The Small Unit Tactics SMARTbook (Leader's Reference Guide to Conducting Tactical Operations) for complete discussion of offensive and defensive operations. Related topics include tactical mission fundamentals, stability & counterinsurgency operations, tactical enabling operations, special purpose attacks, urban operations & fortifications, and patrols & patrolling.*

Rifle companies tend to attack in single column along a 300-meter front, typically an assault lane just a single city block wide. The rifle company is reinforced with a platoon of tanks, and may be assigned engineer teams to remove enemy obstacles.

# III. Defense in Urban Areas

RTA forces prefer to engage enemies outside of urban areas where weapons have a maximum effect on enemy forces. However there are multiple reasons to defend a city within its limits:

- The defense of seaport, airport, and/or train depots
- The defense of critical industry or economic base
- The preservation of key political structures
- To maintain gains after the culmination of an incomplete advance

RTA forces form strongpoint defenses in urban areas. The defensive line is dense without gaps, and is built in depth. A rifle company in urban areas defends along a 200-meter frontline and is supported by a tank platoon, engineer teams, and possibly even artillery units employed in a direct-fire role.

The intent is to canalize the enemy advance into carefully prepared kill zones and attack by fire from multiple angles simultaneously. To achieve this effect, streets may be barricaded and bridges destroyed. Firing positions are prepared from virtually every building, window and doorway.

If an enemy column manages to penetrate a strongpoint defense, RTA forces move quickly to both flanks and continue to attack by fire. The defense of urban areas becomes, in effect, a series of pulsing swarm attacks and baited ambushes.

# IV. Logistical Support

Whether attacking or defending, operations in urban areas demand sustained rapid rates of fire. Ammunition is consumed at astonishing rates. Logistical support must stockpile munitions in prepared cache along the breadth and depth of the operational front.

Likewise, the stockpile storage of water, food, medical supplies and batteries is critical – all the more so if there is a threat of chemical, biological, radiological or nuclear attack.

# (Urban & Regional Environments)
# II. Mountain Operations

*Ref: FM 100-2-2 The Soviet Army: Special Warfare and Rear Area Support (Jul '84), chap 7.*

Historically speaking, it is safe to say that Red Team Armies (RTA) have experienced less success in mountain warfare. While the Jinggang Mountains are regarded as the birthplace of the Chinese Red Army, even Mao's forces had to come down from the mountains to seek victory.

Indeed, mountain warfare has more often been the Achilles' heel for RTA. Anti-communist resistance fighters held up in the Romanian mountains for more than a decade until the early 1960s. Mujahideen guerillas put up troublesome resistance

*RTA forces are rarely able to achieve surprise or speed in mountain operations. Due to their emphasis on armored vehicles, RTA are often relegated to canalized lines of maneuver through low terrain where they are vulnerable to enemy fires. To offset this, RTA use vertical insertion of heliborne units, and sometimes airborne units, to seize high ground. Yet even then regimental commanders do not favor mountain operations because missions are decentralized at the company command level.*

in the mountains of Afghanistan throughout the 1980s. During the Second Chechen War of 1999-2000, guerilla fighters successfully sought refuge in nearby mountains.

Yet the experience of mountain warfare has benefited RTA doctrine in significant ways. The tactical concept of the Bronegruppa was borne through mountain fighting, plus RTA regimental and battalion commanders have begrudgingly learned to trust their subordinate leaders at the company and platoon level to accomplish missions previously tasked only to higher echelon formations.

# I. Impact on Maneuver, Fire Support & Command

Maneuver: RTA doctrine leverages surprise, speed, and violence of action to build irresistible momentum and overwhelm enemy opponents. Mountain operations rarely permit any of these three characteristics in fire and maneuver, and virtually never all three at the same time.

This is at least in part true due to the fact that armored vehicles are greatly limited by the steep grade of terrain, narrow maneuver space, plunging angle of enemy fires, and increased wear of machinery plus increased fuel and coolant consumption. RTA doctrine is forced to adapt to the dramatic terrain of mountain regions.

In mountain regions RTA maneuver is greatly dependent upon roadways within the internal lines of communication and airlift capabilities. While RTA forces may conduct offensive action in an area that lacks roads, RTA forces will not remain in the area without building roads and/or landing strips and helicopter pads. This places enormous emphasis on heavy engineer and civil construction assets.

Fire Support: Close air support is often the most expedient means of placing fires on enemy targets in mountain warfare. Attack helicopter and fixed wing aircraft are prized possessions of RTA forces in these regions.

The steep mountain terrain creates dead spaces, masking artillery and tank fires. Issues that may further complicate the effectiveness of artillery include rapidly changing atmospheric conditions, and targeting limitations due to interference of sound and radar during counter-battery fires with enemy artillery.

For these reasons artillery and mortars are placed forward, very near or even within the front line defenses. Mortars are often preferred due to their high-angle of fire and greater mobility by helicopter airlift.

## Command & Control

Line-of-sight radio communication is greatly restricted in mountainous terrain. High altitude electromagnetic storms and heavy snowfall further complicate communications.

RTA doctrine adjusts for these limitations by establishing retransmitting stations along the internal lines of communication. Yet these stations are fixed sites. That is problematic because they do not lend to mobility, and must be diligently guarded.

This solution also means that RTA commanders must position themselves closer to the frontline for better control of the unit.



# II. Offense in Mountain Regions

Mountain warfare assumes a very different schedule than any other operating environment. Mountain passes may be impenetrable in winter months. And at all times of the year the mountainous terrain canalizes routes of advance, creating a situation in which consumable supplies are exhausted at unsustainable rates – water, fuel, ammunition, food, even batteries wear out quicker.

Mountain operations require a great deal of effort for relatively small gains. So while offensive action is certainly the preferred means of victory in mountain operations, the offense is best described as sporadic in application.

# Mountain Operations (U.S. Military Doctrine Perspective)

*Ref: The Small Unit Tactics SMARTbook (2nd Rev. Ed.), The Lightning Press, pp. 7-44 to 7-48.*

## A. Offense Operations

The principle element of surprise dominates the mountain battlespace. Surprise requires either lightning fast maneuver or slow stealthy movement to achieve unexpected advantage in positioning combat power. Such operations regularly demand a lengthy planning and preparation period.

Offensive action in mountain operations commonly assumes the Movement to Contact (MTC), ambush or raid. These forms of offense do not require follow-up missions such as pursuit or exploitation, and indeed rarely are these conducted. That is, the MTC and special purpose attacks such as the raid and ambush are intended to achieve tactical success for limited operational advantage.

## B. Defense Operations

The primary intent of defense in mountain operations is to deny enemy use of key terrain while maintaining friendly lines of communication.

This presents an apparent blurring of the offensive-defensive dynamic in that the establishment of an outpost defense in order to secure friendly lines of communication is a form of operational offense into the enemy's territory. In short, key terrain assets denied to the enemy may be viewed simultaneously as operational offense and defense.

Mountain defense is established through a series of strongpoint defensive nodes. Each defensive strongpoint maintains 360-degree physical security, yet also overlaps its primary defensive fires with other strongpoint defensive nodes. This is typically achieved along the peaks of a single ridgeline running parallel to the engagement area, or along multiple high points of various terrain features that face into the engagement area – along the lines of communication.

## C. Enabling Operations

Enabling operations in the mountains are as numerous and diverse as any other environment. As discussed previously, high altitude weather conditions and the impact on personnel and equipment must be weighed carefully.

However it is the mission of reconnaissance that is paramount for all offensive and defensive planning. Reconnaissance may be conducted by screening patrols, and often this is the case for gaining situational awareness of the local area. However, for situational awareness beyond the engagement area and rear areas, reconnaissance assets must be planned, managed and employed continuously.

Unmanned Aerial Vehicles (UAV) are effective for looking into defilade canyons for enemy presence, and all the more so when operating above the high altitude tree line. At the small unit level, vehicles like the 4x4 quad motorcycle aid reconnaissance teams in rugged but low-grade terrain conditions. But for the most difficult terrain dismounted patrols are necessary. Scout teams qualified in assault climbing compose valuable reconnaissance asset in such case.

*Refer to The Small Unit Tactics SMARTbook (Leader's Reference Guide to Conducting Tactical Operations) for complete discussion of offensive and defensive operations. Related topics include tactical mission fundamentals, stability & counterinsurgency operations, tactical enabling operations, special purpose attacks, urban operations & fortifications, and patrols & patrolling.*

Mountain warfare is very much like a game of chess. RTA forces spend most of the time in defense, protecting interior lines of communication along a system of mountain outposts. The offense is an opportunity to seize key terrain and test the mettle of an enemy opponent.

When it is time to conduct offensive action, even large-scale offenses, the operation uncharacteristically involves a series of decentralized small unit action guided by centralized command. Nowhere else, other than perhaps jungle warfare, does RTA doctrine employ such an offense. And again, this is due to the nature of the terrain.

The RTA mountain offense seeks to bypass and isolate less valuable enemy positions in order to maneuver into a series of "hammer and anvil" attacks against enclaves of enemy outposts. These often include multiple simultaneous objectives as shaping and feign attacks that disrupt the enemy's defense plan.

Vertical envelopments by RTA heliborne or even airborne units are common. Yet even in the mountains RTA forces will most likely leverage armored formations with intense artillery fires and close air support during offensive action.

Once the objectives are seized or destroyed, RTA forces will defend the conquered territories and establish supply routes along the internal lines of communication, or they may retreat to protected territory within the frontline. The waiting game repeats, in part to test the enemy's resolve, but also because sustained operations in mountain terrain are so costly that to push forward to culmination may risk a loss of all gains if the enemy counterattacks when supplies and resources are depleted.

# III. Defense in Mountain Regions

Defensive operations in mountainous terrain offers RTA forces excellent detection of advancing enemy and effective plunging fires from positions on high ground. The strategy is perhaps best viewed as a siege blockade that is periodically interrupted by extremely violent fire and maneuver.

It is only in mountain warfare that RTA doctrine concedes to the legitimacy of the defense. Indeed, RTA doctrine views the establishment of defensive outposts near or within enemy territory as a form of offensive action!

In effect, any defense along higher terrain becomes a de facto fortified position. As long as each strongpoint defense places effective covering fire on the canalized route of approach, the enemy is forced to weigh the unfavorable option of an uphill battle against a fortified defense. The situation is even less appealing for the enemy when two or more defensive outposts interlock fires along the route of approach.

# IV. Logistical Support

Roads in mountainous terrain are few in number. Engineer support is required to build and repair roadways capable of supporting resupply and reinforcements. Mountain roads are also vulnerable to enemy ambush and seasonal snows that can shut down roadways.

Airlift resupply is planned as part of the RTA solution to logistical support, however weather and the number of aircraft available limit airlifted resupply. Inevitably, roads form the main means of logistics.

Mountain warfare consumes more supplies. The caloric and water intake for each troop is increased in high altitudes. Extreme cold weather equipment is required. Equipment breaks down more frequently and requires more frequent maintenance. Plus ammunition, fuel and batteries are consumed quicker in steep terrain, cold weather and high altitudes.

Such demanding logistical requirements contribute significantly to the limited scope of objectives and the siege blockade nature of mountain operations.

# (Urban & Regional Environments) III. Desert Operations

*Ref: FM 100-2-2 The Soviet Army: Special Warfare and Rear Area Support (Jul '84), chap 8.*

Red Team Army (RTA) operations in desert regions permit maneuver units at the division and corps level. The desert is the one region where large tank battles are still feasible today – not just feasible, but expected. It is in desert warfare that RTA forces commit massive armored formations to achieve surprise, speed, and violence of action in the purest form of RTA doctrine.

Desert regions include 20 percent of the Earth's landmass. As such RTA forces anticipate warfare in the open vastness of the desert.

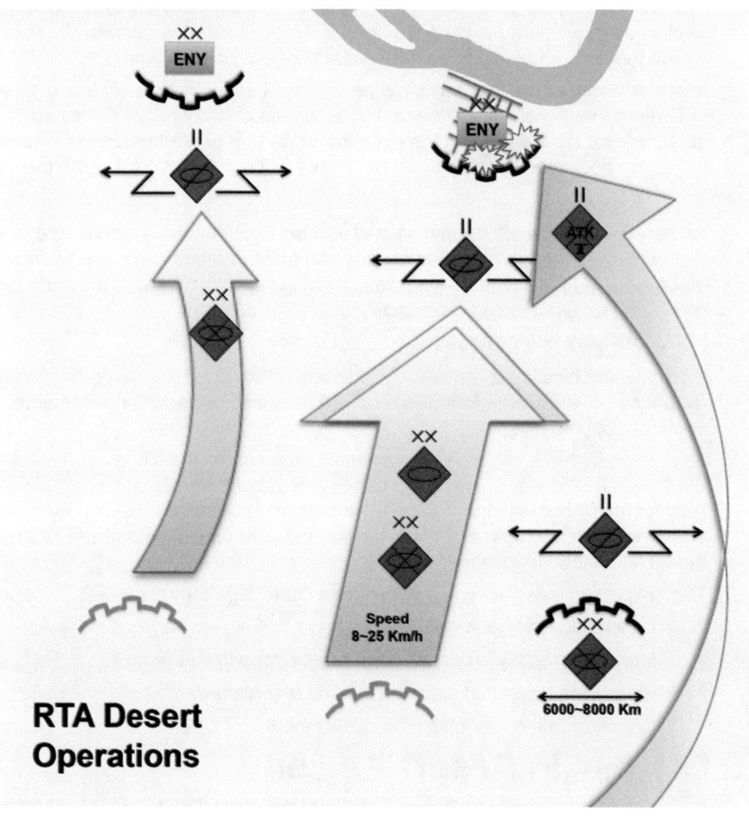


*Desert environments include wide-open areas of visibility and maneuverability with sparse civilian population and a great emphasis on water sources. The desert lends well to the RTA doctrine of surprise, speed, and violence of action. Desert operations involve large formations. A division may defend along an 8-kilometer front, and a corps may defend up to a 50-kilometer front. Rocket artillery and aerial artillery delivered by attack helicopter or fixed-wing aircraft are commonly employed.*

The 1973 Arab-Israeli War offered considerable shaping of RTA doctrine in desert operations. In the initial days of the conflict the Egyptian Army was able to mitigate sophisticated Israeli air attack through an established umbrella of air defense. In fact, it was only when Egyptian Army units deliberately risked moving outside of the umbrella of air defense that their armored columns fell prey to Israeli Air Forces.

Additionally, the 1973 Arab-Israeli War proved the remarkable effectiveness of Soviet-built anti-tank guided missiles such as the AT-3 Sagger in desert warfare.

RTA doctrine in desert operations makes use of such lessons and technology today.

# I. Impact on Maneuver, Fire Support & Command

Aside from the discomfort of temperatures reaching extreme heat and then rapidly cooling at night, the single greatest threat to RTA operations in the desert is inclement weather – specifically the sand storm. These storms can be prolonged for days at a time, and so dense as to limit visibility to just 1 meter. Maneuver, fire support, and command and control come to a complete halt in these conditions.

## Maneuver

A lack of developed roads coupled with the hard, rocky desert floor compels RTA forces into movement across open terrain. Tracked vehicles perform exceptionally well in this environment and easily maintain speeds up to 25 kmph.

Wheeled vehicles are less agile, but perform well enough except in loose sand or soil where there is significant hazard of becoming stuck or rolling the vehicle. In such cases the advance may need to slow to as little as 5 kmph unless wheeled vehicles are dedicated to established roads as follow-on forces behind the main attack.

## Fire Support

Artillery fires can be effectively massed in desert operations. There is little to limit indirect fires, although presence of sand and fine dirt requires constant maintenance of weapons and machinery. Also, navigation is difficult in flat, characterless desert plains and requires the adjusting artillery fires.

## Command & Control

Radio communication is remarkably effective in the desert, however the increased distances between large formations of RTA forces places additional demands on the communication network.

Navigation is also a challenge for command and control of RTA forces. Satellite GPS goes a long way in aiding the movement of both ground and air forces. Yet so significant is this challenge that close air support and artillery fires are rarely ever employed at danger-close ranges. Instead they are used a safe distance ahead of the RTA frontline or advance.

The difficulty in navigation across the desert demands control measures including:

- Designation of attack axis
- Marked assembly areas, rally points, and routes of approach
- Battle formations that ensure flank and rear security
- Communication networks planned in tandem

# II. Offense in Desert Regions

RTA offenses in desert regions involve grand, set piece battles. Corps or divisions engage in decisive action, with entire regiments and battalions conducting shaping actions such as reconnaissance.

Speed is a form of surprise in the desert. The human eye aided by optics can see as far as 32 kilometers (20 miles) across flat terrain under the best conditions. Yet a massive armored column can move that distance in just one and a half hours – meaning that even with excellent visibility the speed of ground combat can quickly mass at locations where the enemy is unprepared to defend.

# Desert Operations (U.S. Military Doctrine Perspective)

*Ref: The Small Unit Tactics SMARTbook (2nd Rev. Ed.), The Lightning Press, pp. 7-28 to 7-29.*

Desert operations establish highly centralized control from commands of higher unit formations. Missions take place in vast geographic areas, yet the command team in the Tactical Operation Center (TOC) commonly monitors and influences the battle as it progresses through a network of ISRC4 capital.

This means tasks to subordinate tactical units at the fireteam, squad, platoon, company, and even the battalion level are often little more than a series of well-executed battle drills. Subordinate units are given an identified objective, a distance, direction and time hack. Each unit will accomplish the mission by employing unit SOP.

## A. Offense Operations

In the desert the offense is swift, powerful and violent. It combines mechanized forces with highly synchronized combat engineer, artillery and Close Air Support (CAS) assets. Engagements frequently begin at the maximum effective ranges of the weapon systems employed, well beyond the range of visual recognition.

## B. Defense Operations

The defense, too, is a large affair in desert operations. On rare occasions an outpost can be established as a strongpoint defense of key terrain. Otherwise, an area defense may extend continuously in breadth over hundreds of miles or kilometers. Alternatively, a mobile defense or retrograde may extend an equal number of miles in depth. For the largest task forces in desert operations, both an area defense and a retrograde are developed simultaneously.

The desert presents few flanking obstacles with which a defense may tie into. If impassable terrain features – the sea, plateau, mountain canyon, sand dunes, or the deep silt of a dried salt lake – cannot be established on the flanks then flanks may be secured with massive minefields to deny the enemy maneuver.

## C. Enabling Operations

The defense requires coordinated planning and sustainment. Combat support and service support units shape the success of any operation. Tactical units must be prepared to provide security for supporting units.

Reconnaissance in Force (RIF) is the primary form of ground reconnaissance in the desert. RIF swaps stealth for speed, and values timely information over catching the enemy unaware. Thus, RIF is typically conducted by mechanized or motorized mounted patrols. And unlike other operational environments that might dispatch a squad or fireteam to conduct reconnaissance, RIF typically involves platoons or entire companies for each reconnaissance mission.

Screening patrols and local area security patrols are conducted as a means of counter-reconnaissance to disrupt enemy activity. This is particularly effective when supporting sustainment operations or a relief-in-place.

*Refer to The Small Unit Tactics SMARTbook (Leader's Reference Guide to Conducting Tactical Operations) for complete discussion of offensive and defensive operations. Related topics include tactical mission fundamentals, stability & counterinsurgency operations, tactical enabling operations, special purpose attacks, urban operations & fortifications, and patrols & patrolling.*

RTA attacks in desert regions are conducted at the march and in depth, most often under the cover of darkness. The front of the attack may be large and tolerates gaps when bypassing enemy strongpoints. These strongpoints can be flanked or even left isolated as targets for artillery or aerial bombardment.

Generally RTA forces do not seek a frontal assault until the enemy defenses have been disrupted and suppressed. Gaps in the enemy line permit smaller formations to envelop the enemy and attack the rear area to disrupt coordinated defenses or trap retreating enemy units in their routes of egress. Under these conditions a frontal assault by fast moving armored formations conducts a defeat in detail.

RTA airborne forces, and less often heliborne units, may carry out vertical envelopment when gaps in the enemy's frontline are not apparent. This again is the classic RTA offensive doctrine of "hammer and anvil."

# III. Defense in Desert Regions

The RTA defense is a temporary condition in desert warfare. The preference for offensive action is paramount. Yet the defense, too, is part of the set piece battle.

RTA ground forces in desert regions form into strongpoint defenses that are developed in depth. Regiments and battalions form forward vanguards armed with guided anti-tank missiles. The division maintains a regiment or battalion in reserve.

Artillery batteries complement the RTA defense with interlocking arcs of fire.

The most critical aspect of the RTA defense in desert operations may be the establishment of the umbrella of air defense that protects all ground assets. Air defense includes three layers – the outer, middle, and inner arcs.

The outermost arc is composed of air defense missiles capable of altitudes above 25 km (80,000 ft.) and striking enemy aircraft at distances of 240 km (150 mi.) and/or enemy ballistic missiles at 60 km (37 mi.). This includes missile systems such as the S-300/400 Triumf, known in NATO as the SA-20 Gargoyle and SA-21 Growler, or the older but still effective S-75 Dvina, known by NATO as the SA-2 Guideline.

The midrange arc of air defense includes missile systems reaching altitudes of 3 km (10,000 ft.) and striking enemy aircraft as far away as 20 km (12 mi.). The Pantsir-S1, also known by NATO as the SA-22 Greyhound, has such missile capability.

The inner arc of air defense is composed of anti-aircraft guns and short-range missiles with similar altitude engagement at 3 km (10,000 ft.) and able to destroy enemy aircraft at distances of 4-5 km (2.5 to 3 mi.). The Pantsir-S1 system includes 30mm cannon with such capabilities. Additionally, the shoulder-fired Igla air defense rocket, known by NATO as the SA-18 Grouse may be attached assets down at the rifle company level.

# IV. Logistical Support

The greatest logistical demand for RTA forces in desert operations is potable water. A single battalion consumes up to 4,500 kilograms (5 tons) of water per day. This considerable weight must be procured and transported daily to some 15 battalions per each division. The demand for food, water and fuel places even greater demand on roadway and railway to and from port of entry.

The impact of sand on machinery, vehicles and in particularly helicopters means sustained maintenance supplies must be sustained through logistical resupply. The effect of extreme heat on electronic devices such as communication and navigation systems further pressures logistical support.

All of this material supply must be transported deep into the desert from entry seaports and airports because desert regions are sparsely populated, and even then primarily along coastal areas and river basins. There is little opportunity for RTA forces to forage off the population or land.

# (Urban & Regional Environments) IV. Cold Wx Operations

*Ref: FM 100-2-2 The Soviet Army: Special Warfare and Rear Area Support (Jul '84), chap 9.*

Depending on their location, many Red Team Armies (RTA) are well suited to military operations in extreme cold environments. Much of Russia as well as parts of China and North Korea experience arctic conditions during the year, and so these forces are compelled to master cold region operations.

The RTA emphasis on the armored vehicle as the core of the fighting unit means that RTA forces can be kept reasonably warm by vehicle heaters while traversing otherwise difficult terrain in forbidding weather conditions.

However, cold region operations come with numerous and significant limitations. Extreme cold temperatures present a unique danger to humans and equipment. There is greater demand for logistical support, placing greater value on roadways and railways from airports and seaports.

Cold regions are remarkably sparse in human population. Townships are small in size and number. They are often centered on seaports, airports, train depots, or critical road junctions. This means that cold region operations are often focused on capturing or defending townships – which also offer protection from the elements.

## I. Impact on Maneuver, Fire Support & Command

### Maneuver

RTA forces tend to be quite capable in cold regions; yet ideal maneuver conditions are significantly limited to specific seasons with solid permafrost ground and roughly 30cm (12in) or less depth of snow.

Tracked vehicles can navigate snow as deep as 1.5 meters (58in) reasonably well. Yet in such deep snow dismounted troops cannot keep up with tracked vehicles. In that case the troops must be towed in a skijoring technique leaving them vulnerable to enemy fires, or they must complete the entire assault while still inside their tracked vehicles, unable to effectively employ their small arm weapon systems.

If the weather is too warm, the open terrain turns into a grassland marsh that is impassable for most tracked or wheeled vehicles. Even foot patrols can get stuck in the grassland marshes.

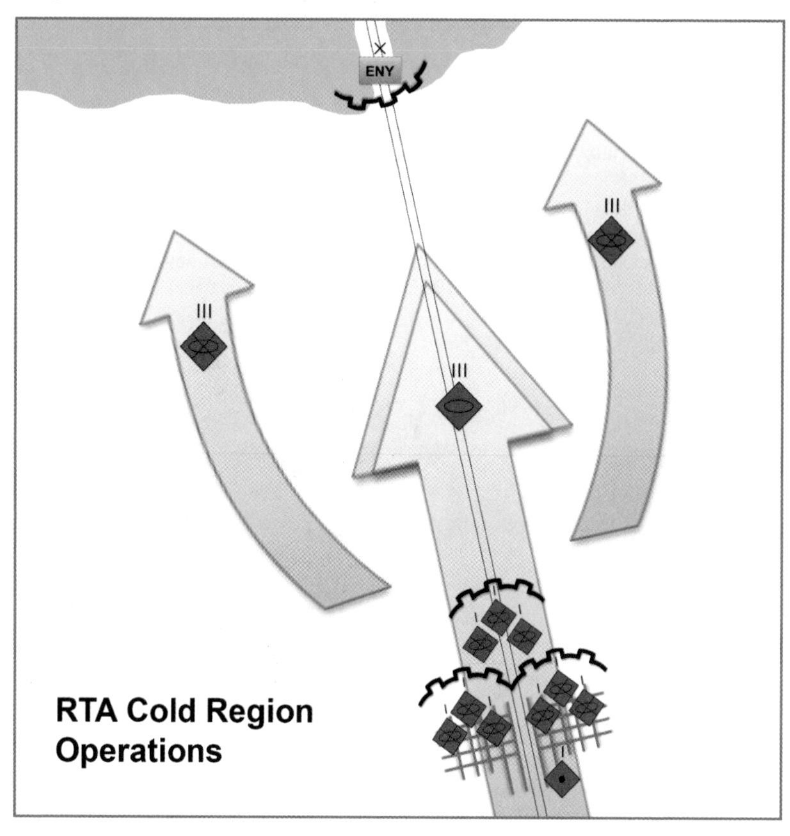


*Cold region operations are characterized as a waiting game interrupted by brief moments of lightning fast strikes when weather conditions permit. Main supply routes and port cities are key assets in cold regions. The defense is densely formed into an inverted stronghold with 1/3rd of the force on the line while 2/3rds are kept warm as a ready reserve in tents or buildings. The defense is maintained even during offensive actions. Offensive action is similarly densely formed due to impeded maneuverability and shorter ranges of fire for weapons systems.*



## Fire Support

Close air support is advantageous in cold regions, yet "peer" enemies place as much emphasis on a multiple-layered umbrella of air defense – the same as RTA forces in cold region operations. If so, close air support may not be regularly available.

Artillery ranges and rates of fire are impacted in extreme cold temperatures. Additionally the effect of artillery is reduced because deep snow absorbs much of the shrapnel and directs the bursting radius upward. Artillery bombardment requires more rounds to destroy a target.

Rates of fire are slowed because extreme cold temperatures turn metals brittle, and more likely to break. Until the weapon system appreciably warms to temperatures at which breakages are less likely to occur.

Small arm weapons, too, are affected in a very similar manner. Cold weapons must be warmed, most commonly through slow but sustained rates of fire, before they can be employed at rapid or cyclic rates of fire. And effective ranges are noticeably reduced.

### Command & Control

Radio communication is affected by routine electromagnetic anomalies of the Aurora Borealis. RTA commanders overcome this limitation by locating units much closer together in dense formations, both for the offense and defense.

Theater areas of operations in cold regions tend to be long and thin, predicated on protecting interior lines of communications along main supply routes. Again, while there may be considerable distance between major units, RTA forces tend to be formed densely and in depth in cold regions.

## II. Offense in Cold Regions

RTA offensive operations in cold regions tend to be medium-to-large affairs that are remarkably dense in formation, and necessarily short in duration due to limited seasons with optimal ground and weather conditions.

RTA forces in cold regions attack in dense formations along narrow fronts for several reasons:

- Enemy targets are densely formed around key terrain, roads or facilities.
- Terrain and boreal forests restrict movement to narrow attack lanes.
- Weapon ranges and rates of fire are decreased.
- Communication range may be limited due to electromagnetic storm.
- Sustainment of the attack depends on supply and warm facilities.

Commanders move very near to or embed with the attack force. Assembly areas are much closer to the attack lanes. And artillery is placed much closer to the front-line.

Artillery is often leveraged as battlefield deception in cold regions. This is because in extreme cold temperatures noise is detected over greater distances. Artillery fire helps to conceal the noise of armored vehicles gathering in their assembly areas and moving into assault positions or lanes.

Other than the noted exceptions, offensive action in cold region operations is conducted in much the same manner as anywhere else. Enveloping units attack the flank and/or enemy rear areas to disrupt enemy frontline defenses, aided by artillery fires and close air support. Only then will armored formations conduct frontal attacks to defeat the enemy in detail.

## III. Defense in Cold Regions

Most of the year cold region operations include a series of outposts forming picket lines along interior lines of communication. With a few notable exceptions by RTA airborne forces, heliborne forces, or small dismounted units that may conduct smaller scale offensive operations in warmer wet seasons; armored formations must wait until specific seasonal weather conditions before an offensive strike.

The importance of townships and boreal forests in cold regions cannot be overstated due to their concealment and protective value. Open terrain between RTA forces and enemy positions offers passable maneuver only at certain times during the year.

### Cold Temperatures

Ironically most injuries and death in cold region operations come not from combat action, but from extreme cold temperatures. Chilblain, snow blindness, frostbite, and hypothermia can set in quickly. Body temperature is lost through exposure to cold air and wind, and when in contact with the ground or cold metal surfaces of vehicles. Death can result in days or even hours. Frostbite to extremities can occur in just minutes, and may require amputation.

Proper clothing, equipment, training and personnel management are required for the success of cold region operations. This is certainly true for the defense.

### Inverted Strongpoint Defense

RTA forces form into an inverted formation and rotation of the strongpoint defense in cold region operations. Guard shifts and listening posts form critical elements of the defense.

Whereas under normal battlefield environments RTA forces form a strongpoint defense with between 65 to 75 percent of the combat power on the frontline and rotate just a small fraction back to rear areas, in cold region operations that power equation is reversed. Typically only 33 percent of the RTA force is kept alert on the front line at any given time. The remainder is kept in rear areas with part of them resting and part of them kept in warming tents or buildings as a quick-reaction reserve force.

Regimental defenses may rotate entire battalions to the frontline of the defense, rotating them once every several days. Battalion defenses keep one rifle company forward, with the other two rifle companies kept in the rear, and they are rotated once per day. Rifle company defenses may maintain just one platoon forward, and will rotate platoons as often as every two hours in the worst weather conditions.

### Air Defense

This is a critical consideration of the RTA defense in cold regions. It may be even more critical because unlike other environments in which RTA forces can spread across wide areas, in cold region operations RTA forces are densely formed and are vulnerable to enemy air attack.

The umbrella of air defense is composed of a three-layered arc with outer ranged missiles targeting enemy aircraft and ballistic missiles at 240 km (150 mi.) and altitudes of 25 km (80,000 ft.); midrange missiles capable of destroying enemy targets at 20 km (12 mi.) and altitudes of 3 km (10,000 ft.); and inner ranged missiles and auto-cannon engaging aircraft at distances of 4-5 km (2.5-3 mi.).

## IV. Logistical Support

Roads to and from seaports, airports and train depots are invaluable assets for delivering large amounts of supplies to RTA forces. Roads must be established and maintained by heavy engineer assets.

Cold region operations increase the amount of daily caloric intact per person, as well as placing enormous demand on heating fuels. Also, because extreme cold temperatures negatively impact weapon effectiveness, an increased resupply of ammunition is necessary.

Cold weather equipment must follow-on each new offensive push into the theater of operations. In no other operating environment are tents, sleeping cots, and heaters more essential to success. Plus, each troop must be outfitted with specialized winter clothing, camouflage, and travel equipment such as snowshoes and skis.

Humans cannot survive in such inhospitable environments without considerable logistical support.

# (Urban & Regional Environments) V. Nighttime Operations

*Ref: FM 100-2-2 The Soviet Army: Special Warfare and Rear Area Support, chap 11, and Sasso, Soviet Night Operations in World War II.*

*The nighttime fighting capabilities of RTA forces have waxed and waned over time, but when they are at their best RTA forces are extremely adept night fighters. (Courtesy of Hae-jung Larsen and OP EASTWIND.)*

## I. Nighttime Tactics, Techniques & Procedures (TTPs)

The ability to perform nighttime operations varies greatly amongst different RTA forces, yet here it is commonly the less sophisticated militaries that perform better under such battlefield conditions of limited visibility.

RTA forces appear to go through a transition regarding nighttime operations that may be directly inverse to advances in technology. To be certain, at the close of the Second World War the German Army had an appreciable respect for the Soviet soldier's ability in nighttime operations. Yet by the First Chechen War of 1994-96, in spite of vast technological advances Russian forces proved almost incapable of nighttime operations.

Internal criticism of Russian forces claims that as commanders and troops began to rely more and more on technological advantage, their ability to perform nighttime operations become intricately linked to the limitations of the given technology. The training of nighttime operational Tactics, Techniques, and Procedures (TTP) is commonly abandoned in preference of new technological gadgets.

Too, as noted earlier RTA forces often enjoy their greatest tactical success within the boundaries of their own sovereign nation. Under these conditions RTA forces develop from guerilla forces and into more conventional armed forces. They do so with both intimate knowledge of the territorial lay of the land, and with the implicit or explicit support of the civilian populous. These favorable variables often have a direct impact on the tactical success of RTA forces conducting nighttime operations – long before they develop sophisticated military technologies of their own.

Such home field advantages are difficult to come by when RTA forces projects military power outside the boundaries of their national borders. Under these conditions, it is perhaps understandable that RTA commanders and troops rely excessively on their technological advantage.

Technology must be exploited within the battlespace! This is certainly true for nighttime operations as well. So with the reintroduction of rudimentary TTP coupled with the mature use of technology, nighttime operations improve greatly the capabilities of RTA forces when operating domestically and when projected to foreign campaigns.

## Special Considerations of Nighttime Operations

Of the many considerations regarding nighttime operations, the mission's objective and the disposition of the civilian populous are of central concern.

Due to the enormous burden of coordination for nighttime operations, RTA commanders must account for the mission objective when considering such tactics. Not all missions are suitable for hours of limited visibility.

A solid rationale for conducting nighttime operations is to seek to mitigate an enemy's advantages in daytime targeting – such as when the enemy has air superiority/dominance and can employ effective Close Air Support (CAS). Nighttime operations create new difficulties for enemy targeting systems, particularly when they are avoiding fratricide.

Alternatively, reconnaissance in force may be employed during limited visibility to draw ineffective enemy fires. This gives greater account of the enemy position and disposition while limiting exposure of friendly troops. Also, clandestine infiltration of smaller units through enemy lines is far more feasible during nighttime hours. Infiltrating RTA forces link up in the rear of the enemy formation, creating an enveloping force the night prior to offensive action.

*Low-light devices such as chemical sticks, flashlights and IR strobes can be used to guide troops at night. But they are placed facing away from the enemy! (Courtesy of Hae-jung Larsen and OP EASTWIND.)*

# (Rear Area Operations & Logistics) I. The Rear Area

*Ref: FM 100-2-2 The Soviet Army: Special Warfare and Rear Area Support (Jul '84), chap 12.*

## I. The Rear Area

The Soviet concept of the "rear area" visualizes modern war in an unprecedented spatial scope. This rear area concept stretches from the forward edge of the battle area (FEBA) back to the national capital.

To the Soviets, there are two aspects of the rear area concept: broad and narrow. The broad aspect includes the entire country, its population, economy, government, and its political structure. It is the production base for necessary war materiel, the mobilization base for personnel replacements, and the control center for the complete war effort. The narrow aspect includes the activities of all military units that supply technical, materiel, and medical support to combat forces in established theaters of military operations (TVD).

Soviet rear area support has a dual task: peacetime support and wartime support. In peacetime, rear area support maintains the Soviet armed forces in a high state of preparedness for commitment on short notice. Soviet military doctrine requires that the armed forces and the entire population constantly be prepared for the sudden outbreak of a major war. In wartime, rear area support provides technical, materiel, and medical support to forces engaged in combat. The Soviets think a major war in Europe is likely to be a short highly intense conflict with conventional or nuclear weapons disrupting the flow of service support. They expect logistic requirements to be quite large when their offensive is in the initial stage. After the penetration, logistic requirements will lessen because attacking forces will encounter less organized resistance deep in the enemy's rear.

Soviet rear area support is organized on three different levels: strategic, operational, and tactical.

### Strategic

Strategic rear area operations are conducted at the national level by the Ministry of Defense. They extend into the theater of combat operations during wartime. Strategic rear area operations procure personnel, materiel, and services needed by the military. These operations prepare the Soviet economy and the Soviet people to provide sustained support in case of war. Also, central rear services,which is the highest logistic organization of the armed forces, serve both to link the national economy and the armed forces and to directly support operational forces.

### Operational

Operational rear area functions are conducted by front and army rear area support elements. Military districts, groups of forces, and army support elements are the principal points of delivery for materiel and equipment contracted by the Ministry of Defense. Most items are received, stored, and prepared for release to combat units directly from industry. Support activities in the operational rear area are conducted mainly from fixed or semifixed installations.

### Tactical

The tactical rear is at division and lower. Tactical rear area operations meet the immediate combat needs of supported units. Divisions carry about 3 to 5 days of supplies.

The Soviets also recognize the need to prepare for a long conflict and to support combat forces that attain and hold deep objectives. Service support units in the operational (army and front) rear and the Soviet central logistic system provide this in-depth, follow-on support. Service support is organized to keep pace with rapidly advancing frontal forces (mechanized and armored units supported by aviation). The central logistic system may deploy to theaters of military operations (TVDs) and directly support operational forces if required.

## II. Chiefs of the Rear and their Commands

The overall system of rear area support is the responsibility of the Chief of the Rear of the Soviet Armed Forces. He is also one of the Deputy Ministers of Defense. He is the principal controller and coordinator of the many logistic organizations and assets which make up the central rear services. However, the organization of specific rear area operations is the responsibility of each individual unit commander.

The Soviets emphasize the commander's responsibility to organize his own rear area operations at every level of command. The commander delegates this responsibility to his deputy commander of the rear also known as the chief of the rear.

The Soviets stress the important role played by the chief of the rear. He is a rear services officer who is directly subordinate to his commander. There is arear services officer at every level of command down to regiment. He assumes responsibility for rear area details, which permits the commander to devote his full energies to combat operations.

The rear area command and control is based on the commander's operational decisions. The commander may make these decisions or delegate this responsibility to his chief of the rear. Specific rear area decisions include designating deployment areas and direction of movement for rear service elements; determining supply and evacuation points, size of necessary reserve units, and the periods of their forma-tion; specifying medical and technical support; establishing rear area security measures; and designating initial and subsequent locations of the rear area command post.

The chief of the rear coordinates basic rear support matters with the unit's chief of staff and arms and services representatives. He keeps them updated on the equipment status, the availability of reserves, and the medical support.

Rear area command posts (CPs) are established at all echelons from front to regiment. A rear CP must be able to communicate with the parent unit and with subordinate, adjacent, and higher rear area command posts. CP personnel include the chief of the rear, his staff, and the communications, transportation, security, and traffic control troops.

Rear area communications are guided by the same basic principles that are applied to all Soviet communications: continuity, mobility, and redundancy. Communication means include messengers, wire, and radio (single-channel, multi-channel, tropospheric scatter). Radio links are supported by airborne, ground-based, and satellite relays. Data links extend from the Ministry of Defense to at least front rear area command posts. Secure voice communications are established down to regimental rear.

The rear area command post's mobility and survivability are improved by employing an "operations group."The functions of the operations group are to maintain continuous rear area command and control during redeployment of the main rear area CP. The operations group consists of a few rear area staff officers with limited communications who temporarily can maintain command and control of rear area operations while the command post relocates.

# III. Rear Area Levels of Command & Control

Soviet rear area support is controlled at three levels: strategic, operational, and tactical.

## A. Strategic

At the strategic level, the Ministry of Defense is responsible for all rear area activities of the armed forces. Within the Ministryof Defense, the Chief of the Rear of the Soviet Armed Forces accomplishes central coordination of all support activities. He and the rear services staff coordinate support operations of the deputy commanders for the rear of the service components and troop branches, the sixteen military districts within the USSR, and the groups of Soviet forces deployed outside the USSR.

Directly subordinate to the Chief of the Rear are the support directorates common to all services and branches (food, clothing, POL, medical, and veterinary services). The Chief of the Rear coordinates with the service branch directorates as well as with special troop directorates on matters falling within their jurisdiction.

In wartime, central logistics units, resources, and command and control elements may deploy to a theater of military operations (TVD).

## B. Operational

The highest level administrative headquarters in peacetime are the military districts and groups of forces outside the country. In wartime, both have sufficient communications and staff elements to form fronts.There are no fronts as such in peacetime.

The military district is a high-level military territorial administrative command. It includes military areas, recruiting districts, military schools, installations, and garrisons. When units in a military district are formed into a wartime front, elements of the military district staff may provide the basis for the front rear area staff. The military district continues to provide command and control for assigned central rear services missions and other support functions. The peacetime rear area support organization of a group of forces can quickly assume command and control of front rear area operations. The wartime operational combined arms formations are fronts and armies. The rear area operations for these formations is accomplished by a chief of the rear, (also called the deputy commander for the rear) and his support units. Command and control of rear area operations are conducted from rear area command posts. The front establishes its rear area command post 150 to 200 km behind the FEBA. The army locates its rear area com-mand post about 100km behind the FEBA. In high tempo offensive operations, rear area commandposts move frequently.

# C. Tactical (Rear Area Command & Control)

*Ref: FM 100-2-2 The Soviet Army: Special Warfare and Rear Area Support (Jul '84), p. 12-3.*

At regiment and division, the chief of the rear (deputy commander for the rear) supervises a staff which includes deputies for food; petroleum, oils, and lubricants (POL); and clothing. Coordination is made with engineer, signal, transportation, chemical, and ammunition directorates. Vehicle maintenance, repair, and recovery is the responsibility of the deputy commander for technical affairs. The repair of onboard weapons and associated equipment is the responsibility of the deputy commander for armaments. These activities are coordinated with the chief of the rear. Chiefs of the rear at regiment and division have small staffs to coordinate the activities of all combat service support elements at their respective levels. However, their basic command responsibility changes for rear area security. If requirements dictate, tactical units can be assigned rear area security missions under the operational control of the chief of the rear.

Division and regiment rear area command posts are equipped with fully mobile communications facilities. Division rear area command posts will be about 30 km behind the line of contact; regiment rear area command posts will he about I5 km behind the line of contact. There is no chief of the rear (deputy commander for the rear) lower than regiment. The unit commander below regiment is his own manager of rear area operations.

At tank and motorized rifle battalion level, the commander is assisted by the following personnel:

- **Chief of battalion staff** (similar to US battalion executive officer) is the principal assistant for organizing and administering battalion rear area operations.
- **Battalion technical officer** is responsible for organization and control of maintenance, repair, and salvage of both combat and noncombat vehicles.
- **Battalion supply platoon commander** orders, stores, and distributes all supplies and equipment. He commands a supply platoon consisting of a supply section and an ammunition and motor transport section. The ammunition and motor transport section operates the battalion's cargo and POL trucks.
- At company level, a **company technical officer** assists the commander in logistics. The company technical officer supervises weapons crews in field maintenance and light repair. He also is assisted by a company first sergeant who is accountable for company-level supply.

# (Rear Area Operations & Logistics) II. Rear Area Protection

*Ref: FM 100-2-2 The Soviet Army: Special Warfare and Rear Area Support (Jul '84), chap 14.*

In the Soviet view, rear area protection and security comprise the comprehensive coordination of more than just the rear of military forces in contact with the enemy. The Soviets also believe that general war will involve more than the armed forces fighting along established front lines. A future large-scale war, whether conventional or nuclear, will include wide-spread espionage, sabotage, infiltration, airborne and amphibious operations, and massive destruction that will occur throughout the nation. So total war will involve the total population. The Soviets have established an extensive and encompassing program of organizations and procedures to conduct rear area security. Security and protection of the rear area is critical. It includes vital installations, airfields, communications and transportation nets, critical industries, strategic weapons, and large troop formations.

## I. Unit Security

All units, from the smallest through front level, are responsible for the security of their own rear areas. In larger organizations (regiment and up), elements of the second echelon have most of the responsibility for security. Organic personnel and equipment carry out basic security and damage control in the rear area. Appropriate measures include the following:

At army and front level, electronic warfare and air defense elements are located to provide thorough coverage of the entire area of operations. Combat support and combat servicesupport elements also have rear area security responsibilities from the rear area of units in contact to the rear boundary.

# II. Rear Area Forces

*Ref: FM 100-2-2 The Soviet Army: Special Warfare and Rear Area Support (Jul '84), p. 14-1 to 14-3.*

## KGB Troops

Besides its major role in intelligence activities, the Committee for State Security (KGB) is responsible for border security and special communications. In the event of an enemy invasion, the KGB border guard detachments would fight delaying actions until relieved by ground forces units. Conversely, during a Soviet offensive, border guard missions would include securing the operational armies' rear, conducting counterespionage, forestalling desertions, thwarting deep enemy penetrations, and conducting mop-up operations in the rear area.

## MVD Troops

Interior troops of the Ministry of Internal Affairs (MVD) are primarily responsible for maintaining domestic security. Missions in the civilian sector include criminal investigation, motor vehicle inspectionand control, and issuance of visas. In wartime, they also have the missions to suppress insurrection, to conduct counterespionage, and to transport prisoners.

KGB and MVD troops are organized, equipped, and trained much the same as Soviet ground forces, but special attention is given to security functions. In general, KGB and MVD troops are considered to be extremely reliable and are very well trained.

## Military Districts

Although not still applicable, the Soviet Union was divided into 16 Soviet military districts. The 16 Soviet military districts were administrative commands which did not correspond to the political boundaries of the Soviet Union's 15 republics. In wartime, the assets of many military districts probably would be organized into fronts, providing both the command and control structure and units for combat operations.

Military activity within a military district continues, however, even when troop units are deployed elsewhere. Military installations such as schools and garrisons, and operations such as logistics and communications would continue to function, and in certain instances, even be augmented.

Military district mobilization plans cover not only units, installations, and activities of the district, but also the call-up of reserves.Reserve call-up is selective to permit orderly activation and to insure an adequate labor force for critical civilian occupations. Civil defense activities also are conducted through the military district command structure.

## Civil Defense

Overall civil defense of the Soviet Union is directed by a Deputy Minister of Defense. Civil defense troops, numbering approximately 40,000, are a branch of the Soviet military under the command of the Chief of Civil Defense. They are subordinate to deputy commanders for civil defense in the 16 military districts. Most civil defense efforts involve organization and training for survival, rescue, repair, and restoration. The intent is to involve the Soviet population. Civil defense is one of several means of involving the population in disciplined activity and of keeping them aware of the everpresent "threat" posed by the enemies of the Soviet Union. Perhaps 70 percent of workers engaged in vital industry belong to civil defense organizations. Their principal objectives are:

- To prevent panic.
- To maintain law and order
- To maintain agricultural and industrial production
- To insure organized decontamination

Civil defense activities involve over thirty million people and are closely tied to the overall war and survival effort. Organized and trained personnel, controlled by the government, will be capable of at least the following activities:

- Fire-fighting
- First aid
- Camouflage of industrial targets
- Chemical defense and decontamination
- Damage control
- Rescue
- Public order and safety
- Communication and warning
- Evacuation
- Reconnaissance
- Radiological monitoring and decontamination

Civilian civil defense formations insure a potentially valuable laborforce for the Soviets. They are also a source for intelligence gathering, particularly in areas threatened by airborne or seabome attack, guerrilla or partisan activity, or large-scale invasion.

Civil defense receives extensive propaganda treatment in the Soviet media. There is civil defense training in schools, for housewives, and for retirees besides the training given in factories and civil defense formations.

However, Soviet civil defense programs have been criticized for their lack of imagination, heavy ideological (rather than practical) emphasis, lack of realism, poor quality instruction, inadequate planning, and poor coordination. Many mass evacuation plans have not been rehearsed for years, if at all. Nevertheless, the Soviet civil defense program reaches virtually every citizen in the nation with at least minimal instruction and indoctrination.

## Reserves

Soviet conscripts have a reserve obligation until age 50. The total Soviet potential reserve manpower pool is estimated to be twenty five million men. About 6.8 million of these men are young, recently-trained veterans.

Soviet reservists are not organized in specific reserve units. Instead, reservists called up for training report to existing active units. In the event of a large-scale mobilization, reservists will be assigned where required. Many would fill out low-strength divisions and other units.

The Soviet reserve system provides a vast resource of former servicemen. Younger and more recently trained personnel probably would be mobilized for combat service. Older reservists easily could take over numerous garrison, guard, and rear area responsibilities.

Given such vast numbers of men with prior military service plus a citizenry which has received consider-able exposure to civil defense indoctrination and training, the Soviets can count on a population that is potentially more aware and prepared, and that is used to discipline.

## Industrial Survival

The Soviets expect to survive and to win any future war. To do this, special attention has been devoted to protecting the industrial and technological base. Protective measures include dispersion of industrial facilities, physical hardening of factories, stockpiling materials and parts, constructing shelters for workers, and creating evacuation plans. Dispersion reduces vulnerability but it also increases the transportation problem and the security burden.

# III. Operational Area Security (U.S. Military Doctrine Perspective)

*Ref: The Army Operations & Doctrine SMARTbook (5th Rev. Ed.), The Lightning Press, p. 7-13 (ADRP 3-37, Protection, pp. 1-4 to 1-5).*

**Base/Base Camp Defense.** Base defense is the local military measures, both normal and emergency, required to nullify or reduce the effectiveness of enemy attacks on, or sabotage of, a base to ensure that the maximum capacity of its facilities is available to U.S. forces (JP 3-10).

**Critical Asset Security.** Critical asset security is the protection and security of personnel and physical assets or information that is analyzed and deemed essential to the operation and success of the mission and to resources required for protection.

**Node Protection.** Command posts and operations centers are often protected through area security techniques that involve the employment of protection and security assets in a layered, integrated, and redundant manner.

**Response Force Operations.** Response force operations expediently reinforce unit organic protection capabilities or complement that protection with maneuver capabilities based on the threat. Response force operations include planning for the defeat of Level I and II threats and the shaping of Level III threats until a designated combined arms tactical combat force arrives for decisive operations.

**Lines of Communications Security.** The security and protection of lines of communications and supply routes are critical to military operations since most support traffic moves along these routes. The security of lines of communications and supply routes (rail, pipeline, highway, and waterway) presents one of the greatest security challenges in an area of operations. Route security operations are defensive in nature and are terrain-oriented (see FM 3-90).

**Checkpoints and Combat Outposts .** It is often necessary to control the freedom of movement in an area of operations for a specific period of time or as a long-term operation. This may be accomplished by placing checkpoints and combat outposts along designated avenues and roadways or on key terrain identified through METT-TC.

**Convoy Security.** A convoy security operation is a specialized kind of area security operations conducted to protect convoys (FM 3-90). Units conduct convoy security operations anytime there are insufficient friendly forces to continuously secure routes in an area of operations and there is a significant danger of enemy or adversary ground action directed against the convoy.

**Port Area and Pier Security.** Ground forces may typically provide area security for port and pier areas. The joint force commander and subordinate joint force commanders ensure that port security plans and responsibilities are clearly delineated and assigned.

**Area Damage Control.** Commanders conduct area damage control when the damage and scope of the attack are limited and they can respond and recover with local assets and resources. Optimally, commanders aim to recover immediately.

*The protection warfighting function is the related tasks and systems that preserve the force so that commanders can apply maximum combat power to accomplish the mission). Refer to The Army Operations & Doctrine SMARTbook (Guide to Unified Land Operations and the Six Warfighting Functions) for further discussion of protection.*

# (Rear Area Operations & Logistics)
# III. Logistics

*Ref: FM 100-2-2 The Soviet Army: Special Warfare and Rear Area Support (Jul '84), chap 13.*

Comparison of US and Soviet military elements has led to the incorrect view that the Soviet logistic structure is austere and inadequate to support their combat forces. Because of differences in concept and organization, Soviet logistic operations have been falsely referred to as the "Achilles' heel" of Soviet military power. However, Soviet military forces do receive effective logistic support.

*Battles are won and lost for want of water, ammunition, batteries and supplies. A careful plan of logistical support is provided for each mission.*

The Soviets have spent enormous sums of money to develop a modern and highly mechanized logistic support system. The use of pallets, containers, and packages has greatly improved the efficiency of Soviet logistic efforts. The Soviets have increased the depth and range of forward service areas and increased the mobility and range of logistic formations in support of frontline forces. They have developed a tactical pipeline capability and introduced improved transportation assets in great numbers. Also, Soviet capabilities for air delivery to forward areas and the use of helicopters for resupply have shown marked improvements.

*Refer to The Sustainment & Multifunctional Logistician's SMARTbook (Warfighter's Guide to Logistics, Personnel Services, & Health Services Support) for complete discussion of U.S. military doctrine related to logistics. Topics include the sustainment warfighting function, sustainment brigade operations, BCT sustainment, sustainment planning, joint logistics, and deployment, RSOI and redeployment operations.*

# I. Principles of Logistics

*Ref: FM 100-2-2 The Soviet Army: Special Warfare and Rear Area Support (Jul '84), pp. 13-1 to 13-3.*

## Centralized Planning

This principle requires concurrent tactical and logistical planning as well as coordination with civilian industry and transportation. Centralized planning insures coordination of civilian war production with military requirements.

## Tailoring of Logistic Units

This principle allows allocation of logistic resources to the combat elements most essential to the success of the mission. Tailoring allows the Soviet military to assign priorities for logistic support.

Fixed Supply Priorities

The Soviet logistic system operates on the following sequence of priorities:

1. Ammunition of all types
2. POL
3. Technical supplies
4. Rations and clothing

However, these priorities can change with the combat situation. For example, a unit advancing rapidly with no opposition has a greater need for POL than for ammunition.

## Delivery Forward

Higher headquarters handle supply requirements for their subordinate units. Supplies and services are delivered directly to subordinate units using the organic transportation assets of the higher headquarters. For example, an army headquarters uses its own trucks to deliver supplies to its subordinate divisions. In emergencies, one level may be bypassed in supply delivery. A division may deliver supplies directly to subordinate battalions, or a regiment may deliver directly to subordinate companies. This concept does not prevent a subordinate unit from using its assets to obtain supplies from its superior headquarters, especially in critical situations.

## Continuous Supply Base Support

Supply bases and repair facilities are established as far forward as possible to insure the flow of supplies from the central logistics level directly to combat units. These echelons of bases from the homeland to deployed battalions assure continuous support for tactical elements.

## Standardization of Equipment

The Soviet system of standardization is both extensive and effective. For example, of the 3,544 parts that make up the ZIL-131 3 1/2-ton truck, 45 percent may be used on other ZIL-produced vehicles, and 23 percent may be used on other trucks of the same weight class. A T-62 tank and the MAZ537 tank transporter share a common power plant. The chassis used for the amphibious PT-76 light tank has been adapted for BTR-50 armored personnel carriers, SA-6 and FROG-2,-3, -4 and -5 TEIs, the GSP amphibious ferry, the GT-T amphibious tractor, the ASU-85 airborne SP gun, and the ZSU-23-4SP AA gun. Extensive standardization has reduced the volume of repair parts and improved the Soviets' ability to repair forward through cannibalization. Also, obsolete vehicles and weapons can be retained for training purposes without having to keep a large stockpile of repair parts.

## Supply Accountability and Resource Conservation

The Soviet system is stringent in these areas, and penalties for unnecessary waste generally are severe. Soviet military publications continually stress resource consenation and honor personnel who effectively conserve supplies.

## Complete Use of Transportation

The Soviet logistic system uses rail transport whenever possible to move supplies from the Soviet Union to front or army level depots. Other transportation assets, primarily motor assets, are used from that point forward. The Soviet military has three separate groups of transportation personnel- railroad troops, motor transport troops, and pipeline troops. Soviet doctrine calls for using tactical combat vehicles to move additional POL and ammunition stocks, especially in the preparation phase before offensive action.

## Complete Mobile Support

From division to company, materiel and servicing facilities operate from wheeled vehicles. Critical supplies such as ammunition are boxed and uploaded on support and combat vehicles. These measures support a continuous, rapid offensive.

## Forward Positioning of Support Elements

Soviet maintenance and medical facilities operate under similar procedures. Both attempt to locate in areas of greatest need with emphasis on quickly returning lightly wounded personnel and repairable equipment to the combat elements. Personnel and equipment requiring additional attention are evacuated to the next-level facility.

## Use of All Possible Resources

Soviet troops are taught to forage for food in local areas and to use captured stocks of food, ammunition, and equipment. While food preparation and clothing supply procedures have improved, the supply priorities discussed above may require the use of enemy materiel.

## Logistic Stockpiles

The logistic storage of war materials consists of four major categories: state, strategic, mobilization, and mobile reserves.

- **State Reserves.** Foodstuffs, petroleum products, manufactured goods, and other strategic raw materials are stored in special government warehouses. These items can be issued only with the express permission of the State. While these stocks are considered to be separate from the military items held in strategic reserve, military use of at least part of these items is anticipated.
- **Strategic Reserves.** These reserves are stocks of supplies and equipment controlled by the MOD. These stocks are similar to stocks in State reserves and are not planned for early use in a conflict.
- **Mobilization Reserves.** These materials are held for issue to newly activated, large military units and for resupply to combat units in the early stages of a conflict. One directorate in the MOD determines the level and configuration of these stocks. It also is responsible for their accountability and maintenance. The military districts coordinate mobilization measures between military and civilian sectors.
- **Mobile Reserves.** Ammunition, fuel, rations, and equipment are located with deployed ground units and transported by the unit's organic transport. Ground forces maintain these supplies for use in immediate conduct of ground operations. These supplies are distributed throughout the ground forces in both tactical and support elements. Quantities of these supplies are established by published norms. They are constantly checked and kept at proper levels. An emergency reserve of supplies is maintained within these stocks. It can be used only on order of the unit commander.

# II. Operational Logistics

Within the Soviet logistic system, the bulk of logistic units are concentrated at two levels, front and army. This concentration supports the Soviet philosophy of streamlined, highly mobile combat elements at division and below. The responsibility and the primary means for logistic support are maintained at these higher levels. Tactical units are free to engage the enemy in high-speed and highly mobile action. This reduction of logistic personnel at the tactical level explains how Soviet divisions can be smaller than US divisions but have more firepower.

The fmnt is not a fixed organization but is tailored to meet specific objectives based on forces available, mission requirements, enemy forces, and the physical geography of the area of operations. Tailoring affects the number and type of subordinate combat elements and the number and type of assigned logistic units. The logistic operation of the front is extensive and complex, and it serves as the major connecting link between the industrial base of the Soviet Union and forces engaged in combat.

Generally Located between 150 to 200 kilometers from the FEBA, the front rear area is served by air, highway, rail, and pipeline from the USSR. Rail transport bears the burden of movement requirements to the front. Despite improvements in motor transport, rail transport is used to carry the majority of Soviet war materiel as far forward as possible.

The front supply complex has a wide range of fixed and mobile depots and other facilities such as major hospitals and capital maintenance facilities. At this level, depots are administered by each service, special troop directorates, and the various subordinate elements under the chief of the rear. When the distance between front and army rear areas is great, a front logistic base may be formed and located in the forward portion of the front area. This logistic base is situated along a railroad line when possible and also is supported by highway, air, and pipeline.

The army is the highest-level peace time combined arms formation. It has a permanent staff plus assigned combat support and combat service support elements. With the exception of its reduced size, the army logistic base is similar to that of the front. Logistic elements are basically the same for both tank and combined arms armies.

The army logistic base normally is located within 100 kilometers of the forward edge of the battle area (FEBA). Like the front,the armyrear area is served by rail, highway, air, and pipeline when possible. If distances between the army and its subordinate divisions' rear area become great, or the number of units to be supported changes, a forward army logistic base is established. Multiple transport modes service this forward base as much as possible. From this base forward, motor transport is used for the bulk of materiel movement.

*Refer to The Sustainment & Multifunctional Logistician's SMARTbook (Warfighter's Guide to Logistics, Personnel Services, & Health Services Support) for complete discussion of U.S. military doctrine related to tactical logistics. Topics include the sustainment warfighting function, sustainment brigade operations, BCT sustainment, sustainment planning, joint logistics, and deployment, RSOI and redeployment operations.*

# (Rear Area Operations & Logistics)
# IV. Tactical Logistics

*Ref: FM 100-2-2 The Soviet Army: Special Warfare and Rear Area Support (Jul '84), chap 13.*

At the tactical level, Soviet logistic support is fully mobile. Streamlined logistic elements support the respective tactical units with ammunition, POL, and rations to insure continuous combat operations.

Supply elements deliver materials to the rear of combat elements deployed on the FEBA. Medical and maintenance elements deploy as far forward as possible to accomplish rapid return of lightly wounded personnel and lightly damaged equipment to the combat units. Personnel and equipment requiring additional attention are evacuated from the battlefield.

Divisional combat service support elements are completely mobile. The division mobile logistic base normally is located approximately 25 to 40 kilometers from the FEBA in the offense,and up to 50 kilometers in the defense. Logistic elements are organized similar to logistic elements at army level. The logistic base is headed by a logistics officer, assisted by branch depot chiefs, and subordinate to the deputy commander for the rear. Maintenance operations are the responsibility of the deputy commanderfor technical matters. Motor transport, medical, and field bakery facilities are organic to the division. Supplies are delivered to regiments and battalions.

At regimental level, supplies are loaded on vehicles to maintain equal mobility combat elements. The regimental chief of rear services is responsible for all supply actions. There are no branch depot chiefs at this level to assist him. Maintenance functions are the responsibility of the deputy commander for technical matters. Located up to 20 kilometersfrom the FEBA, these logistic elements directly supply subordinate battalions, and also may supply line companies when required.

Battalion logistic support is self-contained. Supplies are maintained with the supply and maintenance platoon and transported on battalion vehicles. Prescribed norms of supply are maintained for all classes of materiel, with replenishment provided directly by regiment or division logistic elements. The battalion chief of staff is the organizer of rear service functions. The deputy commander for technical matters is in charge of maintenance support. The supply platoon commander is responsible for receipt, storage, and delivery of supplies to companies. He also deploys and operates battalion ammunition, fuel, and rationpoints. The battalion fel'dsher (a physician's assistant) is chief of the battalion medical section. He is responsible for gathering and evacuating wounded personnel from the companies and the battlefield.

The company commander is responsible for organization of his rear services. The deputy commander for technical matters is responsible for organization of company-level maintenance. The company first sergeant, who is a warrant officer or a senior non-commissioned officer, is responsible for accountability and maintenance of the unit's weapons, ammunition, fuel, food, etc. Medical and sanitary matters are supervised by the unit commander and the battalion fel'dsher.

# I. Supply

Supply is an operational function of MOD subordinate directorates, of other directorates, and of troop commands at MOD level that handle special-purpose equipment and supply. The Organizational and Mobilization Directorate of the General Staff is reponsibile for management of the uninterrupted supply of all forces in the initial phases of conflict.

Military district commanders have immediate directive and administrative authority for supply matters. They exercise these responsibilities through a deputy commander for rear services.The deputy commander directs the operations of the subordinate logistic elements, warehouses, shops, and other facilities. Military districts and groups of forces are the principal points of delivery for material and equipment contracted for by the MOD and delivered by industry. The weapons, ammunition, and other manufactured goods are shipped directly to the military district or group of forces.

Below the military district or group of forces, army and division staffs reflect the organization of the higher unit in logistic matters. Supply elements at army and division are subordinate operationally to their counterparts at the next higher headquarters.

To simplify logistic planning and to standardize ordering and issuing procedures,the Soviets divide the major classes of supplies into specific quantities or distribution lots. These quantities are called "units of fire" for ammunition, "refills" for POL, "daily ration" for fwd, and "set" for spare pans and accessories. These amounts originally are computed based on physical conditions or limitations.

# Locations of Tactical Logistic Elements

*Ref: FM 100-2-2 The Soviet Army: Special Warfare and Rear Area Support (Jul '84), p. 13-5.*

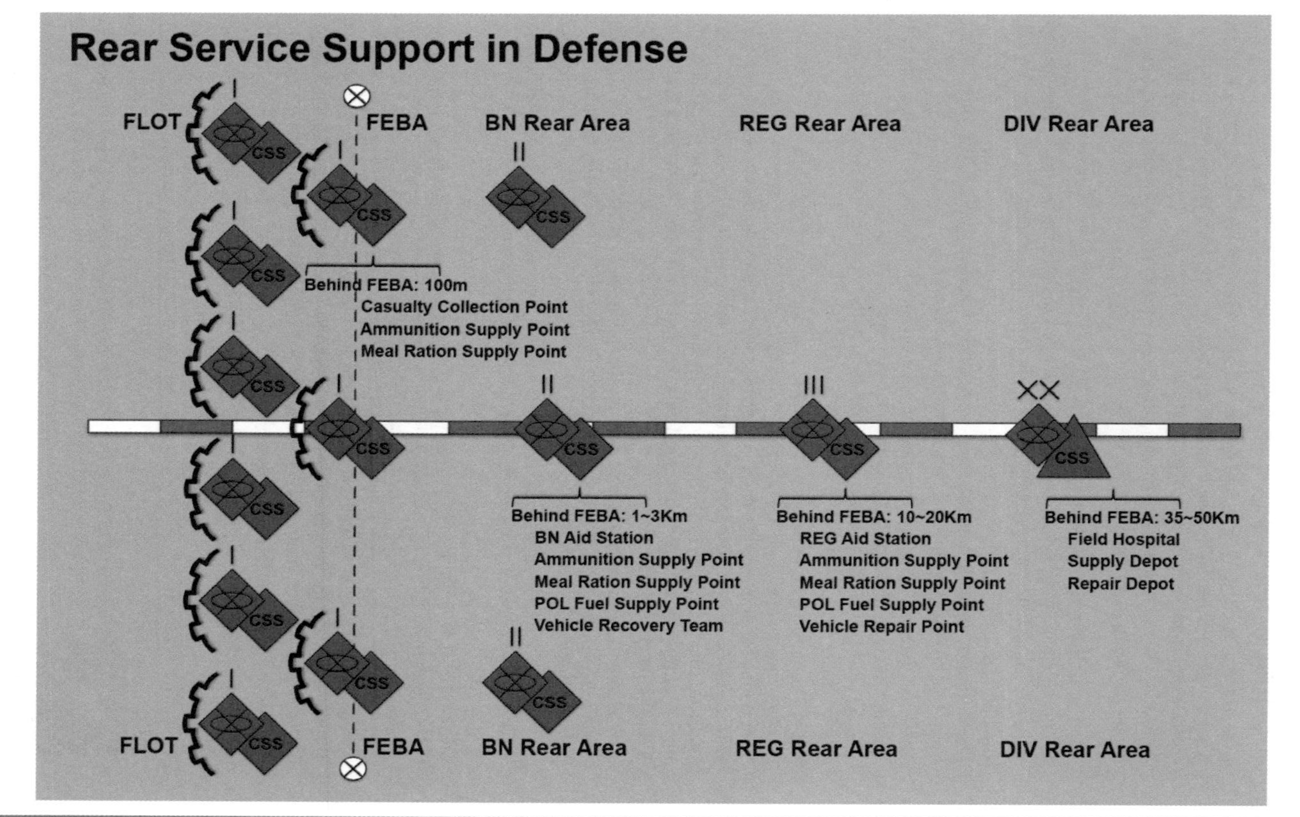

# II. Transportation

The various transportation services under MOD are traffic management, railroad operations, railroad maintenance and construction, highway construction and maintenance, highway regulation, and operation of all transport modes including pipelines.

# III. Maintenance

Maintenance facilities in the field are provided for the following items of equipment: tracked vehicles, wheeled vehicles, artillery and ordnance, engineer equipment, signal equipment, and chemical equipment.

Service for these items is provided by fixed and mobile repair facilities that extend repair capabilities forward into the battle area.

## OrganizationalMaintenance Capabilities

Company Level. Only driver and crew preventive maintenance and routine inspections are conducted at company level.

Battalion Level. The repair workshop contains a shop truck and four mechanics who make routine repairs on tracked and wheeled vehicles. In combat, this repair workshop can be reinforced with a vehicle recovery section.

Regimental Level. The maintenance company performs routine and some medium repair functions. Motorized rifle and tank regiments have both wheeled and tracked vehicle workshops. Each of these elements may form repair and evacuation groups (REGs) to provide support to subordinate battalions.

Division Level. The maintenance battalion is composed of a headquarters company; tracked vehicle maintenance company; wheeled vehicle maintenance company; ordnance maintenance company; and special task, recovery, and supply and service-platoons. Within the companies, there are shop vans, supply trucks, tank retrievers, and tow trucks. Both routine and medium repairs may be performed. In combat, these companies establish damaged vehicle repair and collection points that are similar to regimental REGs.

Army Level. Combined arms and tank armies have their maintenance capabilities augmented by front as required. Army units can provide mobile detachments for forward operations if necessary.

Front Level. Front maintenance units are manned and equipped for capital repairs. These units operate from fixed facilities or mobile detachments.

# IV. Medical Support

The Soviet military medical system provides support to the ground forces under the directionof the Central Military Medical Directorate of the Ministry of Defense. The Central Directorate supervises the supplying of medical equipment and the training of medical personnel. Besides the peace and wartime programs directly related to the active armed forces, the system ties in with the civil sector in screening health records of draft-age youth and in performing natural disaster relief functions.

The two principal missions of the military medical service in combatare the evacuation and treatment of casualties,and the preventionof disease in the area of operations.

*Refer to The Sustainment & Multifunctional Logistician's SMARTbook (Warfighter's Guide to Logistics, Personnel Services, & Health Services Support) for complete discussion of U.S. military doctrine related to tactical logistics. Topics include the sustainment warfighting function, sustainment brigade operations, BCT sustainment, sustainment planning, joint logistics, and deployment, RSOI and redeployment operations.*

# Related SMARTbooks (Opposing Forces/OPFOR)

In today's complicated and uncertain world, it is impossible to predict the exact nature of future conflict that might involve U.S. forces. So the military must be ready to meet the challenges of any type of conflict, in all kinds of places, and against all kinds of threats. This is the nature of the contemporary operational environment (COE), and training for such an environment requires a different type of Opposing Force (OPFOR) than that of the past. An Opposing Force (OPFOR) is a training tool that should allow U.S. forces to train against a challenging and plausible sparring partner that represents the wide range of possible opponents the military could face in actual conflict.

The Lightning Press offers three specific OPFOR SMARTbooks, plus more than a dozen related and supporting "military reference" and "national power" titles:

## OPFOR Smartbook 1: Contemporary Opposing Forces

This OPFOR SMARTbook reflects the characteristics of military and paramilitary forces that may be present challenges for U.S. forces in the contemporary operational environment (COE).

## OPFOR Smartbook 2: The Hybrid Threat

A hybrid threat is the diverse and dynamic combination of regular forces, irregular forces, and/or criminal elements all unified to achieve mutually benefitting effects.

## OPFOR Smartbook 3: Red Team Army

It has been 30 years since a holistic explanation of the Soviet Army was presented in the US Army FM 100-2 series. Through a triangulation of potential and actual post-Soviet threats, an updated and more detailed Red Team Army model is explored.

---

## The Battle Staff SMARTbook (4th Rev. Ed.)

**Designing, Planning & Conducting Military Operations**

Covers the operations process; commander's activities; MDMP and troop-leading procedures; integrating processes and continuing activities (intel, IPB, fires and targeting) ; plans and orders; rehearsals & AARs: & operational terms and graphics.

View, download samples and purchase online at: **www.TheLightningPress.com.** Join our SMARTnews mailing list to receive email notification of SMARTupdates, member-only discounts, new titles & revisions to your SMARTbooks!

---

# www.TheLightningPress.com